THE LAST DAYS
OF FILM

AND THE RISE OF ELECTRONIC NEWS GATHERING

RUSSELL PYNE

Puleo Press
Ponte Vedra Beach, Florida

Puleo Press/The Last Days of Film
Printed in the United States of America

Front Cover Illustration by J. G. Jones, Transactions of S.M.P.E., May 1924.

The Last Days of Film/ Russell Pyne -- 1st ed.

ISBN 9798351571706 Print Edition

CONTENTS

For John Pyne

All the young dudes (Hey dudes!)
Carry the news (Where are you?)
Boogaloo dudes (Stand up, c'mon)
Carry the news

All the young dudes (I want to hear you)
Carry the News (I want to see you)
Boogaloo dudes (I want to talk to you, all of you)
Carry the news (Nowwww)

Mott The Hoople
July, 28, 1972

DUEL AT CENTURY CITY

FRIDAY, OCTOBER 27, 1972

Future Shock

At noon on Monday, October 23, 1972, the 112th Technical Conference and Equipment Exhibit for the Society of Motion Picture and Television Engineers, or SMPTE, (here after 'the Society') officially began with the traditional Get-Together Luncheon at the Century Plaza Hotel in Century City, California. Built in 1966 about nine miles west of downtown Los Angeles and about six miles northwest of Santa Monica and the Pacific coast, it was, at the time of its construction, the tallest building west of downtown. In the fall of 1972, the ocean could still be seen from the top floor of the 19-storey building. The crescent shaped hotel had been designed by the famed architect Minoru Yamasaki, the guy who'd designed the World Trade Towers in New York City. The building was, and still is, considered a masterpiece of the hip, modern New Formalism that was all the rage in the late Sixties. Had attendees arriving that morning

1

at the conference looked to the northwest, they would have seen Yamasaki's newest creation: two 44-storey, triangular-shaped, aluminum-sheathed Century Plaza Towers, going up across the Avenue of the Stars, with the Hollywood Hills as a backdrop, an Edge City being fully realized.

Perhaps some of the Society members felt a twinge of remorse at the price of progress as they walked into the hotel, surrounded by the modern corporate office complex - for the ground upon which they walked had once been the backlot of the 20th Century Fox movie studios.

For nearly 40 years, ever since 1926 when Fox Films purchased the land from Tom Mix, the original cowboy movie star, motion pictures had been filmed nonstop in a curving canyon of artificial facades. More than a thousand stories had been captured in the bright Southern California sun light, with the labor and expertise of more than a thousand motion-picture professionals. They spent their lives on those sets, raising families from their labors. Cinematographers, Grips, Set Designers, and Boom Operators, from sunup to sundown, capturing an endless shot list for a booming industry. Then the movie-making business changed and studios had to sell their theaters, ending the system of block booking, squeezing distribution profits. Huge cost over runs on the film *Cleopatra* a decade later almost bankrupted 20th Century Fox. Three quarters of the studio's 200-acre back lot was sold off to make way for a new development called

Century City, the center piece of which was the Century Plaza Hotel. As to the old outdoor sets from the Thirties? They were flattened to make way for a giant parking lot behind the hotel.

Change, sometimes unpleasant but usually necessary, was a constant in the motion-picture business, but one can imagine the Society members arriving that morning, amid all that aluminum sheathing on the stark, lonely towers, as they walked across the hallowed ground, preparing to take in another week of technical breakthroughs in the realm of image-acquisition, manipulation and exhibition, perhaps feeling a slight hesitancy arising in their hearts, a growing urge to reject the constant rush forward in technology.

Which may explain why, by the end of the week, when faced with the future, they would turn their backs on progress.

Hollywood

The Society had been founded over a half century before by 10 men, meeting in a hotel room in July 1916, in Washington, D.C. In October, they elected the Society's officers in New York City. Upon being elected chairman, the man who had brought the group together in the first place, C. Francis Jenkins, made these remarks in his address to those gathered.

"Every new industry standardizes sooner or later, whether we will it or not. It is our duty, therefore, as engineers, to wisely

direct this standardization, to secure best standards of equipment, quality, performance, nomenclature, and, unconsciously, perhaps, a code of ethics." He went on to say. "*It is an unselfish exchange of views which will make our gatherings interesting, and the discussions of individual investigation valuable.*"

The society met three times during the following year, in Atlantic City, Chicago and New York. By 1918, the meeting schedule was reduced to a more manageable semiannual pattern of every spring and every fall. Chicago would be as far west as they'd go for the first dozen years. By its 10th anniversary, the Society numbered 200 members, only 10 of whom hailed from what at that time was becoming the motion-picture capital of the world ... but that would soon change.

In the early years of the 20th century, the three main centers of motion-picture production in America were Fort Lee, New Jersey, directly across the Hudson River from Manhattan; Chicago, on the shores of Lake Michigan, and at a small but quickly growing arc of studios clustered around the Santa Monica Mountains, between the Pacific Ocean and the city of Los Angeles. This area was named after the small municipality in the southern foothills of the Santa Monica Mountains, Hollywood. Far from the eastern establishment, experiencing pleasant weather year-round, and possessing a certain lawless character left over from the 19th-century Western cowboy mythos, it's no wonder that the district's denizens excelled in creative endeavors. The town already had something of a wild and crazy reputation even at this early date. To a certain extent, it was every man for himself, and consequences be damn.

It is only natural that during this time of exuberant growth that shelter was sought in like-minded gatherings and it is during this period that the kernels of craft groups began to form. In 1923 the International Alliance of Theatrical Stage Employees (IASTE) established a local district. Two years later, a group of Broadway veterans who'd left their stage jobs and moved out west to be players in the movies, established the Masquers Club, the precursor to the screen Actors Guild.

Among the first craft organizations was the American Society of Cinematographers (ASC) which drew up its bylaws in late 1918. In its first decade, the ASC kept up with the technology trends of motion-picture production, but then things started to get complicated. First, sound was introduced into the workflow and the "Talkies" were born, then a new organization emerged, aiming to supplant the alliances, guilds, and locals that were gaining momentum, it was called the Academy of Motion Picture Arts & Sciences.

When Louis B. Mayer, head of Metro-Goldwyn-Mayer's West Coast operation, found out how much money it would cost for IATSE members to throw up a mansion on San Monica Beach for him and his family, it occurred to him that some sort of countermeasure to the growing labor movement in the budding film industry was necessary. So, he formed the Academy.

He installed the nascent organization in the newly constructed Roosevelt Hotel on Hollywood Boulevard, established a suite of rooms in the northwest corner of the mezzanine for its exclusive use, including a 65-foot-by-45-foot club lounge. "In the large ante room leading to the Club Lounge," announced the *Academy Bulletin No. 5*, published on November 25, 1927, "it is proposed to keep on file all motion picture periodicals for the benefit of the membership." One of the first meetings held in the new digs was among the technicians. The proceedings are described in the fifth bulletin. "The new process of lighting for motion picture photography, variously known as tungsten, mazda, incandescent and soft lighting was discussed at some length and it was declared that within a year this process would be in universal use . . . and that not over six or seven cinematographers out of three hundred or more men of this profession . . . were at the present time sufficiently familiar with the new method to photograph a picture by it."

Tungsten was a necessary adaptation. The arc lights, which had been in use up until then, were noisy. With the introduction of sound, new methods of illumination were needed.

It was decided to promote a series of demonstrations of the new technology at the various studios. This was a gracious gesture by the Academy, but the writing must have been on the wall for the cinematographers – they now had competition in the technical arena. So, they called in back up.

On the morning of April 7, 1928, Society members across the United States boarded trains and began the arduous journey across the continent to lend some standardization expertise - *"To secure best standards of equipment, quality, performance, nomenclature, and, unconsciously, perhaps, a code of ethics"* - to the new industry that had sprouted up among the orange groves and barley fields below the foothills of the Santa Monica mountains. To lend further support, the Academy offered its Roosevelt Hotel space and planned a demonstration of tungsten light versus arc light at its own convention, where they would present the findings of its and ASC's research the following week.

The two-week affair was a smash, the biggest the Society had ever held. By the next spring, meeting in New York City, Society membership had nearly doubled. On February 27, 1930, George Mitchell hosted the inaugural assembly of the Pacific Coast Section of the Society at his new camera factory at 661 N. Robertson Blvd., Hollywood, where a demonstration was given of production techniques with the new tungsten light fixtures. Knowledge in the new lighting technology no longer required an invitation to Academy membership.

Society members again travelled to the West Coast for their semiannual gathering in 1931. Then there was a long pause, until 1935 and the advent of the three-strip Technicolor process. After that, the event was held there every two years in the spring. The first Autumn conference in Hollywood was in 1940, when the Society members were given a tour of the newly completed Walt Disney Studios. Hollywood moved into the Society's rotation every 18 months after that meeting. By the fall of 1972, when more than a thousand Society engineers descended upon the Century Plaza Hotel for the 112th Technical Conference & Equipment Exhibit, the conference had been held in Hollywood 26 times. Only New York City had hosted the meetings as many times, Washington, D.C., had hosted 14 conferences, while Chicago had hosted 11.

Such was the significance of the Hollywood meeting of the Society to the film making industry, so it is somewhat ironic that the seeds of the destruction of the physical substance of that industry - cellulose acetate, smeared with a "film" of light sensitive chemicals - were sown in a conference room at the Century City Hotel during that week in October of 1972.

Friday, October 27, 1972

The Advance Program for the 112th conference was published in the September issue of the *Journal of the SMPTE* (hereafter the *Journal*). All the way down at the bottom of the program, on the last day of the conference on Friday afternoon, after a morning presentation by Columbia Broadcasting

System (CBS) on proper coloring on television, a symposium was scheduled. The announcement reads, "Roundtable Discussion: The Great Film-Tape Debate – Coexistance or Conflict." It was reported the following February, in the Society's *Journal*, that "The event ... had one of the largest attendances at the conference."

Wilton R. Holm, president of the Society and research director for the Alliance of Motion Picture and Television Producers, brought the proceedings to order that Friday afternoon. Holm, 58, had been a color consultant on films shot with the Cinecolor process back in the early Fifties. In 1951, he'd been one of the color consultants on the *Sword of Monte Cristo*, the first film shot on SuperCineColor. In his opening remarks, he laid out the question at hand.

"We are here considering two different worlds, generally speaking, the small-screen world of the TV tube, and the large-screen world of the theater projection screen. Film is used in both worlds, and used successfully. Tape is used in the TV world very successfully. It is knocking at the door of the theater world. Some of tape's proponents say it is 'good enough.' Others say it is not. This leaves us with an ever-puzzling question – 'How good is good enough.'"

To answer that question, Holm informed everyone, "We have some film footage and some tape footage to show you and we will let you make your own conclusions subjectively for the time being." Perhaps because he was feeling a bit apprehensive concerning the impending results, he added the following a bit later in his remarks. "I should mention, in all fairness, that what we are comparing here is the Cadillac of the tape-recording technology . . . to the Chevrolet or at least the Pontiac of the film technology, namely 35mm. Perhaps we should be comparing 2-inch tape with 70mm, or even I-Max film." Still keeping Jenkins' words in mind - "*To secure best standards of equipment, quality, performance, nomenclature, and, unconsciously, perhaps, a code of ethics,*" - he stated, "Long Range, it seems that there should be a possible wedding of tape and film, for both TV and theatrical use, in which a film could be made from film and tape, or a tape from film and tape. It would seem, therefore, that standardization should be a concern." With that, seemingly, less-than-ringing endorsement, the unselfish exchange of views which had become the hallmark of the Society's gatherings commenced over the greatest standardization contest the industry had yet known.

Next, Paul Wittlig, of CBS, explained how the demonstration would proceed. "We are going to give two test-demonstrations this afternoon," he stated. "The first will be via closed-circuit television on the monitors and the second will be via direct projection on the screen at the front of the room." As the videotape began playing on 10 monitors set up around the room, a voice-over intoned, "This is the test being shot for presentation here at the Society's one hundred and twelfth Technical Conference. We are shooting an exterior and two interiors. The exterior is this entranceway to the Cutler Union Building on the campus of the Eastman School of Music in Rochester." The interior shots that followed used both low-key light and high-key light in the studio at Kodak Park's Research Laboratories in Rochester, New York. The demonstration ran for three and half minutes. When it was over, everyone turned to look at a projection screen on which the demonstration was run again. The results were reported in the Society's February *Journal.* "On the color monitor . . . the video-tape had consistently better sharpness and color. On the projection screen . . . the tape to film transfers did not compare well to the film negative to film positive clips." When the lights came up, every head in the room would have immediately turned in unison toward the Kodak representative on the symposium's panel, 60-year-old Norwood L. Simmons.

"It would be rather remarkable if I did not have a prejudiced point of view on this subject. I'll try not to let it show too strongly," he began. He'd joined Kodak in 1937 and was transferred out to Hollywood the year Walt Disney Studios produced its first feature-length animated film, *Snow White and the Seven Dwarfs.* By 1964, he was Kodak's general manager of the West Coast division. On Monday, at the Get-Together Luncheon, he'd been presented with the Society's highest award of achievement, the Progress Medal. His words would weigh heavily on those gathered that afternoon. "The title of this symposium suggest that film and tape are on a collision course and only one recording medium may survive. ... We at Kodak believe that these two technologies will co-exist and increasingly complement each other in certain applications." The applications to which he referred were productions such as afternoon soap operas, quiz shows and panel shows. "Keep in mind," Simmons reminded everyone, "that all the action takes place on a fixed set and the creative requirements for the presentation are not demanding. With such uses videotape recording came of age and found its natural niche in the industry. Perhaps because it is a relatively new technology compared to photography, applications are now being sought for video recorders that are perhaps unnatural, such as difficult location shooting." He closed his remarks by saying, "Increasingly, we believe that the nature of the original show will determine which medium is used." In other words, hard-to-get-to field operations would employ film while easily accessible, environmentally controlled sets would employ video.

Besides Holm and Simmons, there was only one other film representative on the panel, 62-year-old Sidney P. Solow, president of Consolidated Film Industries, one of Hollywood's leading film-processing labs. He was also a full professor at the University of Southern California, having taught Photographic Theory since 1947. He observed,

"Regardless of what happens in the big studios where large amounts of money are available for production . . . cameras and film have such clear advantages for the individual film-maker." He Added, "The lightweight, portable, economic, self-contained film camera is incomparable as a tool that will help the creative film artist."

The other five men on the panel represented companies involved in video production. Three were somewhat lesser lights in the motion-picture production world: Hugh Hole, with Vidtronics Corporation, and Jack Cook, president of Video-Tran (both businesses were involved with the transfer of film and video to the opposing format) and Arch Luther of Radio Corporation of America (RCA). Probably the most well-known of the video guys at that time would have been Charles Ginsburg, vice-president of advanced technology at Ampex Corporation in Redwood City, California. Ampex was one of the early Silicon Valley startup success stories. By using copyright-free technology obtained from the wreckage of a defeated Nazi Germany, the company was able to introduce audiotape recording technology in America in 1947. Ginsburg had been brought on soon after to lead a team that had been tasked with developing videotape, which he accomplished to great fanfare in 1956. His opinion on the demonstration, like that of Simmons' and Solow's, would have carried some weight with attendees.

Ginsburg started his remarks by asserting that within two or three years at the most, a color TV camera would be developed that would be competitive, in terms of portability, with film cameras. Then he pointed out, "That of course is not what this discussion is about. What this meeting is really about is electronic production and post-production for thirty-five-millimeter theatrical release." There were three problems he had with this concept. First, the whole TV system would have to be upgraded; second, a camera with much greater capabilities in luminance and color bandwidth would need to be developed; third, a video tape recorder would need to be created that would maintain picture quality while editing without the usual degradation caused by multiple dubs. "All of these requirements are achievable, but I have no firm opinion yet about whether or not they will be achieved," he concluded.

Character of the Happy Warrior

Finally, after six panelists had spoken, everyone's focus turned to the man who'd had the audacity to schedule such a provocative dual on the last afternoon of the last day of the conference, a certain Joseph Antony Flaherty Jr., general manager of CBS-TV's Engineering Development.

He was born in 1930 in Kansas City Missouri, where his father, Joseph Flaherty Sr., was chief engineer at local AM radio station WDAF, owned by the *Kansas City Star* newspaper. When Joseph Flaherty Jr. was 18, the newspaper went into television, erecting a 724-foot-tall antenna south of downtown Kansas City, the tallest man-made structure in the state at the time; next to it, a new building to house the studios was built. On September 11, 1949, WDAF-TV went live, testing the range and quality of the signal from the antenna at a three-day event in the Municipal Auditorium. It was estimated 10,000 people came to see about the new technology on the first day alone. One can only imagine the pride Flaherty felt in his father's accomplishment as the new station's chief engineer.

He must have been bitten by the motion picture bug himself - upon earning a degree in physics from Rockhurst University three years later, he immediately enlisted in the United States Army and joined the Signal Corps, so he could go to the Army Pictorial Center in Astoria, Queens, New York. The APC, as it was called, occupied the former Paramount Studios the Army had purchased a decade earlier, during World War II. Flaherty went to work immediately and built the Army's first television studio on the second floor of the building, in what had been the old special effects room. After his enlistment was up in 1955, and he'd moved on to greater challenges, the Army hired his dad as a civilian in 1958 to be chief engineer in its television division. Reminiscing in 2004 on the APC website, he wrote that it was "a case of 'father follows in son's footsteps.'"

In photos of him taken in the Eighties, when his legend was established, Joe Jr. was always smiling. Even if he wasn't looking directly at the camera, he always had a boyish grin on his face, as if he were about to crack a joke. It's also apparent in his writing from those years that he possessed an extremely refined wit. He would need one for the great standardization war he inaugurated on that Friday in late October 1972.

After the Army, Flaherty the son returned to Kansas City and worked at WDAF for a brief period. He was then sent up to the network in New York, becoming an engineer for the facilities test group at the National Broadcasting Network (NBC). He was at NBC just long enough to meet and propose to his future wife, Janice Hermance; by 1957 he'd moved over to CBS to be a television design engineer.

That same year the Union of Soviet Socialist Republics' Sputnik satellite flew over the United States.

The space race occupied the minds of American engineers, along with everyone else in the nation, for the next 15 years. For engineers working in the motion-picture field, the Holy Grail was a camera in the spacecraft going to the moon. RCA won the honor, sending a camera weighing less than five pounds on Apollo 8, the first space craft to leave Earth orbit and circle the moon. It went up in December of 1968. Four months earlier, at the political conventions held to nominate the presidential candidates that year, all three networks had a version of a compact video camera on the convention floor. The next year, Flaherty won an Emmy for the CBS design known as the Mini-Cam.

At the Society's 107th conference in Chicago in April of 1970, he presented the paper *Trends in Television Recording.* Videotape had, just that year, overtaken film in the network's program production. However, during prime time, from 7:30 p.m. to 10:30 p.m., film was still the dominant medium used. The new camera that had just won him an Emmy could certainly be used to take over some of that production to save money. He pointed out that a typical one-hour film production cost about $15,000 in film stock and processing ($113,000 in 2022) which, over a 26-week shooting schedule, would certainly pay for the initial investment for the video gear, which had a reusable format. The next year, he was at the Society's 109th Conference in Los Angeles, presenting a paper on an editing system designed with prime-time production needs in mind.

Eighteen months later, he brought the visual proof of videotape's value to the 112th Conference, giving a head-to-head demonstration of the latest video camera technology up against the standard in Kodak film.

In his quest for the best small camera to send into space, Flaherty had spent his thirties travelling the world. Unlike NBC, its chief competitor, CBS didn't have the manufacturing arm of RCA, the network's parent company. American

Broadcasting Network (ABC) had made a deal with the Ampex Corporation for its portable video camera, the BC-100. CBS sent Flaherty and Ray Beindorf, head of its station Group, around the globe to share research and look for synergies in technology. They went to London and visited the British Broadcasting Corporation (BBC), to Eindhoven in the Netherlands, where Philips Norelco was located, to Ota City south of Tokyo, home of the Ikegami Tsushinki Company and Akai Electronics and, finally, they went to Darmstadt, along the Upper Rhine River in Germany, where they came across the Bosch-Fernseh KCU – 40 color video camera.

This is the camera Flaherty took to the Research Labs at Kodak Park in Rochester to go toe-to-toe with the predominate motion-picture-capturing technology of the day, Eastman Color Negative Film Type 5254.

It's a famous film stock, in use from 1968 to 1974, at the height of the New Hollywood movement. It was used to film some of the periods most important productions, movies such as *The Godfather*, *Barry Lyndon*, *Cabaret*, and *Bound for Glory*. Type 5254 was, to put it simply, the highest standard of film at the time, and Flaherty, like Peter Cooper a century before accepting the challenge to race his locomotive against a horse-drawn stagecoach, put the newer technology of electronic photography up against the tried-and-true technology of photochemical photography, to find out whether the new technology could keep up with the old.

Film at Eleven

Addressing the gathering at the 112th Technical Conference and Equipment Exhibit, Flaherty began, "As you've gathered, none of us is coming here to predict the death of either the film or videotape imaging systems." Though everyone on the panel seemed focused on "theatrical feature-film production," Flaherty said that there were three other areas in which film and video would henceforth either co-exist or compete. "These are television program production, commercial production and distribution, and news pickup."

News pickup in 1972 had a phrase, "Film at eleven." It was used every evening during the local television news shows at six o'clock. It was a promise to the audience to air the latest news in as timely a fashion as technology allowed, thus demonstrating that newsroom's commitment to inform the public and ensure the continued use of the radio spectrum space licensed to that station. By the time of the Society's 112th Conference, the term had entered the American lexicon to signify crass, overstated promotion, as if to say, "If you think what I'm telling you now is salacious and crazy, wait till you see the pictures." The pervasiveness of the phrase, every night, right after the six o'clock lead story, spoken in somber, august tones by white, male anchors, gave film a patina of near institutional authority. Suddenly, Joe Flaherty had announced an end to film's institutional dominance in news gathering. As it so happened, history had lent a hand that day in October of 1972 to help Flaherty prove his point.

"I have a clipping from today's *New York Times*, October twenty seventh, indicating some of the progress that electronic journalism is making in replacing sixteen-millimeter film for certain applications." He informed his audience near the end of his remarks, surely with a broad grin on his face. "The headline reads, 'CBS Wins Networks Race on Kissinger Briefing.'" The day before, CBS had aired portions of National Security Advisor Henry Kissinger's famous "Peace is at Hand," speech only twenty-five minutes after he'd spoken – more than an hour-and-a-half before ABC got him on the air - by using the CBS Minicam and videotape.

Flaherty concluded his remarks by saying, "Let me point out that the present Minicam, which is six years old and already pretty obsolete, is nineteen inches long, three inches wide and sixteen inches high, and weighs eighteen pounds. The back pack weighs an additional twenty pounds but isn't worn unless one is actually moving. The thirty-five millimeter Mitchell BNC camera, (the standard film camera of the day) with lenses and magazines, is thirty-two inches long, eighteen inches wide and thirty inches high, and it weighs one hundred pounds. The Fernseh camera that was used for this test you saw today is thirty-five inches long, which is three inches longer, ten inches wide, which is eight inches narrower: and fourteen inches high, which is sixteen inches less high, and it weighs one hundred and ten pounds. So the evolution continues and the portability of the electronic and of the film cameras are coming closer together."

With that, Flaherty wrapped up his third stab at sharing the results of his research with the engineers of motion picture production in Hollywood. The verdict of the conference, or at least the last line about it in the February 1973 *Journal*, was that "the nature of the original production will determine which medium is used for the original shooting. Subsequent conversions will then depend on the requirements of the organization distributing the programming."

Norwood Simmons and Kodak had declared that priority would remain on the side of the creator, not the distributor, as to the method of image capture, expenses for film stock and processing be damn. Going forward, most motion pictures and prime time television shows, would continue to be shot on the big heavy Mitchell cameras, or, for the "difficult location shooting," which was an "unnatural," fit for video, the Arriflex 35. But, if no one in the Society acted on Flaherty's findings, others were taking note.

In the weekly trade magazine *Broadcasting*, out the next Monday, the conference was written up with the headline "That tape-vs-film debate is still good for a round at SMPTE." In the article the author wrote, "The controversy over film vs. video tape (do they conflict or can they co-exist) seemed a dominant issue at the conference throughout the week." The article then quotes three presenters on advancing video technology. In January, the producers of the monthly trade journal *Broadcasting/Management Engineering* published their first cover story on the rapid development in video technology. It would become a January tradition for the next decade. At The Ohio State University, in the Spring of 1973, two researchers, James D. Harless and Erik L. Collins, included questions concerning "television news department equipment" in a more general questionnaire concerning work roles in the newsroom, which they sent out to a random sample of three hundred news directors.

As for Flaherty, he began research on a new project at the beginning of 1973.

The CBS network owned and operated local affiliates in five cities: WCBS in New York, KNXT in Los Angeles, WBBM in Chicago, WCAU in Philadelphia, and KMOX in St. Louis. Flaherty and Beindorf put a new second-generation portable video camera in each of the newsrooms. New York, Chicago, and Philadelphia were equipped with the Phillips Norelco PCP-90 made in Eindhoven, Netherlands. The Los Angeles and St Louis newsrooms were equipped with two cameras which had been manufactured in Ota City, Japan.

Located halfway between Tokyo and Yokohama, at the mouth the Tama River and adjacent to Haneda Airport, the air gateway to Japan, Ota City was a large manufacturing center which pioneered *nakama-mawashi*, which translates to "passing something around to friends." The city is, and was at that time, home to thousands of small industrial firms employing at most 10 or 11 people doing very precise designing and manufacturing. It was said that if you threw a paper plane with a design written on it through the window of a small factory in Ota City, you'd have a completed product by the next day.

One such factory, Akai Electric Company, founded in 1933, produced electric motors for film projectors. In 1953, the company began to make tape recorders, expanding into the U. S. In early 1973, Flaherty took a new Akai VT-150 camera and tape deck to St. Louis.

The other new Ota City camera was made by Ikegami Tsushinki. Founded in 1946, the company evolved into producing television studio equipment in 1951; by 1962, it began working on camera design with the CBS Network. That spring, KNXT in Los Angeles took possession its newest creation, the HL-33 portable camera. The 'HL' stood for Handy-Looky, and It would be this camera, and not the Fernseh KCU-40, that would usher in a new era of motion picture technology. The Ikegami Handy-Looky would soon spark the video vs. film revolution - not in the production studios of prime-time entertainment but on the rough unforgiving streets of America – and this revolution would begin the long, slow demise of film-based production.

THE WINTER CONFERENCE
FRIDAY, JANUARY 19, 1973

Key Biscayne

Three months later, on the other side of America, President Richard Milhous Nixon was finishing up a week-long visit to his Southern White House on Key Biscayne, an exclusive island off the coast of Miami, Florida. He'd won re-election the previous November, just 11 days after the Society's 112th Conference ended. Henry Kissinger's "Peace is at Hand" speech, which Joseph Flaherty had referenced, would go down in history as that election cycle's 'October Surprise.' Nixon was spending that third week in January relaxing in South Florida's pleasant subtropical weather, preparing his upcoming Inaugural address and spending some downtime with his friend Bebe Rebozo.

At 8:01 p.m. on Thursday, January 18, he climbed into a helicopter at the Key Biscayne Compound helipad going to Homestead Air Force Base, to board Airforce One and return to Washington, D.C., to begin his historic second term.

His entourage would have packed their luggage and checked out of the only accommodations open to the public on the small exclusive island, The Sonesta Beach Hotel, a few hours earlier. As they left, they may have passed people arriving for the hotel's next event, The Society's Seventh Annual Winter Television Conference.

About that 'T'

The Society's acronym, SMPTE, which appears every month on the cover of its famous *Journal*, hadn't always had the "T" in it. When the original 10 men gathered at the first conference on Monday, July 24, 1916, at the Mayflower Hotel in Washington, D.C., the organization they birthed was known simply as the Society of Motion Picture Engineers, or S.M.P.E. This appellation omitted the word 'Television' - not because television hadn't been invented, however. The theory of radio-transmitted moving pictures had been hypothesized 30 years before the Society's founding. In fact, Charles Francis Jenkins, whose efforts brought the Society into existence and who then served as its first president, spent a considerable amount of time and energy studying the developing technology. He presented the first paper on his findings, *Radio Photographs, Radio Movies, and Radio Vision*, to the Society's 13th Semiannual Conference in Atlantic City, New Jersey, in May of 1923.

Five years later, after the Federal Radio Commission had begun issuing licenses, he established the first television station in the nation, W3XK. Unfortunately for Jenkins, and the 30-plus other experimental stations established throughout America, in the first three years after the federal government had allowed experimentation with the new technology, he used the mechanical method for image capture. That machine, called a Nipkow disk - Jenkin's referred to his design as a "scanning disc" - was basically a swiftly revolving disk with 48 holes in a spiral pattern which broke the picture down into 48 vertical lines. It was outdated before the station went on the air.

The development of electronic television is beyond the scope of this book. Recounting the multitude of engineers and their herculean efforts in advancing the technology, step-by-miniscule step, require a greater volume. Albert Abramson's two-book set stands as the definitive work at this date. What is important to the inquiry at hand now, however, is the relationship the Society had with the technology during the first three decades of its existence, and what caused the Society in the late Sixties to establish a symposium to address the issues of standardization in the broadcast television industry, in the middle of the winter.

Officially, the 'Inventor of Television' title goes to Philo Farnsworth. When Farnsworth was 14, he drew a design of a theoretical image dissector (a vacuum tube with a lens, a thin slice of light sensitive material and an electron gun) on a chalkboard in his high-school chemistry class in Rigby,

Idaho. His teacher, Justin Tolman, was wise enough to draw his own copy and keep it on file. Years later, that same document proved Farnsworth's paternity as the technology's inventor during a nasty patent dispute. In the end, though, Farnsworth was unable to profit from his eureka moment as much as he might have wished. The history of the development of television is filled with many unforeseen twists and turns. But in September of 1927, when he proudly demonstrated a line on a screen that was captured, transmitted, and displayed, entirely with electricity, he thought he had the greatest invention since Edison's lightbulb on his hands. To advance from a line to a whole screen was going to take some work, though, and that's where things got complicated.

Throughout the ensuing years of research, the Society hosted regular updates concerning the development of television at its biannual conferences. The various presentations were then published in the *Journal*. Starting in 1931 with the paper *An Entertainment City,* Alfred Norton Goldsmith's observations appeared in the *Journal* four times. In the May 1934 issue, Elmer William Engstrom submitted his paper, *A Study of Television Image Characteristics.* The May 1937 *Journal* featured an article by Vladimir K. Zworykin, describing his Iconoscope (camera) and Kinescope (monitor) system for broadcasting images. At the following semiannual conference, the 42nd, in New York, a 25-minute talk on

Vacuum-Tube Engineering for Motion Pictures, was given by a L.C. Hollands and A.M. Glover.

There were two things all these engineers had in common. The first was that they all belonged to the Institute of Radio Engineers (IRE), which predated the Society by four years. Alfred Goldsmith was one of the founders as well as the first editor of its publication, *Proceedings of the Institute of Radio Engineers*. The IRE's *Proceedings* - with a granite-gray cover and published pocket-sized for easy reading on a train - was, as Goldsmith claimed in March of 1928, "to be found on the desk of practically every active worker in the radio field." Certainly, the *Standard Terms and Symbols*, published in 1913, 1915, 1922 and 1925, and handy for reading a schematic diagram, was always within the reach of a professional radio engineer. By the end of 1928, the Society, having doubled its membership after its first foray into Hollywood, counted almost 400 hundred members. The IRE had more than 4,000 members - most of whom were from the United States – but more than 700 hundred people were from other countries. The majority of that group were from England, at 276 members, Canada's representation numbered 184, Japan was fourth with 33.

On Tuesday, May 14, 1929, the IRE met at the Mayflower Hotel in Washington, D.C., for the symposium "Photo Radio." It was the first of its kind in America. Jenkins was there, with his scanning disc, having joined the organization the year before. Goldsmith's contribution to the symposium, published in the *Proceedings* four months later, opens with these words: "The purpose of this paper is to introduce a series of papers in which are described specific methods whereby transmission by radio of stationary images or moving pictures can be effectively carried out. Accordingly, it has seemed desirable to establish the position of image transmission by radio in the general engineering technique of this field rather than to discuss individual methods or specialized apparatus." With those two sentences, the *Proceedings* editor declared that the new technology of television would be placed in the realm of the radio spectrum, and not just in the domain of the tools and machinery of motion picture production. Published in the same issue, the article *The Selection of Standards for Commercial Radio Television* by Julius Weinberger, Theodore A. Smith and George Rodwin.

The second commonality the engineers shared, besides IRE membership (except Jenkins), was that they all worked for Radio Corporation of America (RCA). RCA was run by David Sarnoff, and he ruled the airways.

The Boy Wonder of Radio

David Sarnoff was born on February 27, 1891, in the Russian Empire (now Belarus) town of Uzlany, a small crossroads 20 miles south of Minsk, about halfway in between Moscow and Warsaw, Poland. He immigrated to New York City when he was nine and immediately went to work to help support the family, selling newspapers before and after classes at the local yeshiva. Hawking papers was a competitive field, if portrayals of young men shouting on street corners in movies are to be believed, that kept one abreast of current affairs. At 15, Sarnoff sought work on the cutting edge of news and communications, landing a job at Marconi Wireless Telegraph Company of America in 1906.

The company's owner, Gugielmo Giovanni Maria Marconi, succeeded in sending an electric spark a mile through the air by means of radio waves in the foothills of the Apennine Mountains just above Bologna, Italy, in the summer of 1895. Through his mother's connections – Annie Fenwick Jameson Marconi was the Irish granddaughter of the founder of Jameson Whiskey - he was able to demonstrate his invention to the British Royal Navy a year later. This demonstration led to considerable investment in the in the concept of wireless telegraphy. Two years later, he had enough money to build a huge tower, 168 feet tall, on the Isle of Wight off England's southern coast. There, he set to work perfecting a system to send Morse Code messages in the form of electric sparks over radio waves at ever greater and greater distances. In late 1899, Marconi successfully sent a series of coded sparks from a ship 65 miles out at sea to his radio tower on the Isle of Wight. Soon after, the technology was installed on nearly every ocean-going vessel in the world, and Marconi had a multinational corporation on his hands.

In 1906, David Sarnoff was hired as an office boy at the new Marconi Company's American branch. He quickly rose through the ranks; by the time he turned 19, he was the office manager of the wireless station situated on the top floor of the John Wanamaker Department Store on Broadway, between Eighth and Ninth Streets in Lower Manhattan.

Just before midnight on Sunday, April 13, 1912, some 400 miles south of Newfoundland in the North Atlantic, the RMS Titanic hit an iceberg and began to sink. Using their wireless telegraph, crew members sent out a message for help, which brought other ships to their location. As the sun rose on Monday, the last survivors were being plucked from the icy waters. Sarnoff's operation, along with every other wireless station on the East Coast, went into high alert.

For three straight days, Sarnoff supervised his crew working the machines, catching cat naps in his office, troubleshooting crisis as they arose. On Thursday, word came that an operator was needed at the Coney Island station at the entrance to New York Harbor as the ship carrying the survivors of the disaster approached. A hail of messages would be transmitted in a very short span of time and Sarnoff, who had mostly been overseeing operations, had the freshest fingers. He was taken to a hotel, given a Turkish Bath and a massage, and rushed to Coney Island's Sea Gate Station where took control of the key.

A throng of 40,000 people welcomed the ship as it docked at 9:30 p.m. Sarnoff's spot, right at the focal point of information about the survivors of the tragedy, made him a household name. He was soon being called 'The Boy Wonder of Radio.' Afterwards, he was given control of the station at the top of the Woolworth building - the tallest structure in the world at the time - and put in charge of procuring new technology for the company. It was a task he would execute with ferocious energy for the rest of his life.

Marconi Wireless Telegraph Company of America was a wholly owned subsidiary of the British Marconi Company. This setup did not please the United States Navy. At the end of World War One in 1918, the Navy began to rely on updated Transmitters, made in America by General Electric, then sold to an overseas company, then resold back to them. So, the Navy arranged for General Electric to buy American Marconi and make it its own wholly owned subsidiary. The new company was named Radio Corporation of America, and was known simply as RCA.

Four years later, Sarnoff convinced his superiors to invest in the growing trend of mass radio broadcasting. By this time the dots and dashes of Morse Code had evolved into voice and music. Sarnoff saw the new development as an opportunity for the company to go nationwide. A single broadcast could reach an audience that stretched from one coast to the other, all of them equipped with receivers - which

RCA also happened to manufacture. RCA went on the air in December of 1923, with two radio stations that would eventually become the NBC network by November of 1926. Five years later, Sarnoff hired another emigre from Russia, Vladimir K. Zworykin, and set to work on television.

Electric Television

Zworykin and Sarnoff were about the same age, but Zworykin hadn't left Russia until the revolution in 1918. He'd attended the Saint Petersburg State Institute of Technology, where he befriended a professor, Boris Rosing, who also taught at the Konstantinovsky Artillery School across Zabalkansky Avenue from the Institute. Rosing had a lab in the Artillery School and he gave Zworykin a job there, making vacuum tubes to allow one to "see over a distance."

The Imperial Russian Artillery service was rather keen on the possibilities of radio-transmitted motion pictures at the turn of the century. Another Professor, Constantin Perskyi, from Mikhailovskaya Artillery Military Academy, another artillery school across town, travelled to Paris for the Fifth International Electrotechnical Congress in 1900. There he presented his numbers on the speed of rotation needed for a Nipkow Disc. The Congress, held in conjunction with the Exposition Universelle that year was witness to Perskyi's discussion of *Television au moyen de l'electricity*. It was the first recorded public use of the word *television*.

On May 9th, 1911, Zworykin was in the lab when Rosing's efforts at last bore fruit. Four distinct bands were illuminated in a tube. In his biography, *Zworykin, Pioneer of Television*, Albert Abramson described the work Zworykin did for Rosing. "He had to master the techniques of making and blowing the glass bulbs, inserting the various anodes into the envelopes, and distilling the potassium or other photo-electric substance in just the exact amounts. Layers that were too thick or too thin produced inferior tubes."

Once in America, Zworykin applied for a patent in 1929 for an electrical television system based on a cathode-ray tube, which he named a Kinescope. Two years later, RCA had a working model. A transmitter was placed at the top of the Empire State Building, rigged up to one of Jenkins' scanning disks, which had its lens pointing at a test pattern. During the first six months of 1932, RCA engineers travelled the entirety of the New York City metropolitan area with Zworykin's receiver tube and executed a propagation study - a study of radio waves and how they behave in the atmosphere, by analyzing the image received from the transmitter on the Kinescope. A couple of years on, Zworykin produced the Iconoscope to replace the spinning disk and the test continued. By the end of the decade, RCA had a system ready to sell to the public. It was unveiled at the New York World's Fair in April of 1939.

The weekly industry magazine *Broadcasting* covered the fair's opening ceremonies in an article with the headline:

"Television Motif Marks New York Fair." The story followed: "The exposition's opening on April 30 also marked the advent of the country's first regular schedule of high-definition television broadcast." To carry the event live, RCA built two 26-foot-long buses on Mack truck chassis, and polished them up with an Art Deco design, which was all the rage in that era. One bus was for cameras, a switcher, and a 10-man crew. The other was for the 177-megawatt transmitter, with an antenna mounted on the back. President Franklin D. Roosevelt spoke at the opening ceremony, becoming the first president to be broadcast live on television. RCA's pavilion, a 9,000-square-foot building designed to look like Zworykin's tube when seen from above, afforded the public a tour of the whole process of television production. In his remarks at that pavilion's dedication, 10 days before the fair opened, Sarnoff announced that television receivers would be going on sale that very day in stores across New York City.

There was only one problem. The whole thing - the trucks, the cameras, the pavilion, and even the television receivers - was a patent infringement.

For 10 years, Sarnoff (who became RCA president in 1930) and Farnsworth fought a seemingly never-ending legal battle over the patents for the electrical television system. It was only when Farnsworth's lawyers found Justin Tolman, the chemistry teacher who'd sketched out on paper what his student had drawn on the chalkboard years before; and then brought him into a court room to present that piece of paper in person, that finally Farnsworth's priority over Zworykin was guaranteed. But the "Boy Wonder of Radio" introduced electrical television to the world anyway, at the biggest stage attainable at that time, the New York World's Fair. It finally brought Farnsworth to the table.

It took all summer, but by September, Sarnoff agreed to pay Farnsworth a million dollars for rights to his main patents, plus royalties on every television set sold for the remaining seven years of Farnsworth's priority. Unfortunately for Farnsworth, Germany had invaded Poland on Friday, September 1, 1939, beginning World War Two.

Though the United States was not involved in the early part of the war, the beginning of hostilities did curtail the spread of television technology. Certainly, by the spring of 1941, Sarnoff and RCA had other things on their minds, if reporting in the March 24 issue of *Broadcasting* about hearings before the six-year-old Federal Communication Commission on the advent of a national commercial television system are any indication. The article read, in part, "P. J. Hennessey Jr. NBC-RCA counsel, proposed no changes in technical standards recommended by the National Television System Committee (NTSC) and offered no technical testimony. It caused such consternation that Chairman Fly immediately called a ten-minute recess that lasted nearly a half-hour."

Radar research concerned shortwave radio transmission, just as television did, and lend/lease was introduced in the same month as that hearing. There is no question factory floors were being retooled.

Eight-and-a-half months later, on Sunday, December7, 1941, the Imperial Japanese Navy Air Service attacked Pearl Harbor in the U.S. territory of Hawaii. President Franklin D. Roosevelt's six-minute *Day of Infamy* address, just after noon on Monday to a joint session of Congress, was broadcast live to the largest radio audience in American history. One half-hour later, the United States Congress declared war on Japan. On Thursday, December 11 at 3 p.m. Berlin time - that time slot for the speech was chosen because it would be 10 p.m. in Tokyo and 8 a.m. in Washington, D.C., so both nations' leaders could hear him live on the radio on the same day - Adolph Hitler delivered a nearly 90-minute rambling diatribe filled with paranoia and grievance from perceived slights to the Teutonic past of the Fatherland. Then he ticked through an exaggerated list of German successes on the battlefield meant to right those wrongs, though he neglected to mention the enormous reversal the Wehrmacht had experienced during the previous seven days on the frozen steppe of the Moscow Oblast. In the final half-hour of the speech, Hitler declared war on the United States. The U.S. Congress reciprocated two-and-a-half hours later. All eight industrialized nations of the world were now in a state of war ... one which eventually involved a total of 30 countries.

By April of 1942, the United States' new industry of manufacturing cathode ray tubes for use in televisions halted altogether.

For more than four years, television was dormant. Farnsworth's patents were up in 1947, just as postwar demand for television was starting to pick up. Television's rapid advance left Farnsworth behind. The days of the lone inventor, such as Edison and Jenkins, were over. Going forward, corporations would establish labs and hire engineers to think up new patent ideas.

On April 7, 1947, at the Society's 61st Conference in Chicago, Society President Loren L. Ryder delivered his opening remarks, stating about television: "The Society is not now and does not contemplate overlapping in the activities of other societies in the fields of radio and radio transmission." That declaration would soon change. In a report by the Society's Progress Committee, published two years later in the *Journal*, it was asserted, "Any review of progress within the motion picture industry during 1948 must take into account the much greater progress of television throughout that period. The phenomenal rise of the new medium of entertainment is a social change." Further, the report states, "The year was marked by a series of dire predictions as to the closing of thousands of motion picture theaters."

The pace at which the new technology was adopted by the post war American public was breathtaking, an early example of the exponential growth curve. So, somewhat reluctantly, it would seem, on Wednesday, April 6, 1949, speaking at the Hotel Statler in New York City at the Society's 65th Conference, Society President Earl I. Sponable - early pioneer in sound in film, having built the first motion-picture studio for sound for 20th Century Fox in 1926 - announced as he ended his talk, "We are concerned with television whether we all like it or not." Further, he said, that while the development of the new technology was firmly in the wheelhouse of radio engineers, "there is, never-the-less, a very large area of common interest in the two fields," and "(w)e have, therefore, much incentive to offer to the television engineer to join us."

The next conference was in Hollywood, back at the Roosevelt. On Thursday, October 13, a Field Trip to Mount Wilson was planned for 2 p.m., featuring the presentation *Television Transmitters and 100-inch Telescope*, followed by the inaugural *Television Session*, to be held in Carnegie Assembly Hall inside Mount Wilson Observatory. Three months later, the inaugural issue of the *Journal of the Society of Motion Picture and Television Engineers* was published.

The number of television sessions at Society conferences increased from there, peaking with the 83rd and 84th, themed *Films for Television*, and *Films and Television in Industry and*

Education. The conferences had five and six sessions on television, respectively. Those were the last conferences planned before Sputnik I, the Soviet Union's first artificial satellite, appeared overhead in low-earth orbit.

The space race required an abundance of image gathering technology. The National Aeronautics and Space Administration (NASA) required cameras for lift-off, splashdown, surveying the moon and tracking objects in space. NASA required cameras in satellites to look down on Earth to see cloud distribution and type. It needed cameras to capture human reaction to various stress test. It needed high-speed image-capture and low-scan image-capture. And it needed this stuff now, it needed to be good, and it needed to be standardized. Of course, the image-gathering technology everyone was chasing was the ability to capture and transmit live what was going on inside the Command Module.

Monday afternoon, on September 28, 1964, at the Society's 96th conference in New York, J. L. Lowrance and Paul Zucchino, from RCA's Astro-Electronics Division, presented a paper on the company's design of a seven-inch-long, three-and-three-quarters-inch tall, and three-inch-wide video camera, weighing four-and-half-pounds without a lens, that could withstand the abuse of being hurled into outer space atop an Atlas rocket. The paper, published in the February issue of the Society's *Journal*, began with the words, "The Apollo mission to the moon will be covered by television."

Color Television

At about the same time, research was landing on the desks of the three network bosses. This research was going to cause serious disruption in the television industry and force the Society to the forefront in directing standardization in that field in the future.

The headline in the third column on page 32 of the March 1, 1965 issue of *Broadcasting* read, "Pay-off for NBC color next fall?" The story followed: "NBC researchers estimate that next season color alone will give NBC-TV and its advertisers the equivalent of a 1.4 rating-point advantage over the other networks in terms of average audience." A 1.4 rating-point advantage translated to a huge financial payoff for the network. The numbers that NBC researchers came up with were based on the preliminary results of a study done in November 1964 by the American Research Bureau. Underwritten by all three networks, the study compared the viewing habits of 4,600 color TV households to 4,600 monochrome TV households. The study also noted that 14 of the 15 highest-rated shows were aired in color.

David Sarnoff had turned 74 years old a couple of days before that article broke. He was RCA's chief executive officer by that time; his son, Robert, was president. RCA was becoming a dynasty, the House of Sarnoff. Everyone addressed the old man as "General" because he'd received a brigadier general's single star during World War II. In his lifetime, he'd seen radio pictures go from a schematic diagram all the way out into outer space. Still, with the Space Age dawning all around him, most of the network's programing - a majority of which was shot in color and therefore had higher production costs = was being watched on black-and-white television sets across the America, because no one could agree on how and when to execute the transition to full color. Most of the U.S. color sets, about three million at the start of 1965, were made by RCA, but demand for those was dampened because almost half of all programing was in monochrome. By the summer of 1965, CBS was producing half of its programming in color; while ABC was only running a third of its shows in color. Sarnoff had had enough. He had the research to prove color TV was a money-making proposition. He didn't need congressional approval or an agreed-upon set of standards. The market had spoken, so he pulled the trigger and unilaterally went full color at the beginning of the 1965 fall TV season.

The impact this decision had on local broadcast stations all over the United States was illustrated in a quotation from the June 1965 issue of *Broadcast Management/Engineering* (hereafter called *BM/E*) An article headlined, "COLOR TV on the Local Scene" showed a boxed-off section of text posing the question, "Are Local Stations Ready for Color?" It read, in part: "To find out, BM/E made inquiries across the country. We learned that most stations are not yet equipped to originate live studio and remote programs [in color]. Most stations cannot, at present, tape color network shows for rebroadcast. Some stations still can't even transmit commercial spots and movies in color." To say that Sarnoff's sweeping decision caught most of the country off-guard is an understatement.

In October 1965, the Society held their 98th conference in Montreal, Quebec. Canada had scheduled its official launch of color television for September 1966, so the conference had been planned to address the issues of color television and television in general. As such, there were sessions on television every day. One of the 36 papers presented was by Canadian Broadcasting Corporation's P. Corio, who was at that time working on mobile transmission units.

The next two conferences had only two TV sessions each; all told, five papers were presented, and a single panel discussion was held, on the impending color transition. One of the papers, *Color Fidelity in TV Camera Systems*, was by General Electric's Joseph F. Wiggin.

Both Corio and Wiggin then appeared on a list of presenters in the December *Journal*. In the section *Education Industry News*, a "Color Television Broadcasting Conference and Workshop" was announced, which began with "The Detroit, Chicago, Rochester and Toronto Sections of the SMPTE, in cooperation with the University of Michigan Extension Service, will hold a joint two-day conference on

Color Television Broadcasting in Detroit, January 27-28." Though the conference was announced only a month in advance, 600 people signed up to attend.

The workshop's topic chairman was 37-year-old Frederick Remley Jr. He was born in Washington, Pennsylvania in 1929, and enrolled in the University of Michigan in 1948. He earned a physics degree in 1951; three years later he was the chief engineer of the university's first television production center on the Ann Arbor campus. He stayed at UM for the next 42 years, overseeing, amongst other things, construction of all the university's radio transmitting facilities, including a television station in Flint, as well as three FM radio stations and the University Hospital's color television system, being used for medical procedures.

The workshop was to be held at the Horace H. Rackham Educational Memorial Building, just north of downtown Detroit, in the city's art center. The Rackham was home to the headquarters of the Engineering Society of Detroit and the University of Michigan Extension Service. Built in 1937, the building's late-Art Deco style, representing that prewar celebration of technological advancement which was in vogue at the time, makes for an imposing sight. Upon approach, one sees four columns separating five bronze double doors at the main entrance, drawing the eye to the crown of the building where four reliefs are carved into the Indiana limestone in an interpretation of Aztec style. Representing

education, sciences, engineering, and structural steel workers, the reliefs lend the building an austere air of rigor and
precision mixed with a primitive exclamation of wonder and
awe.

On the morning of Thursday, January 26, 1967, the
day before the workshop, an unexpected snowfall began in
Chicago. It didn't stop for more than 24 hours. As the storm
headed east, it dropped more than two feet of snow on the
ground in some places, leaving towns paralyzed and people
stranded on roadways in Illinois, Michigan and Canada. This
storm went down in history as the worst blizzard to ever hit
the Midwest. Reminiscing a quarter-century later, Remley
described the 35-mile drive from Ann Arbor into Detroit on
the cold Thursday night as "really harrowing!" Furthermore,
he related, "Ice and snow made it a miserable experience.
Travel into Detroit by air, rail, and car was difficult at best,
and impossible for some registrants." Joseph Wiggin, in fact,
was one of the presenters who couldn't make it in; P. Corio,
from the Canadian Broadcasting Corporation, did.

One can imagine the scene at daybreak on Friday morning as 368 attendees, who'd braved snowdrifts and icy roads
travelling the day before, walked south along Woodward
Avenue from their warm Park Shelton Hotel accommodations. To the left, they observed Rodin's well-known statue
of "The Thinker," perpetually hunched over, his chin on
his hand, in front of the Detroit Institute of Arts. Then the

intimidating limestone block of the Rackham Building came in view, its soaring piers and Aztec reliefs proclaiming that naïve reverence in modern industry that was so prevalent in the late Thirties.

It was only 15 degrees Fahrenheit outside; the engineers were trudging along through a foot of snow and still the stuff fell from the sky. They must have wondered: "All of this for color television?" Yet the effort these broadcast engineers made to get to the Rackham Educational Memorial Building that morning to learn the latest in best practices for standardized color television illustrates the magnitude of what was at stake in the industry that day.

The workshop was such a success that another was planned for the following year. A total of 400 showed up for that one. Then, in June of 1968, the Society permanently established the conference on its calendar, renaming it the SMPTE Winter Television Conference. The first to officially bear that name was held in Toronto, Ontario, in recognition of the efforts of the Canadian Broadcasting Corporation at the inaugural event - 500 attendees were expected. The next three assemblages were in Atlanta, San Francisco and Dallas, respectively. A mere 200 people showed up in Dallas in early February 1972. How many conferees went to the Seventh Annual Winter Television Conference held on Key Biscayne in 1973 is unknown. There was no summary report about the conference published afterward - one of the few times that would happen. It can be surmised, however, that the attendance at the seventh conference did not exceed the sixth.

A pre-conference announcement, published in the December *Journal*, listed the films scheduled to be shown at the start of each of the three sessions. Friday morning's film was *Kite Flying*, Friday afternoon's offering was *Destination the Beach*, and the final session on Saturday would open with a film called *Serpent's Gift*. There was no way the general manager of a broadcast TV station was going to pay for two nights at the pricey Sonesta Beach Hotel just so the station's chief engineer could watch *Destination the Beach*.

There were no pressing issues facing the television industry that January, but the wheels had started to move again and were, in fact, about to pick up considerable speed. Once again, the Society's Winter Television Conference would bear witness to the unselfish exchange of views concerning individual investigation to solve an urgent crisis, to *"wisely direct the standardization, to secure best standards of equipment, quality, performance, nomenclature, and, unconsciously, perhaps, a code of ethics."*

THE DIGITAL REVOLUTION

MONDAY, MARCH 26, 1973

Sheraton Park

On Monday morning, March 26, 1973, Senator Samuel Ervin Jr., a Democrat from North Carolina, left his home and headed to the Sheraton-Park Hotel in northwest Washington, D.C. The 76-year-old World War 1 veteran who'd earned two Purple Hearts before attending Harvard Law School was marking his 19th year in the Senate. A month before, he'd been assigned the Chairmanship of the Senate Select Committee to Investigate Campaign Practices, which would go down in history, simply, as the Senate Watergate Committee. He had been given this responsibility because it was common knowledge he wasn't going to run again in 1974, when his third term in office would be up, so he wouldn't be bothered to maintain a good image. Right before the assignment, he'd put the final touches on another project in which he'd been involved. It was called *"S.917 – A bill to protect the people's right to know by regulating the testimony of newsmen."*

The previous four years had been fraught times for some media companies critical of the Nixon Administration. One in particular, *The Washington Post*, owned the television station WJXT-TV, which broadcast out of Jacksonville, Florida. In September 1972, President Nixon had been taped in the Oval Office on his secret White House recording system referring to that station, saying "The main thing is the Post is going to have damnable, damnable problems out of this one. They have a television station ... and they're going to have to get it renewed." On that Monday morning in March, everyone in the television broadcasting industry was watching this license-renewal drama play out before their very eyes in the halls of the U.S. Capitol. There was concern among various television and radio station managers across the America - what precedent would the feud bring about? Ervin's bill, to protect the confidential sources of news reporters, would be a welcome assist from Congress in the ongoing imbroglio. So, on that day, Ervin set off to give a speech at the opening luncheon of the three-day convention of the one organization of motion-picture production professionals that had the pull and the power to stare down an American president: the National Association of Broadcasters, or more familiarly, the NAB.

Self-Regulation

Initially, the National Association of Broadcasters, unlike the Society of Motion Picture and Television Engineers, did not have a *Journal*; nor did it have a *Transactions* like the Institute of Radio Engineers (IRE). Because of this, the precise inception of the association is somewhat murky. In the April 3, 1972, issue of *Broadcasting*, on page 64, a small article headlined "NAB 50" outlines some basic facts concerning the association's first meeting. "Fifty years ago, a group of 23 pioneer broadcasters met at the Commodore hotel in New York for the first convention of the year-old National Association of Broadcasters ... on Oct. 11, 1923." Those elected to launch the new association at this meeting were Eugene F. McDonald Jr. as president, Frank W. Elliott, the organizer who was eventually elected to be the second president, in 1926. Also in attendance was one of two vice presidents, J. Elliott Jenkins.

The problem, obviously, is that October 1923 was 48 years and six months prior to April 1972. Why hadn't the March 26, 1973 meeting been considered the groups 50th gathering?

Some clues can be ascertained in the August 1923 issue of *Radio Broadcasting*. On page 271, There's a photograph of six men, the cutline below reads: "Some of those responsible for the National Association of Broadcasters." In the center of the photo is the distinguished visage of Eugene F. McDonald, of WJAZ, standing opposite Henry Ramsey of the Chicago Board of Trade. Gathered around those two are J. E. Jenkins and Thorne Donnelly of WDAP, Frank J. Elliot of WOC in Davenport Iowa, and a W. Johnson of WFV. The presence of a Chicago Board of Trade official places this early get-together in that city. Jenkins' and Donnelly's WDAP, by that time in the Drake Hotel on Michigan Avenue, would have provided the best accommodations for the Association's inaugural meeting.

Jenkins, though, was a member of an organization that had begun even earlier, the National Broadcasters' League, which had been set up on October 11, 1922, by George S. Walker of Western Radio Corporation, and Frederick A. Smith, publisher of *Radio Age* magazine, among several others. The April 1926 *Radio Age* issue featured a letter Frank Elliot, then NAB president, had written, congratulating the magazine on its fifth anniversary. It read, in part, "The National Association of Broadcasters is the outgrowth of two or three [nebulous even then] associations, formed in different parts of the country, to get the broadcasting interest into one unit." This indicates the connection of several groups in 1922 which coalesced at the Drake in early 1923 to establish the NAB. What was the catalyst that brought about the unification of these groups?

On November 15th, 1922, radio station KYW, one of the first in the United States to broadcast music, had to cancel a show when the copyright holder for Puccini's *La Boheme* refused to allow the station to transmit the performance. This put the handful of radio broadcasters operating at the time in a bit of a pickle. In the December *Radio Age*, Frederick Smith wrote an editorial asking, "Will the author of the 'bedtime time story' arise to demand his fee?" The answer appeared, as the new year began, to be "Yes."

The American representative of the copyright holder of Puccini's, *La Boheme,* was, in 1922, the American Society of Composers, Authors and Publishers (ASCAP). This organization, with its copyright challenge to radio broadcast profit margins, would continue to vex the NAB for the next half-century.

There were other problems that needed tackling in 1923. The growth in radio transmitting sites for broadcasting had grown so fast in the early Twenties that the United States Department of Commerce, which in those days, regulated radio licenses, was forced to go from three-letter designations to four. The crisis was so immediate and disruptive, Secretary of Commerce Herbert Hoover convened the first federally sponsored radio conference in February of 1922. One outcome of that assembly was the creation of a finite number of stations operating at a higher wattage and on a different wavelength. Separated in the ether from other broadcasters around them, these "Class B" stations' signals could go further with no interference. One caveat: they couldn't play phonograph records - performances had to be live - and they could transmit for only a couple of hours within a 24-hour period. KYW was just such a station, so calling a halt to a live operatic performance was a serious threat to the station's future. The creation of an aristocracy of the airwaves, however, tended to cause division among the operators. The formation of the NAB was intended to heal those divisions and get everyone on one game plan.

By 1925, the handsome visage opposite the Chicago Board of Trade's representative in the aforementioned photograph was on an expedition to the Artic establishing radio communications from Etah, Greenland. Using the latest in short-wave radio technology, McDonald succeeded in communicating back and forth, hosting a concert of Inuit music and doing business with his company, Zenith, which was 1,000 miles away in Chicago. Zenith had manufactured a mobile transmitter and various staffers had been driving around Chicagoland testing transmission sites and giving public demonstrations of the promising new technology. In the process, McDonald's engineers had figured out the ideal location for a new transmission tower for his station, WJAZ, 22 miles northwest of Chicago in the town of Mount Prospect. By the time McDonald got back home, the station was ready to go on the air.

On Saturday, December 19, 1925, WJAZ started broadcasting nationwide on a frequency the Department of Commerce had promised to Canada. In the resulting lawsuit, *United States v. Zenith Radio Corporation*, it was alleged that the station had violated the 1912 Radio Act when it

"used and operated certain apparatus for radio communication, as a means of commercial intercourse among several
states of the United States, to wit, from Mount Prospect, Ill.,
to Seattle, Wash,; which apparatus was so used and operated
not under and in accordance with a license such as described
in the act; and that defendant McDonald aided, abetted, and
procured the commission of the offense."

Suddenly, the NAB started to push back.

Turns out, the Radio Act of 1912 didn't, in fact, allow
Secretary of Commerce Herbert Hoover to regulate radio
operations that way. Federal Judge James Herbert Wilkerson,
Northern District of Illinois, ruled that "administrative rul-
ings cannot add to the terms of an act of Congress and make
conduct criminal which such laws leave untouched."

This forced Congress to act. The next year, the *Radio Act
of 1927* was signed by President Calvin Coolidge. The Act
provided for a commission to be formed to handle radio issues, one that would be independent, acting apart from the
White House and the Department of Commerce. It was
stipulated that the commission would be in force for only
one year, a limitation that may have been the impetus needed to get Hoover on board. At any rate, the Federal Radio
Commission (FRC) held its first meeting on Tuesday, March
15, 1927.

Organizing the AM radio spectrum was going to take
longer than one year, so the commission timeline was

extended. Hoover was elected President in 1928; he aimed to move broadcasting regulation back into the Department of Commerce but, as so often happened in the development of broadcasting technology, historical events intervened.

Monopoly

Film and radio weren't the only things experiencing spectacular growth during the Roaring Twenties. When Warren Gamaliel Harding was sworn in as the 29th president of the United States on March 4, 1921, promising a "return to normalcy," no one could have predicted cigarettes, speakeasys, or the Thompson submachine gun (also known as a "Chicago Typewriter" or a "Tommy Gun) would dominate certain sects of society. That was the new normal, though, along with aviation, automobiles and electrical appliances. Consumer demand for these new marvels of modern manufacturing went through the roof. The sons and daughters of the American Heartland rose from their parents' dinner tables and headed into the great cities to take jobs in the factories, mills, and assembly plants to meet that demand. After working a twelve-hour day, this group would fill a flask with illegal liquor and hit the dance halls and speakeasys for a few hours to enjoy the new high-energy dance craze, called the Charleston, which went well with the soundtrack of the era, Jazz.

They also got into investing in the stock market, not because they had expendable money lying around, but because fortunes were being made and they wanted in the game. So, they borrowed the money. Credit was easy. Everyone had to borrow money to buy the new cars, the new ovens, and the new refrigerators: why not borrow money to buy the stock certificates? No one envisioned that the good times might come to an end. They'd just witnessed the conclusion to the War to End All Wars and a worldwide pandemic. What else could possibly go wrong?

Herbert Hoover was inaugurated in March of 1929; three weeks later, the stock market suffered a minor crash. It was stopped two days later only when banker Charles Mitchell, president of National City Bank (now Citibank) put up $25 million in credit. Immediately the frenetic pace of the boom began apace.

In late September 1929, Clarence Hatry, an English financier and promoter, was caught using two sets of the same bonds his brokerage had issued to a municipality as collateral at two banks, trying to get two separate loans. He was seriously short of cash because the photobooth company he'd started, Photomaton Parent Corporation, in which he'd coerced London's upper-crust investors to buy into, had been up and running for about a year and, despite hundreds of locations around the United Kingdom, hadn't done the business he'd anticipated. On September 20, he declared bankruptcy. And on that very day the London Stock Market began a descent of its own.

The Hatry affair shook the confidence of American investors. In the next month, the U.S. market began to display what is known in the business as *volatility*, described as an occurrence when large sell-offs are followed by investors going on short buying sprees, only to see the bottom fall out again and selling continue - all on the same day. As the month went on, this uncertainty jangled everyone's nerves and lead to a further loss of confidence in the market. Things started getting bad on Thursday, October 24, and then, five days later, $14 billion in market value just vanished from the books. The Great Depression had begun.

The resultant economic downturn had an adverse effect on advertising in newspapers, magazines, billboards and even on the sides of buses. Meanwhile, radio advertising had increased a whopping 89 percent and it showed no signs of slowing down. Allegations of a radio monopoly in advertising started flying and newspaper publishers began to lobby Congress to follow the European model of broadcasting, specifically the United Kingdom's BBC and Germany's Reichs-Rundfunk-Gesellschaft (RRG), both of which were state-run and devoid of any advertising. The RRG in particular was even more attractive to newspaper publishers because it didn't allow news reporting to be sent out over the ether. This squared well with two other powerful groups, the National Committee on Education by Radio, and the National Advisory Council on Radio in Education, both well-funded and both eager for Congress to legislate into existence huge 50,000-watt clear channel radio transmitters, strategically located around the U.S., for educational institutions and governmental agencies.

At noon on Monday, October 26, 1931, President Herbert Hoover addressed the ninth annual NAB convention, held this time in Detroit, using a microphone that had been installed in the White House. He was able to do this through a network of telegraph wires spanning the Midwest, linking him to Detroit's Hotel Statler, a little more than a mile south of the site where the Rackham Building would be built six years hence. The speech was also broadcast over the brand-new radio networks NBC and CBS, to every radio in America. According to the inaugural issue of the weekly magazine *Broadcasting*, the NAB had not been doing well for the last few years. An editorial on page 18 revealed that the convention came about at the agency of "Philip G. Loucks, the association's capable young managing director who in less than a year lifted that organization from a state of desuetude to real aggressive activity and performance." *Desuetude* is an old Latin legal term describing inactivity or disuse.

Hoover began his speech by reminding everyone that he'd arranged the first few national conferences concerning radio in the early Twenties and had appreciated, even then, the work of the NAB in the early days of broadcasting. "The decisions reached at that early date," he continued, "have been of unending importance. The determination that radio channels were public property and should be controlled by the government; the determination that we should not have governmental broadcasting supported by a tax upon the listener, but that we should give license to use of those channels under private enterprise where there would be no restraint upon programs and excellence of service without cost to the listener. This decision has avoided the pitfalls of political and social conflicts in the use of speech over the radio which would have been involved in government broadcasting. It has preserved free speech to the country."

By recognizing the role of the NAB in establishing the first rules of broadcasting on a national level, then assigning a role as important as that of the defender of the First Amendment, Hoover had put the organization on par with the Radio Commission.

The NAB was about to emerge from the wilderness to take a leading role in self-regulating the broadcasting industry.

That Hoover had plucked the association from obscurity demonstrated just what was at stake in the power struggle playing out at that time. Hoover knew he had little chance of being reelected in 1932. He'd declared himself a Republican back in 1920 because he knew that after the Woodrow Wilson's presidency the Democrats were certain to lose. A shrewd political observer, he sought a private partner to stand up to Congress and the never-ending Radio Commission.

Franklin Delano Roosevelt was sworn in as President on March 4, 1933. He wasted no time setting up an interdepartmental committee to study electronic communications. Its recommendations were passed on to the legislative branch in February of 1934. The resulting Act of Congress was drafted by Representative Samuel Rayburn, a Democrat from Texas, and Senator Clarence Dill, a Democrat from Washington. It was passed and signed into law 15 months into the new administration. The *Communications Act of 1934* created a new independent agency which over saw all electronic communication, including radio, telephone, and a cherub named 'television.' When the act passed it made the commission of 1927, the FRC, a permanent entity which became the lead authority over the new agency, The Federal Communications Commission. Unlike the Commerce Department run by an appointed secretary, the FCC was to be run by a committee of appointees each serving five-year terms. No more than three appointees could belong to the same political party or have any financial interest in business that involved the agency.

The Communications Act of 1934 was the law of the land for the next four generations: Silent, Boomer, X, and Millennial. The National Television System Committee (NTSC) operated under the auspices of the FCC. It wasn't until 1996 that a new act was drafted, once again during a time period of significant change, change that was quickly eroding film's preeminence in image acquisition.

On Monday, September 17, 1934, at the first NAB convention after the Communications Act went into effect, Senator Dill addressed the opening session at Cincinnati's downtown Netherland Hotel. The title of his speech, announced in the preceding issue of *Broadcasting*, was *News by Radio*.

Broadcasters were in a tight spot that fall. Newspaper publishers had forced two news agencies, United Press International (UPI) and the Associated Press (AP), both of which depended on newspapers for most of their income, to allow only very short periods of time to broadcasting news. It was also dictated that no spot news and no sponsorship of news would occur. The next issue of *Broadcasting* featured a photograph of Dill at the podium, at the top of page nine, smack-dab in the center. Above this photo, the headline read "MINCES NO WORDS." In his speech Dill declared, "Either the press associations must change the terms of the agreement so radio stations can give their listeners up-to-the-minute news and for longer periods of time, or radio stations will find or create means and methods for securing news entirely independent of the press associations. This is not only their full right. It is their duty. It is a part of that public service which they are bound to give if they are to justify the use of the radio frequencies the government has granted them." By the time he finished that pronouncement, the audience was on its feet cheering and clapping.

Since broadcasting was thus endowed with the responsibility to deliver the immediate news by any means necessary, Dill's speech (like Hoover's three years earlier) to the NAB members ennobled the association as the main liaison between the government and the private interest of broadcasting.

ASCAP, radio stations' class divisions, news production, advertising and the FCC – and, before long, television – all these and a myriad of other issues continued to challenge those interests and the NAB.

In the Spring of 1973, 39 years later, broadcasters still had a lot on their plates. Cigarette advertising had been banned from the airwaves two years before, a proliferation of sex talk radio had materialized and was in serious need of self-regulation, and just two weeks before that year's annual NAB convention began, the Nixon Administration introduced a license-renewal bill to Congress to, in the words of Clay T. Whitehead, director of the White House Office of Telecommunications Policy, "guard against 'elitist gossip' and 'ideological plugola'." These were just a few of the concerns facing the NAB that Monday morning as Senator Ervin arrived to speak about *S.917*, the bill to protect news reporters from having to reveal their sources. Before Ervin even took the stage, though, rumblings had begun among attendees about something else at the convention, something that was about to steal all the attention for the rest of the week.

The Show

At the 1934 convention, there were no broadcast equipment exhibits or demonstrations. There had been, however, a single small announcement at the bottom of the back cover of the preceding *Broadcasting*. It read: "NAB MEMBERS, While in Cincinnati see the RCA equipment at the World's Famous Station, WLW." At the next convention, held in July 1935 in Colorado Springs, there were four press services plus equipment manufacturers, including RCA Victor, Graybar-Western Electric, World Broadcasting System, and others, each showcasing their wares. From that time on, the number of exhibitors only increased. Even in the depths of World War II, when the NAB refused to participate in the exhibit process, manufactures still showed up, displaying their machines' newest iterations. At the first postwar convention in 1946, the NAB officially reinstituted exhibits and established an engineering program to run concurrently with the other programs.

There had been some big announcements about breakthroughs made at the exhibits through the years. In 1956, Ampex introduced videotape; in 1967, RCA introduced its new color camera; in 1969, RCA showed the cartridge tape machine, which was easier to operate than the clunky reel-to-reel tape machine. But in March of 1973, a black box was put on display that would change everything.

There were 154 exhibitors filling four large halls on hand that week. The NAB convention itself was spread out among a group of hotels in northwest Washington, D.C. To get from one locale to another, one had to get on a shuttle bus and ride there. The equipment show was spread out in two different hotels, the Sheraton-Park and Omni Shoreham. But the black box that was going to change the world couldn't be found on any of the four main show room floors. Instead, as described in the ensuing issue of *Broadcasting*, it was "to be found in an obscure suite somewhere in the most outlying region of the sprawling Sheraton Park." In the May *BM/E* issue, the location of the display was more specific: "to see it, you had to go to Suite K708." The article then describes getting there. "The K-wing in the Sheraton Park is not the easiest place to find, but soon all one had to do was follow the crowd. Word spread quickly – 'it's revolutionary,' 'mind boggling,' 'biggest thing since the introduction of the VTR [videotape recorder] itself'."

The black box was officially called the CVS-500 Time Base Corrector. 'CVS' stood for Consolidated Video Systems, a small startup company from the incubator of small startups, Northern California's Santa Clara Valley, which at that date was increasingly being referred to by the sobriquet 'Silicon Valley.' The CVS labs, at 3300 Edward Ave., Santa Clara, were 12 miles south of the garage where Hewlett-Packer got its start and 16 miles south of Ampex's headquarters in Redwood City.

The company's president was William B. Hendershot. He'd spent a couple of years working on an idea he called

'High-Speed Thermal Duplication of Videotape.' He'd presented a paper on his findings at the 111th Semiannual Society Conference held in May 1972 at New York City's Hilton Hotel.

Unfortunately, he had been late to register for exhibit space at the NAB Show at the Sheraton-Park and was forced to unveil his company's new invention up in his room, K708, far away from the action on the main exhibit floors. To get folks to drop in and examine the CVS-500 Time Base Corrector, he printed invitations describing what he'd brought. They read: "A Digitalized Video Signal Corrector that will enable reproduction of broadcast quality signals from relatively inexpensive helical videotape recorders."

Tape to tape editing, no matter what tape you were using, it was Jenkins' Holy Grail - standardization.

The videotape recorder, or VTR as it was commonly referred to in the technical writings, was unveiled to the world on Sunday, April 15, 1956, at the Conrad Hilton in Chicago, on the eve of the NAB's 34th Convention. People were surprised when they discovered which company had accomplished this feat. *Broadcasting* ran a story, headlined "Little Ampex Steals Show from Electronics Giants." It had been expected that either RCA or the BBC would develop the VTR, so when Charles Ginsburg and his team, including a 23-year-old Ray Dolby, introduced a machine that could transfer a stream of electrons carrying the pictorial information of each one of the 525 lines of a monochrome television picture onto a thin plastic strip coated with magnetizable material, they were entering a crowded marketplace. Of the 70 machines the company sold that week, generating a cool $4,000,000 in orders, one went to RCA's labs in Camden, New Jersey.

It didn't take long for the engineers in Camden to reverse-engineer the thing and add color to the design. On August 15, 1957, RCA invited Ginsburg and Paul Flehr, Ampex's patent attorney, to visit its labs between Rutgers University and the Delaware River, across from Philadelphia, to witness a demonstration of the RCA color VTR. So impressed were Ampex engineers, they agreed to share patents with RCA for a mere $100,000.

In the subsequent technical report, published in the February/March 1958 Issue of *RCA Engineer*, Anthony H. Lind, manager of Audio and Mechanical Devices Engineering at the Camden labs, wrote a brief review of RCA's efforts at developing a VTR, "During a period of several years of research several methods of recording wideband electrical signals on magnetic tape were explored." What the RCA engineers learned from that research was combined with the reverse-engineered Ampex monochrome VTR, creating the world's first color VTR. The name they gave this new color recording product? The "Quadruplex System."

Albert Abramson, the Theodor Mommsen of television history, was not impressed. On page 81 of the second volume of his tome, *The History of Television, 1880 to 2000*, he wrote of Lind's patent claim, "... he was making a distinction that truly did not exist. It is strange that nowhere in the prior literature is there ever any mention of an RCA Simplex, Duplex, Triplex or Quintuplex recorder. So what did the term 'Quadruplex' mean? Where did it come from?" It didn't much matter. On Monday, April 28, 1958, when David Sarnoff Dedicated NBC's $1.5 million VTR operation in Burbank on the first day of NAB's 36th convention in Los Angeles and said Ampex was monochrome and the RCA 'Quadruplex' was color, the name stuck. RCA color videotape took on the name Quad in a couple of years to differentiate it from the monochrome Ampex system. After Sarnoff's color transition in 1967, all tape was color, so all two-inch-wide videotape became known as Quad.

Quad was the NTSC standard, the Committee having been empowered by the Act of 1934, thus was endowed with the power of the law. Hence, the format manufacturers achieved a monopoly over the industry for the next two decades.

The other kind of videotape was called Helical-Scan. It was introduced to America at the Society's 87th Biannual Technical Conference on Thursday, May 5, 1960, by Toshiba of Tokyo, Japan. Toshiba was in Minato City, Tokyo's port district, about six miles north of Ota City and its thousands of micro-factories. It's generally credited with having produced the first practical helical-scan VTR, though Ampex claimed to have a working model at the time. At any rate, helical-scan tape was recorded on while moving slowly by a single, rapidly spinning head set at a slight angle, creating a near horizontal line on the tape, whereas Quad moved faster by four slower-spinning heads, each going vertically across the tape or, as the engineers called it, transverse. With a slower speed and fewer heads, a user saved tape, space and, most important, money. But helical-scan didn't meet broadcast standards, so it wasn't used at any of the American television stations. Instead, it caught on among businesses and educators. That's how things remained throughout the Sixties: two parallel video recording worlds, condemned never to meet.

Dueling formats were not the only challenges facing video recording. It seemed, as time went on, that no two tape machines operated at the same speed. If one was duplicating a tape from quad to quad, or helical to helical, the slightly different pace of the tape speed from one machine to the other manifested itself in the image as waves near the top and bottom of the screen. The waves, called "flagging," or "skewing," were the bane of broadcast engineers the world over.

Now, however, all those glitches had been solved. Simply put, CVS's black box took a videotape machine's electrically generated signal, which carried the image information of the 525 lines of the standard NTSC TV picture, converted it into the binary 0s and 1s of digital language, then held this information in its memory before converting it back to an electrical signal at just the moment the recording head was starting its run across the tape. This digital "time out" allowed the slow-moving helical-scan tape to be duplicated onto the fast-moving two-inch Quad tape, eradicating the flagging and skewing caused by tape machines moving at different speeds.

The time-base corrector saved a substantial amount of money, but there was yet another way it affected the videotape format which aroused little discussion in any of the publications at the time: videotape could now be edited.

From the start, Quad could be edited. It took a razor blade, a microscope and a very highly paid professional a long time to do it, but it could be done. Helical-scan tape couldn't be edited at all. Well, it *could* be done, but it was challenging. The whole production had to be recorded in the order it would appear in the final cut before being dubbed tape-to-tape. Shooting the production in order was vital – otherwise, the sync on the source tape wouldn't match the record tape, and that dreaded flagging and skewing would appear.

Suddenly the CVS 500 Time Base Corrector, or TBC as it came to be known, changed all that. Material could be recorded in whatever order was necessary. Just like film exposed in a camera. It was a paradigm shift for videotape. An edit now happened digitally, at the speed of light, leaving the old mechanical film-editing process in the dust. Soon, Sergei Eisenstein's theory of montage, the ability to communicate ideas through the sequencing of images, executed at the speed of the imagination, was going to hit the streets of America, and every local news shooter, in every local news market, would have the new tool at their disposal.

IKEGAMI HL-33

WEDNESDAY, OCTOBER 17, 1973

The Rag Shop District

Sunday, October 14, 1973, was a beautiful 70-degree day in Boston. It was also very dry; it hadn't rained in a month, and a 40-mile-an-hour west wind was blowing, occasionally sending leaves and light debris swirling skyward. Conditions were perfect for a fire.

North of downtown, across Boston Harbor, in the city of Chelsea, the salvage district was deserted. Many of the structures in this neglected area, old weather-beaten wooden buildings, had been slated for demolition, and so only 300 people were living in the area. There were no workers in any of warehouses which made up the bulk of the remaining structures in what was the largest recycling hub on the Eastern Seaboard of the United States at that time. So, when the fire ignited that day, it had a considerable head start before anyone noticed. By the time the first firefighting apparatus arrived, not long after an alarm had been pulled at

3:56 p.m., the fire was really going. The first fire fighters on scene worked diligently and efficiently - as only that particular breed of humankind can - attaching one hose end from their fire engine to the nearest hydrant, then moving as close as they could to the fire with the other end from the engine. When they pulled the brass handle back on the nozzle of their hose the water pressure from the hydrant was so weak, most of the water blew back in their faces.

By that time, the inferno had jumped behind them, from embers that had blown across the street above. They had to fall back. Soon, a second crew joined the first, and the exercise was repeated, with the same results. The firefighters continued to fall back as warehouse after warehouse, each full of paper and oily rags, was engulfed in the rapidly expanding blaze. Ninety minutes later, firefighters were trying to keep their own station from being consumed, and every fire company in the Boston metropolitan region was onsite, struggling to get the conflagration under control. Hoses had to be run out for more than a mile to get to a supply source with stronger water pressure. It took 90 minutes, and a heroic stand in the broad front yard of a school building, before the fire was finally contained. It would take another three days to get the fire completely extinguished.

On the first day citizens were allowed back into the blackened wreckage of what locals referred to as the Rag Shop district, a 24-foot, six-inch recreational vehicle (RV), one of the ubiquitous Winnebago Indians on American roads then, rolled in along with the returning crowds. Proudly emblazoned on the RV's side was the logo of a television station, WCVB – TV. The 'C' stood for Channel, 'V' for the Roman Numeral five, and the 'B' for Boston. The station's channel number was shown in a uniquely stylized numeral 5, with an arrow circling inside, in a bright shade of red. The RV was parked in a spot from which the crew in it knew they could see the 52-story Prudential Tower in Boston's Back-Bay area, about four miles south-southwest of the salvage district. Two-crewman exited the van and climbed up on its roof, where they stood up and secured a round, four-foot-wide, parabolic dish antenna and pointed it in the direction of the tower. One man climbed back down, went inside the RV and contacted the station with a radio telephone, or Telco as it was known. Then he flipped on the power switch of a Microwave Associates 2.1-gigahertz (GHz) radio transmitter. Electronic News Gathering (ENG) had begun in Boston.

WCVB-TV

The 1973 Chelsea fire was, indisputably, a preventable manmade disaster. It was the second extreme firestorm in almost the exact same spot. It was fewer than 200 yards from where another major conflagration had erupted back in 1908. Piles of oily rags and paper were a high fire risk - that was no secret. Still, the fire fighters in that area didn't have the necessary tools to control such a dangerous situation. The main flaw hindering any success had been inadequate water pressure and the general disrepair of the water supply system. In hydrant inspections before the fire, it had been discovered that one in six hydrants in Chelsea was inoperable. The ground was practically at sea level and the pipes were disintegrating in precisely the place where pipes in good condition were most needed. It was a gross failure of civic leadership, and there was a considerable outrage throughout greater New England. If a television news operation wanted to prove its commitment to a local community, getting to the bottom of the Chelsea catastrophe would go a long way toward demonstrating it.

WCVB – TV was just the operation for the job.

The ABC-affiliate station, with its choice number-five channel position, had been on the air for only 19 months. It was owned by Boston Broadcasters Incorporated (BBI), a grass roots organization formed to bid on a broadcast TV station's license when that had spun into legal jeopardy. In this case, the license was held by the *Boston Herald-Traveller* newspaper, which owned WHDH – TV. The *Herald*, as locals called it, owned an AM radio station with the same call letters. It had gotten its TV broadcast license back in 1949 and went on the air in 1957. Unfortunately for them, Publisher Robert B. Choate, and the paper's lawyer were seen having lunch at the Statler Hotel in Washington, D.C. with

FCC Chairman George C. McConnaughey during a licensing renewal period.

Soon after, a House Subcommittee on Legislative Oversight found that another FCC commissioner, Richard A. Mack, had raked in $40,000 beyond his salary that year. In the ensuing investigation, Chairman McConnaughey admitted under oath that *Herald* publisher Choate had broached the subject of his broadcast license renewal during that lunch at the Hotel Statler. Choate was then called to testify; he refuted that account. While the *Boston Herald-Traveler* wasn't accused of any wrongdoing, lawyers for contenders to the license argued before the Circuit Court of Appeals that in assigning the license to an established newspaper and radio company, they were in fact going against the FCC's stated policy of diversity of ownership. So began the longest court battle in American history over a television station's license.

It took 15 years, but on March 19, 1972, at 3:05 am, WCVB replaced WHDH on the coveted channel 5 spot on the television dial and began to broadcast from a former International Harvester dealership next to Interstate 95, which had once been route 128, up on the heights west of the Charles River, in what was the Route 128 Tower Complex, nine miles southwest of downtown Boston.

BBI had gone a long way toward winning its license by promising to air more local programming than any other local station in the country, 50 hours a week. This, at a time when most TV stations didn't even stay on the air after midnight. It was a major undertaking. In the precious 7:30 to 8 p.m. time slot, locally produced content ran instead of *The Newlywed Game* or some other syndicated show - programs like *Miller's Court*, which featured a Harvard law professor discussing legal issues.

The month before the fire in the Rag Shop district, the station launched a two-hour morning show, airing from 9 to 11 a.m., aptly named *Good Morning*. Two years later, the ABC network stole the name as well as the format with the production of *Good Morning America*. WCVB renamed its show *Good Day*. The show made the promise to travel the greater metro region every day, going live from different locations. To do so, the roving crew would need to be able to transmit a radio signal from a mobile platform. In June of 1973, the station management team - Dr. Leo Beranek, president, Robert Bennet, general manager and Steve deSatnick, director of engineering - started looking around for ways to accomplish this. Their options were few, though - after all, they were a scrappy start-up and they couldn't afford to go big.

The RCA Color Bus

If you wanted to see big back in 1973, you needn't look any further than the RCA color bus. It had only been two years since another Boston startup, WSMW – TV, on channel 27, owned by the deep-pocketed State Mutual Life Assurance Company, had promised more "local live television." They went to RCA to fulfill that promise. The results were written up in the June 1971 issue of *RCA Broadcast News*. That issue's cover art includes a small photograph of the mobile unit. The truck was a monster: 30 feet long, 12 feet tall, "a virtual production center on wheels." It was equipped with five video cameras, associated tripods, camera control units, viewfinders, a big reel-to-reel quad-tape recorder, and a control room for switching from camera to camera. Finally, the transmitter, the TT-50FH, which cost more than $200,000, was actually two transmitters - an extra one had literally been built in, in case the first one failed.

RCA had been in the mobility game from the beginning of course. The American public first saw Franklin Delano Roosevelt live on television in 1939, at the opening ceremonies of the World's Fair in New York. This was accomplished with the two 26-foot-long Art Deco-styled buses on Mack Truck chassis which RCA had designed two years earlier. By 1946, the Type TJ-50A Television Mobile Unit was in use. This truck became ubiquitous at local NBC affiliates across America during the late Forties and early Fifties. It was just over 21 feet long, eight feet wide, and nine feet tall, built on a one-and-a-half-ton Chevrolet chassis and equipped with three cameras, a switcher for cutting from one camera to another, and all the necessary cable to connect it all together.

To get a power supply, the truck required access to either a big three-amp wall socket, the kind used for large appliances, or a generator, which could be towed behind the mobile unit. The truck needed that much power to run the cameras, monitors and control panels - and an actual oven, called a radio transmitter.

The early mobile radio transmitters were basically the same kinds of devices as electric ovens. In a transmitter, just like in an oven, electricity is sent through a black body; nickel is a substance commonly used to create energy radiation. The difference between an oven and a radio transmitter is that the energy emanating from the black body in an oven is used to heat food and the transmitter's energy is used to create a focused beam of electrons and then prepare that for transmission.

In the radio transmitter, a series of glass vacuum tubes take the picture from the image dissector, or the Iconoscope, and turn it into a radio signal. First, a gap is created in the nickel baking coil and an airtight glass envelope is created around it. Then a wire grid is placed is placed in the gap. When the 220 volts of electricity are sent through the coil, the electrons shoot across the gap between the cathode and the anode, until a signal from the camera creates a negative charge in a grid. Then everything stops. Suddenly the signal from the image dissector goes back to positive, and the stream across the gap in the coil instantly goes back to full-on light speed. Thus, amplified, the stream of electrons encoded with the picture information moves on to the modulator and the oscillator tubes, and more 220-voltage-induced electrons give the existing stream a wave form. This form is measured in terms of the number of peaks which take place in one second. The frequency of maximum amplitude, or height, of the wave in each period is known as a hertz and is expressed in kilohertz, megahertz, and gigahertz.

This measurement of wave frequencies is named for Heinrich Hertz, the man who first demonstrated their existence to his new girlfriend on one of their early dates back in 1879. His untimely death at age 36 in 1894, and the subsequent publication of all his papers, caused a widespread uptick in interest in his work - which the 20-year-old Guglielmo Marconi became swept up in.

At the 1939 World's Fair, RCA, the American offspring of Marconi's company, pumped 220 volts into the big Mack truck bus equipped with the radio transmitter and cranked out an electron beam with a dipole antenna that had a wave frequency measured in kilohertz. By the late Forties, the Type TJ-50A Television Mobile Unit sent out a signal from a parabolic dish with a microwave frequency in the megahertz range. By 1964, the transmitters in the large RCA color buses were cranking out signals with a wave in the gigahertz range, a million-plus increase in the frequency of maximum amplitude over the Kilohertz range. As frequencies climbed, more energy was needed to produce the hertzian waves, causing the transmitters to get hotter and hotter. A large air conditioner was necessary to keep everything cool and this, in turn, required a huge generator to provide power, which itself needed to be water cooled. So, the trucks kept getting bigger and bigger to accommodate the increasing workload and its concomitant gear and, accordingly, kept getting more and more expensive.

Microwave Associates

Beranek, Bennet and deSatnick, looking around from their WCVB offices in the former Harvester dealership along I-95, were understandably skeptical of dropping more than a million dollars on a five-camera monstrosity like the one used at WSMW. They'd all invested quite a big chunk of their own money into the station's operating budget and surely weren't interested in blowing it.

Fortunately, there was another remote television system in the field that year, the second-generation CBS Mini-cam, the one that had given Joseph Flaherty his Emmy win, combined with a small helical-scan videotape recorder and a transmitter that used transistors instead of tubes, made by Microwave Associates, a company right up the road in Burlington.

Microwave Associates had spent the Fifties and early Sixties providing microwave solutions to the United States Defense Department, specifically designing rugged little steel boxes which were mounted in the nose cone of supersonic jet fighters, such as the McDonnell Douglas F-4 Phantom, which would provide a high-frequency radio signal to function as a radar. Those steel boxes did not need air-conditioning to keep them cool - a heat sink and a fan would suffice - because their radio transmitters were solid-state. Invented in 1947 by John Bardeen, William Shockley, and Walter Brattain, in the labs of the Bell Telephone company, the sole provider of phone service at the time, and later improved upon by Mohamed Atalla and his colleague Dawon Kahng, the transistor is considered one of the major technological achievements of the 20th century, for the most part because it replaced the delicate power-hungry vacuum tube.

Transistors don't require 220 volts as tubes do; they get sufficient power from a standard 110-volt wall socket. Instead of a vacuum, transistors have doped-up silicone, which is a recipe of atoms in a particular electron arrangement which allow a weak signal from a camera to stop and start the electron flow. The rest of the device is made of plastic and metal, instead of glass, and doesn't get as hot. The transistor is also solid, not hollow like a vacuum tube. This "solid state" makes the transistor far more dependable.

With the fan-cooled steel box for a transmitter, a small helical-scan video tape recorder, Consolidated Video's time-base corrector, and the second-generation CBS Mini-cam, a

Norelco PCP – 90, the WCVB crew could stay out on the street twice as long for half the price it would take to keep WSMW's 30-foot-long, five camera, double-transmitter, monster color bus with more than 10 crew members in the field. An added Plus: they were nimble.

Senator Edward Kennedy toured the wreckage on Thursday or Friday that week in October. After his tour he justified the need to declare the site a disaster area under the Federal Disaster Relief Act of 1970 (departing for the first time from the usual practice, reserving that federal relief level for a natural disaster) by pointing out that the 300 now-homeless residents were "for the most part ... poor and elderly and did not have a lot of money or insurance in many cases. When they wipe out they just wipe out completely." WCVB, with its Winnebago RV, could get that sound turned around faster than anyone else, and do it day after day. This all-encompassing coverage made the station a ratings leader in news.

A decade later, BBI sold WCVB to Metromedia for more than $2,000,000 and Beranek, Bennet and deSatnick became rich. In the news coverage of the day, the station's innovations in content were celebrated - the situation comedy, the morning show, *Miller's Court*, and other local community shows. Nobody recalled the 24-foot-plus-long Winnebago Indian and its Microwave Associates solid state 2.1-giga-hertz microwave transmitter, but there is no doubt these factors led to more than a few of the station's incredible early successes.

In 1973, WCVB was one of only six local television stations in all of the United States practicing Electronic News-Gathering. There was no way the people there could have foreseen that their bet on the stripped-down remote live truck would pay off so spectacularly. Nobody could have known, not even Joseph A. Flaherty, inventor of the new system.

Ikegami Tsushinki HL-33

On the Wednesday WCVB's Winnebago RV rolled into the blackened, charred remains of Chelsea's Rag Shop district, about 180 miles southwest, Joe Flaherty left his office inside CBS's black granite building in midtown Manhattan, walked 800 feet up 52nd Street to the Hotel Americana, and presented his latest research on electronic photography to the Society's 114th Semiannual Technical Conference. It had been a year since the duel at Century City, now he was introducing a newer version of his Emmy-winning camera, this one made in Ota City, the Land of a Thousand Factories. His presentation, *Television News Gathering*, announced findings gleaned from 10 months of experience with the new camera system, which had been placed in the CBS-owned-and-operated local stations in New York, Los Angeles, Chicago, Philadelphia and St. Louis.

Though the words of the Society of Motion Picture and Television Engineers' founder, C. Francis Jenkins, *"Every new industry standardizes sooner or later, whether we will it or not"* were always on the minds of Society members, one can still wonder if Flaherty supposed it was going to be later rather than sooner if or when his second-generation mini-cam would be an industry standard.

In his report, Flaherty described some of the basic problems involved in gathering motion pictures for television news. CBS, he told those in attendance, had 400 "stringers," a term then used to designate freelance film camera operators, spread out not only across America, but throughout the entire world. Its competitors, NBC and ABC, had similar numbers of camera operators, bringing the total number of camera crews chasing news for the networks worldwide to about 1,200. This assessment, though, amounted to fewer than half of what the 600 local television stations in the United States had on the streets on any given day shooting motion-picture news coverage. All combined, local stations employed nearly 3,000 camera crews, which altogether used more 250,000,000 feet of film every year, at a cost of approximately $40,000,000, in excess of $2,500,000,000 in 2022 figures.

The most severe limitation to successfully cover the news was, as Flaherty explained, "the gathering of 'hard' news – i.e., current, fast breaking and often unpredictable news events." Electronic News-Gathering went a long way toward alleviating those problems.

He then broke down the new electronic system of image-gathering into two categories: 'Record Mode' and 'Live Mode.'

In Record Mode, film and tape were much the same until the crew returned to the station. Once in-house, there was no time for processing the videotape like there was for film - the images could go straight to air. Flaherty observed, "The time thus saved will enable more thoughtful editorial judgements to be made and offer greater immediacy in broadcasting news stories." Of course, as to the question of the actual quality of the picture or, more succinctly, how Joe's minicam picture compared to the film picture, he stated unequivocally, "no degradation in quality can be observed, and indeed the electronic photography has a somewhat crisper appearance."

Flaherty then moved on to Live Mode. "This mode is particularly appropriate for local television news gathering," he stated. He'd even brought illustrations, which were projected on a screen for everyone to see. There was a diagram of vans with antennas on top, pointing toward tall buildings with receivers on the roofs and squiggly lines connecting them. He showed a photo of Chicago's WBBM – TV's Ford Econoline Van, with its round, four-foot parabolic dish up on the roof aimed at the 62-storey John Hancock Tower. This was followed by a shot of a crew member unloading the PCP-90 minicam; then a picture came up of the van's interior, showing the racks of electronic equipment, including the Microwave Associates transmitter and CVS time-base corrector.

He also displayed a bar graph which he'd made. Time was the Y axis with three bars, each representing a different type of news-gathering technology. The "Film Camera" bar had three segments and therefore took up the most time. The segments were "Transport to News Center," "Processing," and "View, Edit, Prepare for air." The second bar, labeled "Mini-Cam plus VTR," had two segments, "Transport to News Center," and "View, Edit, Prepare for Air." The third bar, labeled "Mini-Cam plus Microwave," had only one segment, labeled "View, Edit, Prepare for Air."

"The 'Live' mode of operation has a number of practical advantages," announced the guy who'd built the first television facility for the United States Army. "First, the real-time live broadcasting of 'hard' news events is possible." Further, he said, "the news editors can actually watch the incoming live coverage as it is being recorded. They can make initial news value judgements as the story takes place and visualize the main edits that they will make on the recorded coverage." Finally, he summed up the benefits of Electronic News-Gathering with this: "It has been found in practice that the ability of a news director to communicate directly with a crew during coverage of a news event is of great assistance in composing a news story which will require less editing later because editorial judgement is exercised while the story is being covered."

Flaherty then presented his results. First, regarding "Immediacy," he stated, "Of 184 assignments given to electronic news gathering crews in one trial period, 93 percent were completed successfully. Further, 56 percent of these assignments were late-breaking news stories which could not have been covered on film in time for the film to be processed and made available for timely broadcast on the next scheduled news program."

As to "Cost," he said, "while the initial capital cost of cameras, microwave links and video tape recorders, are higher than the capital cost of film cameras and processing equipment, the direct operating cost is much less than with film. This is so mainly because of the cost not only of film stock but also of processing labor and materials, which have no counterpart in videotape. And, of course, videotape is reusable, while film is consumed."

Then he explained how these two factors led to an improvement of the overall quality of the news product. "As a result of the greater immediacy provided by electronic news gathering, it is found that part of the time saved can be used to upgrade the quality of content of news stories, by providing more time for thoughtful news value judgements and editorial decisions."

Near the end of his presentation, Flaherty introduced his new electronic news camera to the world, the Ikegami HL 33, the Handy Looky from Ota City, Land of a Thousand Factories. "These results have been obtained," Flaherty told those gathered, "with available equipment which has been adapted to the needs of news-gathering. While this first-generation equipment has served to demonstrate the reliability of the system, a second-generation system has been devised specifically for the needs of news gathering." He then displayed a photo of the camera in action, recording an interview with a firefighter at a spot news event, positioned on the shoulder of the photojournalist, in just the same way small portable film cameras had been handled. He ticked off the camera's specifications; 12-and-one-half inches long, seven-and-one-half inches tall and four inches wide. The camera weighed 12 pounds and required a 22-pound auxiliary backpack.

He wrapped up his remarks with the observation that "the invention and development of the time-base error corrector has made it possible to use simple, lightweight and inexpensive helical-scan videotape recorders." So, while the present outlay of capital for the camera was $40,000, that price would only drop, ushering in "a period of dramatic growth in electronic news gathering, both domestically and abroad."

Whether Flaherty truly believed that last bit is open to debate. He didn't send the article about his research to the Society's *Journal* to publish for another six months. That delay does not indicate a dramatic uptick in interest in ENG surrounding that year's technical conference. It's easy to imagine him heading back to work after introducing a second camera in just 12 months, casually catching up with old friends, exchanging wry observations, always with that boyish grin, then walking the 800 feet back to his office in Black Rock, absentmindedly tossing his presentation materials to a corner of his office, finished with them for the time being.

It would have been obvious to him on that October 17, 1973, that he may have revealed the next great technological breakthrough in motion-picture image-gathering, one which would change the world - as an important advance to image-acquisition as the steam engine was for transportation - but the world wasn't ready for it. In the meantime, game four of the World Series was being played at Shea Stadium that night, and it's not unreasonable to think that he and a few Society buddies took in the game. The next morning, back to work, he went about his business, maybe focusing on the tight ratings race in the St. Louis market.

After introducing his second of two different cameras made to gather imagery electrically at a tremendous cost savings compared to film, then being completely ignored by the industry each time, he must have felt like his was the lone voice crying out in the wilderness. Perhaps that's why he held off sending the research into the *Journal* for another six months.

Economics

We can take this historic leap of imagination because we happen to know what news directors across the country were thinking about electronic photography at that time, as well as the overall economic conditions of the period, and the general malaise that was slowly spreading across America in the early Seventies after the successful completion of the Space Race and the less-than-successful denouement of the Vietnam War.

Back in the Spring, not long after the 112th Society Conference, James Harless and Erik Collins of The Ohio State University had sent a survey to 300 news directors at TV stations throughout the United States. These inquiries had questions concerning whether "portable electronic camera and recording equipment" was going to be part of future capital purchases. That October, they were preparing the results for publication in *Work Roles, News Gathering Equipment, and Newscast in Current U.S. Television News Departments*. They referenced a 1966 study by the head of the Photojournalism Department at the University of Minnesota School of Journalism, R. Smith Schuman, *Visual Aspects of Television News: Communicator, Message, Equipment*. Schuman had written about the results of his survey, that five percent of stations reported having portable electronic cameras and that "Miniature hand-held electronic cameras and portable recording equipment may become important in the next few years."

Seven years later, however, after recording the results of the 192 responses they'd received, Harless and Collins found that the number of stations using video cameras in the field had grown by only 9 percent. Not only that, but "less than 1 percent of all current news directors see portable VTR equipment in their future."

So, no one was banging down Flaherty's door wanting to hear all about the new Ikegami HL-33 that fall. There's a reason why only 20 stations nationwide were even considering purchasing electronic cameras and videotape recorders in 1973: the United States of America was not in a good place.

NASA's Apollo 17, the last moon mission, had splashed down in the Pacific on December 19, 1972. A month later, the Paris Peace Accords had been signed, officially bringing an end to the fighting in Vietnam. Three weeks after that, the first prisoners of war started coming home. There were no parades, and the days of parades after going to the Moon were long past.

In April, two top White House aides, Chief of Staff, H.R. Haldeman and White House Counsel John Ehrlichman, resigned their high-level post after being charged with obstruction of justice. Vice President Spiro Agnew pleaded *no contest* to a felony charge of tax evasion on October 10; he resigned as well. While the Nixon White House unraveled the stock market did the same.

On January 11, the market began to trend downward slowly and didn't let up until August. By that time, it had declined 18 percent. It went up all through September and into October - then Agnew resigned, and the downward trend resumed.

Meanwhile, things were coming apart in the Middle East. On Saturday, October 6, 1973, Egypt and Syria attacked Israel on Yom Kippur, Judaism's holiest day. In the 11 days leading up to the Society's Technical Conference, a fluid state of hostilities played out. By Monday, October 15, Israeli forces had crossed the Suez Canal into Egyptian territory and were approaching Damascus, Syria's capital. Israel's military had rapidly turned the tide of war due in large part to an infusion of arms and ammunition from the U.S. to counter the Soviets' supplies to Egypt and Syria. In retaliation, on Tuesday, October 16, six Persian Gulf nations raised the price of a barrel of oil from three dollars to five dollars. The next day, Wednesday, October 17, the day Flaherty introduced the HL-33 to those who attended his presentation at the Society's conference, officials from 10 Arab countries met in Kuwait and decided to start cutting oil production by five percent each month from then on. The Arab Oil Embargo had begun.

Everyone knew that the price of gasoline was going to increase, but no one had any idea by how much. Americans had no clue about the crisis on the horizon. These were, economically speaking, highly uncertain times. And Joe Flaherty knew, as he was walking back up 52nd Street after giving his report, that no one was going to be looking to buy one of his exotic new Ikegami cameras, designed and built in Japan, in the Land of a Thousand Factories. So it could be debated whether he truly believed that there would soon be a "period of dramatic growth in electronic news gathering, both domestically and abroad." As it turned out, however, in the end, he was right.

PRIMARY SOURCES

FRIDAY, FEBRUARY 1, 1974

Oil Shock

Three weeks later, on November 8, 1973, President Richard Nixon sat before the TV cameras in the Oval Office and addressed the nation.

He announced that the United States was facing a shortfall of two million barrels of oil by the end of the month. Then he decreed: "We, as a Nation, must now set upon a new course." He outlined six steps all Americans had to take to avoid certain catastrophe. One step: Cut the supply of home and office heating oil by 15 percent. He continued, "We must ask everyone to lower the thermostat in your home by at least six degrees," He announced that he was going to try to get the governors of each state to lower the speed limit on highways to 50 mph but, as it turned out, none of his efforts that November were enough. In the days before Thanksgiving, Nixon asked all American gas stations to stop selling gasoline on weekends. This led to long lines at the pumps the other five days of the week, which in turn led to actual physical altercations breaking out among impatient motorist waiting in line, sometimes for hours.

In economics, a recession is declared when a basket of indicators starts going downhill. Such indicators may include the number of people working, the amount of money they're spending, the amount of goods made, and cost of investments to make more goods. As oil became increasingly scarce, there was a definite drag on all those fronts. At some point that month, those indicators began to decline. The 1973 – 75 Recession, or Oil Shock, as it became to be known, slowed down the entire country. That November, in fact, marked the end of the Great American Post-WWII Economic Boom. To say that the United States of America was literally at a standstill as the new year dawned was not an overstatement.

Eighth Annual Winter Conference

Despite the lousy economy, the Society of Motion Picture and Television Engineers members carried on. On Thursday, January 24, 1974, the Winter Television Conference convened in Denver. Its theme centered on the quickly growing cable and satellite method of distributing electrical content, otherwise known as CATV, an acronym for Community Antenna Television. It's now referred to simply as 'cable.' In 1974, cable television had made some rather large strides in growth. R. Edward Turner III, aka Ted Turner, had just begun transmitting to subscribers from his monster broadcast antenna in downtown Atlanta, the 10th-tallest structure in the world when it had been built five years earlier, Charles F. Dolan and Gerald M. Levin, of Sterling Manhattan Cable, had been sending out Home Box Office to their subscribers in Lower Manhattan for a little more than one year. And one week before, on Wednesday, January 16, Director of the White House Office of Telecommunications Policy (OTP) Clay Whitehead, he of "guard against 'elitist gossip' and 'ideological plugola," fame, released the Nixon Administration's policy proposal for cable television. It stated: "The committee has concluded that programing, advertising and other information and services on cable channels can be allowed to develop on a free and competitive basis, with no more regulatory power exercised over the content of this communications medium than is exercised over the print or film media."

January 1974 was a big month for cable, and the industry was about to get a major boost. Applications Technology Satellite-6 or, simply, ATS-6, was set to launch in May. It would be available to a cable system servicing public schools in remote areas like the Appalachian Mountains, Alaska, and the Rocky Mountains, to broadcast *Time Out*, a junior-high career education series. The Federation of Rocky Mountain States Inc., a public/private concern working to improve the quality of life for its small population (only four percent of the nation's total) of widely scattered residents, had just completed the groundwork needed for the diffusion of ATS-6's radio signal. The system would serve 56 communities spread out over eight states, 860,000 square miles of mountainous terrain. The Federation had built the ground receiver stations and the rest of the distribution and viewing infrastructure in what could only be called a very challenging environment. On Thursday, January 24, the Federation's principles gave a series of reports on its progress at the Society's Eighth Annual Winter Television Conference.

In the conference report, printed in the Society's February *Journal*, the reason given for holding the event in Denver was because of a "heavy concentration in the Colorado area of cable and closed-circuit television interest" and the fact that Denver was the Federation's base. More likely, though, the conference was in Denver because that was where Robert William Daniels Jr. lived. And Bill Daniels was widely seen as "the father of cable television.".

Daniels had been a fighter pilot in World War II and the Korean War. Legend has it that on his way home from Korea, he happened to be in a Denver bar, where he watched a boxing match on television. He'd been the Golden Gloves Champion for the entire state of New Mexico at age 21, so he saw at once the huge potential for broadcasting live sports. He was so enthusiastic on the technology and its impact that he immediately went to work researching microwave transmission. In 1952, he set up one of the first CATV services for the remote town of Casper, Wyoming, from a tower in Colorado. By the mid-Sixties, he was a millionaire – as were his employees. Bill Daniels was a generous man who believed in ethics and integrity. His speech at the conference luncheon on the second day was featured in the February *Journal*.

He began his remarks by noting, "There are some very interesting parallels in the growth of cable television and that of broadcasting, parallels that are most striking." He then compared the resistance to cable as quite similar to the way newspapers had resisted the emergence of radio. He noted that the film industry had considered television to be a serious threat but, he pointed out, everyone had survived. It would be the same with cable, he assured them. "As leisure hours grow, Americans will be looking for a wide selection of information and entertainment at the flip of their 35-channel TV switch."

In the conference report, which included Daniels' speech, the number of attendees isn't mentioned. There's a photo of the registration desk which shows three people posing off to the side, yet there is no one waiting in line to sign in. It's unlikely there were more people there than the 200 that attended the Dallas conference in 1972, or the author of the report, writing anonymously – a rarity in the *Journal* - would have mentioned it. It's also unlikely general managers at TV stations throughout America were willing to finance a trip to

Denver so their engineers could hear how the competition was advancing. Money was tight - no need to witness how the space race was benefitting a 1,000 percent increase in available TV channels.

The cover of January's *BM/E*, the second annual issue comparing film to video, featured a photo of each medium's reels side-by-side with the headline "Use Both Now ... Watch Tape's Future." A seven-page article briefly mentioned "News Gathering." The writer admitted "we can discern [the] handwriting on the wall that, again, points toward a big future for electronics in news." The CBS system, with the Norelco PCP-90 and Microwave Associates transmitter, was mentioned, but the writer hedged their bets with the possibility of "film remaining as an auxiliary or companion method."

That was it, one page, in one magazine, discussing the new portable video camera and its possible impact on news-gathering.

It is in this lull, this calm before the storm, that the three main primary sources for the events about to transpire over the following 30 months should be introduced, they are Joseph Roizen, Frank Beacham and Robin Hirsch.

The Engineer

Joseph Roizen was born on September 9, 1923, in Kishinev, Romania, about 100 miles north of Odessa on the Black Sea's northern coast. At the tender age of three months, he made his first of many Atlantic crossings, immigrating with his family to North America. He grew up in Sainte-Agathe-des-Monts, Quebec, Canada, a resort town about 80 miles north of Montreal. His father died when Joe was 12 and, despite his academic talents – particularly in science and electronics - he was forced to quit school in the 10th grade, to work to help his family survive during the Great Depression. In 1939, when World War II began, he lied about his age and tried to enlist in the Royal Canadienne Air Force. He was unsuccessful, but he did get a job as a back-seat rider in aircraft to test radio systems.

After the war, he went to work for the newly founded Trans-Canada Air Lines, again in radio technology. As a perk, he was able to travel far and wide for free. On one trip, he visited Los Angeles and fell in love with its warm weather. He decided to move there, first working for a television manufacturer and then for KTLA-TV. He soon discovered Lake Tahoe and bought land there to build a cottage. To be closer to this summertime retreat, he and his family moved to Palo Alto, where he was hired by Ampex.

Two years later, on April 24, 1958, at the Society's 83rd Semiannual Technical Conference, held at the Ambassador Hotel in downtown L.A., he gave his first presentation on his company's new videotape editing system.

A little over a year later, he was in Moscow for the opening of the American National Exhibition, at the controls of a video camera when Vice President Nixon arrived at the Ampex pavilion to give Soviet Premier Nikita Khrushchev a look at the new Ampex color videotape equipment. It's unlikely Khrushchev was aware of the possibilities of the new videotape technology paired with a free press, so his impromptu diplomacy session is understandable. The colorful debate began in front of the cameras and continued throughout the tour of the exhibition before climaxing at the display of a "typical American home," specifically, an American kitchen. This historic exchange would go down in history as the Kitchen Debate.

The part Roizen shot was smuggled out of the Soviet Union by an Ampex executive; it aired on all three major networks' news shows three days later, with a lower third translation of what the Victor of Stalingrad told the Vice President of the United States. "As we pass you by, we'll wave 'hi' to you," he said, while actually waving in Nixon's face, getting a good laugh from everyone in the audience. Then he said, "and then if you want, we'll stop by and say, 'please come along behind us'." Nixon, ever the polite host, smiled all the while, waiting for the translation.

Roizen would eventually win an Emmy Citation for videotaping the Kitchen Debate.

By 1966, he'd risen to the position of International Video Consultant for Ampex International, circling the globe to explain how videotape recorders worked and how to edit the big, fat Quad tape. In 1969, Roizen struck out on his own and started Telegen, a company that provided international markets with technical help, market research, and editorial services relating to TV. Then, in January of 1973, he shows up on the editorial board of *Broadcast Engineering* magazine, and starts explaining video technology to anyone who picked up an issue.

It seemed, at first, that the magazine didn't know what to do with him. In the first four months of 1973 he only appears on the Magazine's masthead on alternating months, each time as one of the publications two the CATV editors. Then suddenly, in May, in the NAB convention review issue – which inexplicably omitted the introduction of the CVS Time-Base Corrector, the biggest thing at the show – he was assigned the position of "video" editor. His first article, "The Sensuous Test Pattern," ran in the next issue. It's worth the time and space here to share its first four paragraphs.

"No dyed-in-the-wool television engineer can ever resist the siren song of a television test pattern, calling out to fondle the knobs of the receiver and assess the performance of the television system being scrutinized.

There is an uplifting joy to setting the fine tune at the crispest picture point, a hairsbreadth away from dropping off the end of the allocated RF channel and losing everything. Then, a little clever tracking and trimming of the brightness and contrast controls sets up the pattern for a leisurely and soul-satisfying evaluation.

Sight – that precious sense – is nurtured by the symmetry of linear circles and squares, visual acuity is satisfied by converging wedges of horizontal and vertical resolution, reason looks for a progressive gray scale and logic deduces the intrinsic deficiencies from the miniscule evidence of small element ringing and low frequency bar smear. Add to this the Lorelei of a clear 1000 cycle tone and the overall effect can be a severe case of 'picture tube passion.'

The purist will roll the vertical and check for the presence or absence of VITS and the cynic will drive up the contrast and listen for intercarrier buzz in the audio. But, whatever the inclination, the true engineer will leave the set walking a little taller, smug in the knowledge that one has met the interpretive challenge. Test patterns are not just technical – they are sensual as well."

This was not your typical broadcast engineering language and it's sheer luck to have had such a clever, observant witness take us through the next two-and-a-half years of turbulence in the broadcast industry.

The Journalist

Frank Beacham was born on April 1, 1948, in Honea Path, a small South Carolina town, about 25 miles south of Greenville and 25 miles east of the Georgia state line. He spent his childhood watching the brand-new invention called television, which showed up in his home when he was six years old. Thereafter, he developed a fascination with broadcasting. He also spent time assembling electronic Heathkits, soldering the vacuum tubes into the circuits, taking over the family kitchen for days at a time.

One weekend in 1964, he drove north to Belton, a nearby small town, walked into the radio station, and asked how he could get a job there. It wouldn't be the last time he used such an approach to get where he wanted to go.

By his junior year in high school, Beacham was running the station on his own every Sunday. A couple of years later, he enrolled in the University of South Carolina, majoring in Journalism. At USC, he landed a job at WIS-TV as a studio-floor camera operator during the great monochrome-to-color changeover. In 1968, he transferred over to the news department. During the summer break, he convinced his superiors to send him to Chicago to film the Democratic National Convention. At one point, exiting the International Amphitheater to shoot some footage of violent protest out on the streets, he passed a Japanese video crew with a Sony DV-2400 Video Rover, the first in their line of Portapak minicams with a portable helical-scan videotape recorder. It was a sight he wouldn't forget.

When he returned to Columbia, he went to the Broadcast Chair of USC's School of Journalism and asked if his coverage of the convention would earn him any credits toward graduation. After a discussion, Dr. Richard M. Uray informed Beacham that he could forgo his senior year.

After a brief stint in Law School, he dropped out of college, which made him eligible for the Selective Service System draft. In order to avoid combat, he signed up for the Coast Guard and was sent to Cape May, New Jersey, for recruit training. Holding strong antiwar beliefs and chafing at the military regimen, when an opportunity arose for him to disqualify himself, he leapt at the chance. While taking a hearing test, Beacham was sitting in a position that enabled him to see the controls for the test. His background in radio and television technology helped him understand how the equipment worked. By watching a VU meter, which was marked with a point of failure, he was able fake an insufficient hearing ability to serve in the military and was honorably discharged.

Having defeated the federal government so handily, in possession of an honorable discharge and a semester of law school, Beacham figured he'd work in the media in Washington, D.C., and he figured the best guy to work for there was Senator Edward Kennedy of Massachusetts. So, one Friday, he made the drive from South Carolina up to Washington, D.C.

Employing the same method he'd used six years before at the small Belton radio station, he arrived unannounced, with no appointment, at the senator's office and again, boldly asked for a job. Having openings only for volunteers, Kennedy's staff informed him that another Democrat, Senator Robert Byrd of West Virginia, had an opening for a Press Aide.

The very next Monday, Beacham was hard at it, toiling nonstop at his new position. He wrote press releases, a West Virginia newspaper column, "Byrd's Eye View," as well as some the senator's floor speeches. Since he was the aide with the most knowledge about TV and its workings, he was given the responsibility of prepping Byrd for Sunday morning news program appearances.

He was 22 years old, sitting in the green room at NBC or CBS, sweating out the performance his 53-year-old boss gave on the prime national political platform of the 25-year-old technology, and never getting a day off. In the end, Beacham realized he didn't really enjoy the nebulous nature of political horse-trading. About six months into the job, he saw another opportunity with a renowned news agency, United Press International (UPI), and grabbed it.

Beacham was dispatched to Mississippi to cover Charles Evers, brother of the slain activist Medgar Evers. Charles was campaigning for governor - the first African-American governor of that state. One day, in Philadelphia in Neshoba County, 30 miles north of Meridian, where Civil Rights workers James Chaney, Andrew Goodman, and Michael

Schwerner had been murdered seven years before, he was refused service at a gas station. He smiled and politely left town.

A year later, in the Spring of 1972, Al Neuharth, president of newspaper giant Gannett Company, offered him a job at *TODAY.*

TODAY was a morning paper that Gannet had started in 1966, with Neuharth at the helm. Neuharth had convinced the publishers of four afternoon papers - the *Cocoa Tribune*, the *Titusville Star-Advocate, Eau Gallie Courier* and the *Melbourne Daily Times* - to sell out to Gannett. Neuharth then started printing a morning edition, on the presses at the four papers, to compete with two existing regional morning papers, the *Miami Herald* and the *Orlando Sentinel.* Eventually, Neuharth launched *USA Today* as a national paper, but in early 1972, when Beacham went to work for him, that publication was a dream in progress. Neuharth was still in the process of building the team to make it a reality.

The main newsroom of *TODAY* was in the *Cocoa Tribune* building, a few blocks north of the city's small downtown and a block from the banks of the Indian River. Between downtown and the paper's headquarters, the Hubert Humphry Causeway heads east across the river, then across Merritt Island and the Banana River, before delivering motorist into Cocoa Beach on the outer banks. To the north, the cape juts out into the Atlantic Ocean. Along that shoreline are lined up the launch pads of the Kennedy Space Center. The newsroom Beacham walked into that Spring was fewer than 20 miles from where the last few Apollo missions were launched to explore the moon.

In his autobiography, *The Whole World Was Watching, My Life Under the Media Microscope*, published in 2018, Frank Beacham described the newsroom of 1972. "It seemed that nearly everyone at *TODAY* did drugs of some kind – from marijuana to psychedelics. Drugs of all kinds were ample and cheap to buy." Beacham traveled the state covering politics and came home to his ocean view beach house to get high and watch the behemoth Atlases blast off into the eastern sky.

By the summer of 1972, he was back reporting on the big national political conventions. Both parties had scheduled to hold their rallies in Miami. He stayed at the Miami Beach Convention Center's hall until 2:48 a.m., well past his deadline, "[u]nder the influence of mescaline," to hear Senator George McGovern's acceptance speech after his nomination for the Democratic presidential candidacy. One month later, Beacham was tear-gassed while covering war protestors rioting on Collins Avenue in Miami Beach. Al Neuharth himself picked up Beacham in his limo after that harrowing experience. Not long after that he was flying to Tallahassee in Neuharth's private jet to cover Florida state politics.

It could be assumed Beacham had it made at that point, but the man wasn't one to stand still for too long. Maybe it was because he missed broadcasting and working on the Heathkits, or maybe he wanted to report in a longer form, as opposed to the short, tight *TODAY* style of reporting - whatever the reason, he started talking to a TV station up in Jacksonville about working for the investigative unit.

The station was WJXT-TV, the same station Nixon had been recorded talking about in the fall of 1972, on the secret White House recording system, saying, "The main thing is the Post is going to have damnable, damnable problems out of this one. They have a television station ... and they're going to have to get it renewed." This had been followed by the administration's license renewal bill to, in the words of Clay T. Whitehead, director of the White House Office of Telecommunications Policy, "guard against 'elitist gossip' and 'ideological plugola,'." WJXT had spent the next year defending themselves in Congress from this bill.

By early 1974, Beacham was about to get a haircut and move from behind the camera to on-air position at one of the nation's top investigative newsrooms that had just stared down a president ... checking off yet another box on an already impressive resume and earning priceless experience for the coming storm.

The Artist

Robin E Hirsch was born in Miami, in 1951, to Rose Rabstein Hirsch and Samuel Hirsch. His book, *The History of Image Gathering: An oral history of technology and technique,* published in 2016, is (as he writes in the prologue), "the story of my generation's incredible image gathering journey." It is a shared oral history, fitting for a generation of image-gatherers, collected over a long period of time. The author felt no need to provide his autobiographical details, so one must look elsewhere for information about Hirsch's youth. This quest leads to his father, Samuel Hirsch.

Samuel Hirsch grew up in New York City, graduated from the University of North Carolina, and earned a graduate degree from the Neighborhood Playhouse in Midtown Manhattan. In 1950, he took a position as a professor of Theater Arts at the University of Miami. Robin was eight when his father moved the family to Boston, where he joined the theater department at Boston University. In January 1964, his article, "Theatre of the absurd (made in America)," was published in the *Journal of Social Issues.* Another article, "Drama as Theater," was featured in the *Journal of Education* in December of 1965. By that time, he was the chairman of the university's theater department and was looking for greater challenges. In 1967, he became the theater critic and editor of the Sunday entertainment supplement of the *Boston Herald-Traveller.* His competition for readership in the crowded Boston newspaper market included the legendary critic for the Hearst-owned *Boston Record American*, Elliot Norton, and the critic at the *Boston Globe*, Kevin Kelly.

In January of 1972, he published an article in the *Herald-Traveller*, titled "Curtain Call for Henry," which was reprinted in the April issue of the *Dartmouth Alumni Magazine*. The introduction to the reprint read, "The following article about Henry B. Williams, Professor of English and Director of the Experimental Theater, who ends his long Dartmouth career in June, appeared in the *Boston Herald Traveler* of Sunday, January 23. Mr. Hirsch, who has had a professional interest in the Dartmouth drama program over the years, is the father of Robin Hirsch '73, who is spending his junior year at the University of Israel."

It is apparent from this brief summary that Robin grew up in a household that valued work, academic rigor, and a strong appreciation for the arts, particularly the theater arts. It was something he would get called on as he began his professional career in image-gathering.

In between Samuel Hirsch's review in the paper and the reprint in the alumni magazine, the *Boston Herald-Traveler* lost its case with the Supreme Court, and WCVB had taken over its TV license. The *Herald-Traveler* didn't last for too long after that. The Hearst owned *Record American* purchased the paper that spring. It's easy to imagine that by the time Robin Hirsch returned from his year of study abroad, his father was no longer working at a newspaper/television conglomerate, so it may not have been as cheerful a home coming for Robin as he could have wished for. As it turned out, however, this setback didn't slow down the Hirsch clan, as demonstrated in the next year when Samuel shows up at WTVJ – TV in Miami to be the on-air theater critic. Not long after, Robin joined the staff there as a news photographer.

WTVJ was, in 1973, a CBS affiliate on Channel Four, owned by Wometco, which began in 1925 as the Wolfson-Meyer Theater Company, named for brothers-in-law Mitchell Wolfson and Sidney Meyer. They built their first theater at 310 North Miami Avenue, modeling it after the grand Capitol Theater in New York City, built seven years earlier at a time when giant movie palaces were becoming popular all over America, in big cities and small towns. In a quarter-century, the company had mushroomed into the largest chain of movie theaters in South Florida; it was also given the new abbreviated name, Wometco.

On March 21, 1949, Wometco began broadcasting a television signal from the theater building on North Miami Avenue, the first in the state of Florida. One of the first hires at the station was a 20-year-old recent graduate of the University of Miami, Ralph Renick. On August 26 of that year, he took a film camera out to the streets around the theater and rolled on the Category 4 1949 Florida Hurricane, marking the inauguration of that annual ritual in news-gathering. Soon he was news director and the main anchor of the daily news segment, a position he held unopposed for the next five years.

By the time Robin Hirsch walked into WTVJ 24 years later, it was still the dominant Number One news operation in town and Ralph Renick was still the news director. The station itself had grown considerably, expanding to cover the entire west side of the 300 block of North Miami Avenue. On the website for Cinema Treasures, a guide to old palace movie theaters, in the comment section concerning Miami's Capitol Theater, an anonymous poster describes the facility in the early seventies: "In 1971 the Wometco complex at 316 North Miami Avenue was a group of old buildings (including what had been the original theater) connected internally, with the floor at different levels, termite infested, claustrophobic, without windows, a veritable fire trap." Into this teeming cauldron of activity, the fresh-faced Robin Hirsch got to work on his image-gathering career. It wasn't long before the theater kid ran afoul of the grizzled news veteran who ran the show.

In Part One, Chapter four of his book, in the second paragraph – there are no page numbers in his self-published manuscript – of the "Recollections – Shut Your Mouth: Tales of an Old Pro," section, Robin wrote, "As the new guy on staff, I used to work by myself a lot covering the more nonessential type of stories, I got into the habit of telling people to walk over here, sit down there, please do that again, you know a little directing so I could get the shots I needed quickly and easily." Then, on an early assignment with a reporter, he recalled, "The first time I gave a subject some directions, I got a very stern lecture from the reporter about keeping my mouth shut and not directing the action. I was told that news has no place for staged or directed images, I believe that there was mention of going to Hollywood if I wanted to do that or something like that. He was pretty harsh, but not as harsh as the news director who told me if I did it again, I'd be out of there."

It was a timely lesson for young Robin taught by the Lion of the Miami media market, Ralph Renick. But the kid who grew up in the world of theater had a few tricks up his sleeve. As the new year began, he found himself on firmer footing in the newsroom.

In Part Two, Chapter 16, "The Final Payoff," Robin recalled: "I actually still remember my first big success." On the first day of February in 1974, he was sent to a local truck stop to talk to truckers about why they'd gone on strike. By that time, the price of diesel fuel had skyrocketed. That, along with the suspension of weekend fuel sales and the threats from the Nixon Administration to lower freeway speed limits had put truckers in an untenable financial predicament, so they decided to walk off the job.

Robin writes, "I was given the assignment of going out to a local truck stop to see if I could round up a group of drivers and get some reactions to what was going on. The assignment editor sent me out alone, figuring it was not crucial, and not worth wasting a reporter on the low probability that there was anything to get. This was better known as a wild goose chase. I was young and enthusiastic enough to savor the challenge of getting something good nevertheless. I had to take every chance that came my way to make a name for myself."

"Anyway, I drove out and as luck would have it found some truckers having lunch and hanging around the truck stop's café. They agreed to talk to me and I got permission from the café's owner to shoot there. I gathered about five or six guys in a group around a couple of tables, facing the window so I had a great light source. I hid my microphone behind a napkin dispenser. I threw out some questions and encouraged them to talk to each other. In a few minutes I was all but forgotten."

"I shot it all hand held or portable as we called it back then. I worked it for about ten minutes, listening as I shot so I could get some good sound bites. I worked the angle of the window to their faces finding positions where the lighting was just a bit more dramatic than straight on. I also grabbed listening shots, did some rack focus shots, and really worked it getting some great footage. When I was on a roll, I hated to stop. The creative juices just got me going ... When it was all done and edited the news producer really liked the story and moved it up to the top block of the show."

Back in early February of 1974, the only chance a photographer had to see their filmed story on a large TV screen was at airtime. Sure, the show was recorded on a big, fat, Quad tape, but that was archival, a holy relic - the only access one would ever have to view the story again was in the editing booth. So, the cameramen made sure to be in the newsroom when it aired. After all, everyone else was there, too, watching and listening very intently. Robin described the experience that day:

"I sat quietly as it aired on the six o'clock news. It looked even better on the TV monitor than it had looked in my little moviola viewer."

"When the piece finished, well, it was my coming out party. All the guys had great things to say, and for the first time they were asking me how I had gotten some of my shots. Asking me, the newbie!!! Moments like that stay with you for the rest of your life."

The theater kid was suddenly a force to be reckoned with in the hallways of the Wometco complex on North Miami Avenue. His work ethic, combined with his dramatic stage-lighting knowledge, would serve him well in the transition looming ahead.

And looming the transition was. Three days later, on Monday, February 4, 1974, newspaper heiress Patty Hearst was violently abducted from her apartment in Oakland, California. This shocking kidnaping started a chain of events that would bring about a global paradigm shift in the image-gathering industry, and these three gentlemen – Joseph Roizen, Frank Beacham, and Robin Mirsch - saw it firsthand.

Fortunately for us, they each wrote about their experiences so future generations could learn what happened from those who were there, in the trenches. Today, these writings provide the most in depth description of the sudden technological cyclone that swept through the local broadcast news industry in the following months.

PARADIGM SHIFT

FRIDAY, MAY 17, 1974

State of the Art

In the first few months of 1974, at the peak of the 16-millimeter film era, the greatest film camera for field operations of all-time hit the streets of America. It was the Cinema Products CP – 16R, with a through-the-lens reflex viewfinder, a primitive audio mixer, zoom lens, and the ubiquitous 400-foot "Micky Mouse Ears" magazine on top. The body was sturdy, made from magnesium, but light -14 pounds, with a lens, a battery, and a fully-loaded magazine. Based on nearly a half-century of refinement in 16mm camera design, and updated with the latest electronic technology, it was, in a word, perfect. Unfortunately, not that many were made.

Auricon

Kodak had launched its 16mm format back in the Twenties. At first, there were only a few cameras that could use the film. Kodak made one, of course, its Cine-Kodak Special, Bell & Howell produced the Filmo 70, and a Swiss company, Bolex, made the H-16. Each camera was powered by a hand crank or a spring, which was wound up and then released when an operator pushed the shutter button, causing the film to run by the lens, exposing it. The cameras were geared for the amateur film enthusiast market. Professionals didn't pay much attention to these cameras or the new film format and, in fact, occasionally derided them.

By the mid-Thirties, however, things started to change. First, Kodak introduced its famous color film, Kodachrome. In early 1935, two engineers who'd met at RCA's research labs decided to go into business together designing 16-millimeter film equipment for professional use. The company, called the Berndt-Maurer Corporation, made its inaugural appearance at the Society of Motion Picture and Television Engineers' 47th Semiannual Technical Conference, held on Atlantic City's boardwalk in New Jersey, in April 1940. John Maurer introduced the new, all-in-one camera and sound system, the B-M Sound Pro, designed from the ground up to work off electricity. It was the first 16mm equipment made for professional use.

Soon after, his partner, Eric M. Berdnt, and Walter Bach, the company's treasurer, decided to head west and form a new company to go after Hollywood's growing 16-millimeter film market. A little more than a year after setting up shop, the Japanese attacked Pearl Harbor, beginning America's involvement in the second world war.

The war's impact on motion-picture production was huge. For one thing, the very materials necessary for film production - chemicals and celluloid - were immediately rationed, making the smaller gauge 16-millimeter a desirable substitute for 35mm film. Not only that, there were also the new needs a nation at war required from its motion picture production industry - a certain genre of film, namely training films, lots and lots of training films - to get the thousands of volunteers up to speed on their new specialties in the military services.

The United States War Department was going to require a great many cameras to film all the demonstrations, and the location of the image-acquisition wasn't always going to be easy to get to. The new 16mm cameras were portable, lightweight, and easier to operate with a smaller crew - the ideal machine for the job.

Four months after the attack on Pearl Harbor, American Cinematographer Association's magazine, *American Cinematographer*, printed an article that highlighted a new camera system from the E. M. Berndt Corporation. The camera had simplified film-threading, recorded high-fidelity sound, weighed only 37 pounds, and included a rechargeable battery which allowed for field operation where no 110-volt wall sockets were available. The article stated, "In design and construction, the new camera is completely in keeping with today's necessity for conserving critical materials . . . the camera's case, for example, instead of making use of the cast or stamped metal to which we have become accustomed during the years of plenty, is of wooden construction." The camera itself wasn't much to look at - a box with a handle on top, that looked more like a suitcase more than a camera - but its debut was, in the words of the *American Cinematographer* writer, "at precisely the moment when it can be most useful in the making of civil defense and training films by both professionals and advanced amateurs." The new camera system's name? Auricon.

At war's end, Berndt and Bach built a magnesium version of their wooden sound camera, naming it the Auricon Pro. Then, in December of 1949, just as local broadcast newsrooms around the United States were gearing up, they put out their Auricon Cine-Voice.

It weighed only 12 pounds, 6 ounces and cost less than $700. That was $500 less but, more important, 40 fewer pounds than the pro model. It was initially intended for the home-movie market; indeed, its first ad in the December 1949 *American Cinematographer* shows a father filming a toddler saying "Daddy."

Television station managers couldn't resist the lower cost or the camera's portability. Soon, an Auricon Cine-Voice was being used in almost every television newsroom in America.

There was just one problem. The magazine held only 100 feet of film, which meant it could shoot a mere two minutes and 45 seconds of footage - not enough length to get a full story to run on the nightly news programs.

The problem was soon solved, however, by employing that grand old American tradition, the chop-shop. By cutting off the top of the camera and welding on a piece rigged up to accept the 400-foot, Micky Mouse Ears magazines from Mitchell Camera Corporation, located at 665 N. Robertson Blvd., West Hollywood, news-gatherers could film 11 minutes of footage at a cost of only three hundred bucks. An entire cottage industry of retrofitting Auricons with those 400-foot Mitchell magazines popped up overnight.

By August of 1959, in Wisconsin, when D. A. Pennebaker handed Albert Maysles a chopped Auricon with a wide-angle lens on it so he could film Massachusetts Senator John F. Kennedy and his wife Jacqueline arriving at a campaign stop for the documentary film *Primary*, in the process introducing Direct Cinema, or as the French called it, Cinema Verite, to the American viewers, the camera had become the portable news gathering instrument par excellence.

The next year, Berndt left the company to continue researching various methods of making film and cameras smaller and smaller. Both he and Maurer eventually worked for NASA during the Space Race against the U.S.S.R. During the Sixties the company, now known as Bach Auricon, continued its line of 16mm cameras, occasionally updating designs, but not improving the Cine-Voice at all. Meanwhile, in Europe, the German Arri and the French Éclair companies were making considerable advances in 16mm camera design. The cameras they developed would become the preferred tools of documentarians like Pennebaker and Maysles.

In local newsrooms, however, the European cameras – at $2000-plus a pop - were beyond their budgets. Not only that, but the Mitchell magazines didn't fit the Arri and Éclair cameras.

On October 5, 1970, at the Society's 108th Semiannual Technical Conference, Sheldon Nemeyer, manager of NBC's News Film Equipment and Lab in New York, gave the presentation, *Reliable TV News Motion-Picture Equipment Adaptations.* He told attendees, "The National Broadcasting Company has about 600 Mitchell 16mm 400-ft film magazines assigned to about 150 Auricon converted cameras." That meant four magazines for each camera. It can be safely assumed that that ratio was about the same across the country. While locals may not have had as many magazines, the cost was still about 80 bucks for each one, equal to about $600 in 2022, and managers were not enthusiastic about buying a whole new camera system. Enter Cinema Products to the rescue.

CP-16

Cinema Products was owned by Edmund DiGiulio. A 1950 graduate of Columbia University, he'd worked at IBM for 10 years before becoming director of engineering at the Mitchell Camera Corporation facility at 665 N. Robertson Blvd., West Hollywood. He was there from 1963 until 1967, crafting a motor to enable a photographer to execute a smoother zoom. He also invented a way to equip Mitchell cameras made before 1960 with through-the-lens viewfinders.

The problem with through-the-lens viewing in filmmaking was that the film needed to be in front of the lens while filming. This positioning meant the operator couldn't see what was going on in front of the lens. Various contraptions were mounted on the sides of the cameras to compensate for this, but they all suffered from the parallax issue. Arri came up with a solution in 1939: a spinning mirror that would rotate by the lens while the shutter was closed and the celluloid moved to the next frame to be exposed. This was a brilliant piece of engineering, referred to as *reflex*. The camera was called Arriflex. Its major flaw? It was noisy. It wasn't until 1960 that Mitchell Camera Corporation devised a system for its BNC, the most common film camera in motion-picture production. The downside? The system made Mitchell cameras manufactured before 1960 less and less valuable as the decade wore on. By 1967, DiGiulio had concocted a chop-shop solution.

He called it the Silent Pellicle Reflex Conversion System. It had a translucent mirror behind the lens which reflected 30 percent of the light into the viewfinder, allowing the rest of the light to hit the film surface. This light beam split was possible because the new film out that year, Kodak's Eastman Color Negative, type 5254 - the film of New Hollywood – was more light-sensitive than earlier films, so the cameras had extra light to split into another beam. In late 1967, DiGiulio left Mitchell and struck out on his own. His first project was getting his chop-shop up and running.

On the last page of the January 1968 issue of *American Cinematographer,* right across from the index of advertisers, DiGiulio had posted an exceedingly inconspicuous ad for his new company. It read: "MITCHELL BNC CAMERA REQUIRED. Full details including serial number, accessories and price to: ED DI GIULIO, Cinema Product Development."

Nearly two years later, he received an Academy Award for his through-the-lens viewfinder retrofit. Then, on page 61 of the January 1970 *American Cinematographer,* DiGiulio appeared in a full-page ad with the text, "I'll reflex your BNC for $6,000 or buy it, sight unseen, for $20,000." The ad continued: "Used BNCs sold for $12,000 to $15,000 a year ago. Your BNC is worth as much as $8,000 more today, thanks to our SPR. Reflexed, your BNC is probably worth over $30,000. Your money ahead with our conversion. We're No. 1. Over 35 of our SPR's are in use."

If he were able to nab just 10 cameras for $12,000 each after posting his first little low-profile ad on the last page of the January 1968 issue, before anyone knew what he was up to, convert them and then sell them for $30,000 a pop, he'd net more than $100,000. That's quite a tidy sum to build a camera factory. The patents for the Auricon Cine-Voice had just expired, so his next project was to update cameras for the local broadcast news market.

In 1971, at the Society's 110th Technical Conference and Equipment Exhibit, held October 3-8, at Montreal's Queen Elizabeth Hotel, DiGiulio unveiled his CP-16. A month before, he had announced what would be on exhibit at booth 12 of the show in the Society's *Journal*: "presenting first production model of the CP-16, our lightweight 16mm camera for DC operation, with magnesium housing, for shoulder-resting single-system magnetic sound recording, incorporating Bach Auricon centerplate."

DiGiulio's updated, modernized Auricon camera – which could accommodate the ubiquitous 400-foot Mickey Mouse Ear magazine from his former employer, Mitchell Camera Company - the same Mitchell product line for which his retrofit had won an Oscar - sold like hot cakes.

For the next two years, while not working on a particular Mitchell BNC camera he'd sold to Stanley Kubrick, chopping it to use a lens developed for NASA for photographing the dark side of the moon, he created an update for the

CP-16. It was unveiled at the Society's 114th Conference in New York, a few days before Joe Flaherty presented his Ikegami.

The CP-16R (the R stood for "Reflex," as in through-the-lens viewing) used fiber-optics in the viewfinder for indicator lights. The DC battery was small enough to fit in a shirt pocket. The new magazine Digiulio designed to replace those Mitchell Mickey Mouse Ears was made from the same material as pro football helmets. This camera was another enormous hit. The first models were showing up in the field in early 1974, but by then events were already in play that would render the machine obsolete and usher in a new era of motion-picture production.

Berkeley

The person behind these events leading to a paradigm shift in image-gathering technology was 31-year-old escaped convict, Donald DeFreeze.

Born in Cleveland, Ohio, in 1943. DeFreeze was traumatized in his youth by his father, then further traumatized in prison in his teens. He would do everything he could to ensure his liberty from then on, and a keen interest in firearms and explosives developed in his troubled mind thereafter. He moved to New Jersey in 1963, met a woman and married her, fathered three children, then moved the family to California. They settled in Watts, seven miles south of downtown Los Angeles, in 1965. Never able to hold anything more than the odd job, and never able to stay out of trouble (he had 10 violent outburst that required the interdiction of law enforcement during the Sixties), yet he had never been brought before a judge for a disposition in all that time. Whom he informed on during those years in order to avoid a court room appearance was never revealed. Finally, in November of 1969, he was injured in a gun battle with police, went before a judge and was sent to prison.

He spent the next three years being transferred around the California penal system. In the summer of 1972, he ran into a group of young Maoist radicals who'd infiltrated the Black Cultural Association, a self-improvement program sponsored by the University of California, Berkeley, and California State Prison Solano in Vacaville. He was soon leading the association's weekly study group.

In December, he was transferred again, this time to Soledad State Prison. He ingratiated himself with the guards there in order to get a good job with some personal freedom and then he escaped from custody, in March of 1973.

By Summer, DeFreeze was living in a house in Berkeley he shared with two women from the study group, Patricia "Mizmoon" Soltysik and Nancy Ling Perry. Both women had middle-class backgrounds and good educations, but the Berkeley psychedelic scene, the Vietnam War protest, the so-called free love, and the whole miasma of America in the early Seventies had thrown them for a loop. In the process, they became revolutionaries, looking for trouble. Paranoid and isolated in the house, Defreeze never went out, fearing he'd be caught. He and Patricia and Nancy wrote up revolutionary manifestos and communiques. They named their revolutionary group the Symbionese Liberation Army (SLA).

The idea of a liberating front for a symbiotic relationship does not bear further examination, and neither does the title Defreeze bestowed upon himself: Field Marshall of the Western Army. Counting the two woman and their friends, the little group's membership never got much higher than ten.

They were a disaffected lot, only one other was African-American, another was Hispanic; the rest were white, middle-class kids who'd been star pupils in their secondary school years. Two of the group were veterans of the war in Vietnam, and four met through a common interest in the theater program at the University of Indiana. The group's foray into revolutionary action would be violent and short-lived, with a strong component of marketing thrown in from the theater aficionados.

Their first act of terrorism was the assassination Marcus Foster, a gifted educator who was the first African-American superintendent of the large metropolitan Oakland Unified School District. This act of senseless violence does not bear examination, either. It convinced the other African-American in the group to leave, causing Defreeze to reassess the degree of violence he could press for. The 'Army' started to consider kidnapping as a more viable outlet for their revolutionary activities.

In December 1973, a member spotted a newspaper engagement announcement of two students on the nearby Berkeley campus. the bride-to-be was Patty Hearst, the publishing heiress. The name Hearst had been associated with one of the great newspaper publishing houses since the beginning of the 20th century. The theatrical-minded members recognized a good public-relations angle when they saw one. As the new year began, the idea of kidnapping the 19-year-old college sophomore with the high-profile name gained energy in the group. It wasn't hard to find out where she lived - her address was listed in the student directory. Then they started watching her place.

Not long after, there was a setback: two members were arrested. Suddenly an idea occurred to them, a prisoner exchange to free their incarcerated comrades. So, on Monday night, February 4, 1974, the study group staged a violent kidnapping of an heiress to one of America's great newspaper fortunes, and the strange saga of the Patty Hearst abduction began.

Their plan soon came to naught, however. California Governor Ronald Reagan declined any possibility of an exchange and the SLA had to concoct another plan. In a communique sent to a radio station, they demanded a food give away, starting by February 19, to everyone in California on government assistance, courtesy of the Hearst family fortune. This communique spelled out instructions on how the food give away should be done, and included a tape on which one could hear Patty say, "Mom, Dad, I'm OK." The whole package was sent to KPFA, the listener supported Berkeley radio station, so the public heard Patricia's voice at the same time the family and the Federal Bureau of Investigation (FBI) did. The nation was jarred by the recording, and interest in the kidnapping and the SLA skyrocketed. The theater aficionados had been right.

Kidnapping is a federal crime, so the lead investigating entity was the FBI. The Bureau, like much of the rest of America at that time, wasn't in the best shape. J. Edgar Hoover, the Bureau's founding father, had died just two years earlier, and Associate Director Mark Felt who, in effect, ran the agency for the next year during the servitude of two "acting" directors (and who was, as Deep Throat, feeding *Washington Post* reporter Bob Woodward background intelligence on the Watergate investigation) had left the previous June. But state and local authorities were ordered to step aside anyway; the old kidnapping playbook was brought out and dusted off, and the long ordeal of negotiations began.

Soon the public's attention turned from the SLA and their young, vulnerable 19-year-old college sophomore hostage to other events of the day, namely the unraveling of the American Presidency.

Nixon at NAB

By the end of February, Richard Nixon knew that there were seven indictments coming down regarding the cover-up of White House involvement in the Watergate break-ins two years earlier. They were going to be dropped on his administration on Friday, March 1. He was also aware that he was going to be named as an unindicted co-conspirator. To get ahead of the news cycle, he announced two press conferences. The first would be in Chicago on Friday, March 15, at an Executive Club of Chicago luncheon, where he would accept reporters' questions. This exchange would be televised live, nationwide, at two o'clock in the afternoon Eastern Time.

Then, on Tuesday, March 19, in Houston, at the National Association of Broadcasters' 52nd Annual Convention, he would take questions live starting at eight o'clock p.m. Eastern time, just as everyone in America, east of Lake Michigan and Panama City, Florida, were settling in for their evening's TV entertainment.

In the March 11 *Broadcasting*, a preview of the event ran: "Questioning will be done by members of Radio Television News Directors Association invited for occasion. Jesse Jones Auditorium is too vast to permit questioning from audience so RTNDA newsmen will be on stage with Mr. Nixon." Just who these newsmen were was described by the NAB's advance man as "a representative sampling of the broadcasters of America."

If Robin Hirsch or his father were near a television that Tuesday, they surely would have been paying close attention to the press conference, because the Lion of the Miami Media Market was slated to be on the stage that evening.

About 40 minutes into the presser, after reporters from Phoenix, Forth Worth, Nashville, and Minneapolis had asked questions, Ralph Renick stepped up to the microphone, introduced himself, and asked Nixon, "Mister President, at your news conference last October twenty six, you were particularly critical of broadcast reporting. You mentioned network TV reporting, calling it vicious, distorted, outrageous. The National News Council subsequently tried to obtain from the White House specifics on those charges, but those were not provided. Do you still feel tonight that you're being victimized by television reporting, network reporting, and could you be more specific?"

Nixon replied, "Well, as far as network reporting and television reporting is concerned, I realize that bad news is news, and good news is not news. I realize, too, that people don't win Pulitzer Prizes by being for; they usually win them by being against. I don't mean to say that in criticism of those who award the prizes, because that is part of the job of a good investigative reporter. But I don't think that - speaking to my long-time friend from Miami - I don't think any useful purpose would be served by me in talking to many of the Washington press, the regional press, and our friends from the NAB, to discuss the President's problems with the press. Let me just say this: I am not obsessed by how the press reports me. I'm going to do my job, and I'm not going to be diverted by any criticism from the press, fair or unfair, from doing what I think I was elected to do, and that's to bring peace abroad and, I trust, prosperity without war and without inflation at home."

It was the pinnacle of Nixonian noblesse oblige. Most of the exchanges that evening, however, were more in line with the one that took place near the end, between Dan Rather, the CBS reporter in the White House press pool, and the President.

The pool reporters weren't supposed to ask any questions that night, just the local RTNDA guys. But Rather was a local - he'd grown up in Houston, been a newspaper reporter and worked at two of the TV newsrooms there before going network and rising quickly, all the way to the White House. He wasn't going to be denied.

As the applause died down from Nixon's previous answer, Dan Rather appeared at the microphone and introduced himself. "Thank you, Mr. President. Dan Rather, CBS News." There was a sudden burst of applause in the room, the first time for a reporter, followed soon after by a not-too-subdued chorus of boos. As the crowd quieted down, Nixon ask Rather, "Are you running for something?" This elicited a round of laughter, to which Rather responded, "No sir, are you?" which elicited a further round of laughter - as well as some more boos.

Later, according to a report in *Broadcasting*, attendees returning to their hotels were heard "criticizing Mr. Rather severely for the remark; they said it was gratuitous and showed disrespect for the Presidency."

Perhaps Joe Roizen and his wife Donna were in Jesse Jones Hall that evening. A person of his stature would have been provided access, and he would have had a natural curiosity in how the victor of the Kitchen Debate would fare against the stars of local broadcast news. But he mentions Nixon's appearance only in passing in his article in the May *Broadcast Engineering*, in relation to the late upswing in interest in the convention. The article, headlined, "Electronic journalism steals the show," focuses primarily on four areas that caught the attention of "engineering-oriented visitors."

"The first is Electronic Journalism, a catch-all phrase that relates to more portability and greater speed and mobility in gathering the daily local news and getting it on the air," he helpfully explains to readers unaware of the new trend. He goes on, "experiments such as the CBS venture spearheaded by Joe Flaherty and his headquarters group has driven a number of suppliers to rapidly bring to market light weight, lower priced color cameras that can be shouldered by one person and carried out into the action."

The selection of the cameras designed for Electronic News-Gathering had grown from two or three in 1973 in Washington, D.C. to 10 that year in Houston.

The other three areas which Roizen reported grabbing engineers' attention at the convention was the ongoing battle between Quad and helical-scan videotape, making do with old existing Quad tape machines by updating and refurbishing them, and seven new manufactures of the new digital time-base correctors.

But attendance was down in Houston, by 20 percent from one year earlier, 4,825 versus 6,035 in Washington, and even fewer than the 5,006 who were in Chicago in 1972. One can imagine that without the presidential appearance, the numbers would have been even worse, so it's unlikely conferees had come to buy new equipment. News directors and chief engineers were only looking at the new portable electronic cameras in the East Hall of the Albert Thomas Convention and Exhibit Center, not placing a lot of orders. If anything, it's more likely that at the other end of the convention center, at booth 1010 in West Hall, there was crowd around the Cinema Products display, admiring the new CP-16R, and putting in orders to replace outdated Auricons. Either way, most newsroom managers probably thought they could wait to buy equipment until the economy picked up.

A Bank Robbery

On the Thursday after Nixon's presser at the NAB, Defreeze and his Army moved their captive from their suburban hideout into San Francisco itself. He theorized they'd be able to move around easier in the city and recruit more members. Being underground for months had squeezed the SLA's finances, so they needed more revolutionaries to contribute their life savings to the symbiotic cause. They rented an apartment on Golden Gate Avenue, a little more than a mile from FBI headquarters, and began putting up flyers on street corners under the cloak of darkness, in the dead of night.

Unable to procure any funds that way, the Army went with a different course of action: bank robbery. Not just any old heist, though – this one was planned by the theater aficionados with an eye on achieving the greatest amount of publicity possible. They chose a bank equipped with one of the new video security systems just catching on at the time. On Monday, April 14, 1974, at 9:51 a.m., the Hibernia Bank branch manager at 1450 Noriega St. heard a commotion in the lobby and punched the security alarm, which triggered two cameras to shoot a frame of video of the bank's entrance and waiting area every four seconds.

Fifteen seconds into the video, after a security guard and some customers were cleared from the waiting area, a diminutive figure backs into the frame from the upper right corner. Dressed in a long coat and sporting a beret, wielding an M1 carbine, the U.S. Army infantryman's standard semi-automatic firearm, the figure stands guard, the head moving sharply, watching, back and forth. Another armed figure, running in and out of frame, motions for the smaller one to move a bit to their right ... and then it becomes clear. It's the 19-year-old Patty Hearst wielding the M1. The newspaper heiress is assisting her captors in the act of robbing a bank.

When the video hit that evening's newscast, it caused a national uproar. As it's referred to in the news business, it was a talker. How could it be that a child of the elite, high born class would join with her insane terrorist captors?

Looking back, nearly a half a century on, the teenager's actions are a bit less mysterious. The middle of five daughters, she was the rebellious one, attending five Catholic schools in her youth - the last one was where she met her future fiancé, Steven Weed, six years her senior and a math teacher at the school. Their relationship was not to her parents' liking. And eventually not to Patty's liking, either: she didn't get a ring when they became engaged, and he abandoned her the night she was kidnapped - literally jumping out the back window of their apartment. The girl was none too thrilled.

While being held captive, in the spirit of free love, she was assigned a mate from the group, Willy Wolf, the guy who'd started the study group at Vacaville a couple of years before. He was the least prone to violence of anyone - he'd been in the lookout car with Mizmoon during the kidnapping - and

Patty called him "the gentlest, most beautiful man." He was also closer to her age and a product of a prep school education similar to hers. It's no wonder, after a lonely childhood in a gilded cage, that she found a home within the rag-tag study group. Besides, the vaunted FBI hadn't even come anywhere close to rescuing her at any time during the 70 days since her abduction. Living as a captive was becoming the new normal in her young life.

The bank robbery had an unintended consequence the SLA theater buffs hadn't foreseen. The SLA and its famous captive were no longer just a federal law enforcement issue - the local San Francisco Police Department was on the case, too. This turned the heat up on the group - DeFreeze decided to decamp the Army and head south to his old turf, South Central Los Angeles.

A month later, in mid-May, the cohort was getting punchy. Being on the lam in a strange town, moving about only at night, while stuck in a shack with no electricity and no hot water began to fray everyone's nerves. Since they were in a predominantly African-American area, DeFreeze was the only one who could go outside. The rest were cooped up all day, passing time by doing drills and calisthenics. Supply runs out into the wide world were a welcome break from the routine.

On May 16, a trio which included Patty, headed out for a run in the afternoon. Around four o'clock, they stopped by a sporting goods store and one of the crew tried to shoplift a shotgun shell bandolier, and got nabbed in the parking lot. Patty, who'd been told to wait in the van, promptly got out and emptied the clip of a sub machine gun into the store's sign, then grabbed her M1 carbine and shot off a few more rounds.

Store security retreated and the trio got away, abandoning their van and carjacking another, melting back into population. But their actions had awakened the famed Los Angeles Police Department and its new elite Special Weapons and Tactics team, referred to simply with the acronym SWAT. They soon found the abandoned vehicle; inside a parking ticket which led directly to the shack where the rest of the group was hiding.

South-Central Los Angeles

As the sun came up on Friday, May 17, the entire metro region was suddenly fixated on the fact that the SLA and its hostage, the young heiress-turned-revolutionary, were somewhere in Los Angeles.

At 9 a.m., the FBI busted down the door of the shack and found the place was empty. Its occupants had left in a hurry. As the hours passed, things started to move faster than the FBI could handle. The community of South-Central Los Angeles is predominately African-American, and the pale-white revolutionaries stood out like so many sore thumbs.

Soon the neighborhood was pin pointed, and by 4 p.m. the house at 1466 East 54th Street, 140 feet west of Compton Avenue, was on law enforcement's radar. The LAPD SWAT team started quietly constructing a perimeter. Hot on their trail came the local media, including KNXT and its Ikegami HL-33.

On the northeast corner of the intersection of Compton Avenue and East Fifty-Fourth Street stands Slauson Recreation Center. Behind the rec center is a sports field, free of trees and buildings, which offers a nice, clear view of Mount Wilson, and the antenna cluster at its peak, 20 miles in the distance. It was a perfect spot to set up a live shot. Photographer Rich Brito and engineer Ray Hernandez parked the live truck, deployed the parabolic dish, fired up the rugged little solid-state Microwave Associates transmitter and established a signal with the radio tower on the mountain, while the LAPD tightened its knot, as more and more bystanders came by to see if the SLA and Patricia Hearst were about.

DeFreeze had spent the day getting drunk and waiting for the LAPD, bragging to curious visitors from the neighborhood that there was going to be a gun fight. Daryl Gates, head of the LAPD SWAT team, was ready to oblige him. Tactically, once the sun went down, the offense lost its advantage, which put officers in danger. Local law enforcement knew DeFreeze wasn't going to surrender - better to execute a warrant sooner than later, get it over with. At 5:55 p.m., after 10 minutes of demanding the surrender of everyone inside, they shot two cannisters of tear gas into the house. Suddenly the building lit up with an immense amount of return fire.

By that time, the live camera was in position on the east side of Compton Avenue. The actual video is on *YouTube*. The scene is back lit like crazy. There's a tremendous flare across the shot from the setting sun. The reporter and photographer can be heard conversing with one another, the reporter trying to convince the photographer to line up for a better angle on an LAPD officer standing behind the trunk of a palm tree. The practical photographer responds, "I don't know if it's a good idea to interview somebody right now."

Eventually the shot gets lined up and the reporter ask a nearby officer, "That white house with the two windows that we can see there?"

The officer, probably traffic patrol sent down to handle that issue, looks at the news crew with complete disinterest and replies, "As far as I can determine. You've got[ten} as close as I have."

Suddenly shots ring out and the TV crew ducks and runs away, trying to find cover for themselves.

"We just took a bullet," the reporter says before collecting himself and specifying, "A couple of inches or so, 'cause we felt it go by."

"We felt it go by," confirms the photographer. "That's right," he almost gets out before laughing nervously.

All of this was live on the air.

Then, suddenly, the camera's shot went down.

KNBC had shown up a few miles away. The House of Sarnoff, with its monster color bus and its huge, doubled-up, vacuum-tube-filled transmitter, blew the rugged little solid-state 2.1 GHz Microwave Associates transmitter off the air. Engineer Bob Long, back at KNXT, quickly called his counterpart at KNBC and offered to make the feed from the Ikegami pool camera available to all. Soon the live picture from Compton and East 54th was back up on all three affiliates. Then the feed went statewide; after that, all three network news operations broke into regularly scheduled programing and took the picture coming out of the camera live on every television in the nation.

By that time, LAPD SWAT had run out of ammunition and had resorted to shooting every can of tear gas on hand into the building, catching it on fire. Brito was still shooting the scene off his shoulder, and the bullets continued to pop off, while the reporter informed viewers it wasn't yet safe for firefighters to approach to extinguish the flames. It was an especially poignant scene, because no one knew whether Patricia Hearst was inside or not.

As it turned out she wasn't. The trio from the sporting goods store shootout the day before had checked into a hotel in Anaheim, near Disneyland, to hide. She was sitting on clean sheets, fresh from her first warm shower in a month, watching the live shot showing the structure with her closest companion in the world at that point, the "gentle," Willy Wolf, burn to the ground, along with the rest of the country.

As the sun set, the fire fighters moved in to douse the fire's remaining embers and the live shot came down. The networks returned their audiences to regularly scheduled programing. Across America, general managers, news directors, and chief engineers turned away from their television screens that night and came face-to-face with the prospect of their proposed capital budgets also lying-in embers. Everyone in the world of broadcast news had felt the seismic shift, and film had suddenly become an obsolete medium for newsgathering on the streets of America.

KMOX-TV

Portapak

In his book, *The History of Image Gathering*, Robin Hirsch related this story: "The anchorman introduced the story and the director hit play. There was Kissinger stepping out of the plane and getting into his limo. It was one of those great moments that the general public was never aware of. They saw Henry Kissinger walking down some airplane stairs and getting into a limo. No big deal for them. What we saw was an historic moment for TV News. It was the first time our station had aired videotape of a news event less than a half an hour after it had happened. It was basically less time than it would have taken just to get the film out of the lab, let alone edited. Pretty miraculous from our perspective back in the day."

That "day" when Electronic News-Gathering arrived in Miami, Florida, is not noted in Hirsch's oral history of technology and technique. However, a general range of time can be ascertained from the facts that were recounted in the telling.

The story is found in the book's Part 3, "Electronic News Gathering-ENG," Chapter 3, "The Next Step Forward: The Portapak" under a section "Recollections, Video Untethered." It begins, as one would expect an image-gatherer to begin, with the camera.

"The newsroom had just gotten a new Portapak to play around with as a demo from some sales rep. It seemed pretty cool, but nobody paid much attention to it. One day though we got a last-minute tip that then Secretary of State Henry Kissinger was coming to town for some kind of political fundraiser. He was due to land at a small, local, executive airport in Miami, Florida around five o'clock in the afternoon. Now(sic) way to shoot it and get film back and processed to air on the six o'clock news. Then someone mentioned the Portapak. The news director said let's give it a try."

The reason someone tipped off the station as to the time of the United States Secretary of State's arrival at a small executive airport in Miami was because Henry Kissinger was on his way to commit a violation of the *Hatch Act of 1939*, which prohibits federal employees, particularly Senate-confirmed employees, to attend any political event, in particular political fundraisers.

This puts it sometime before August 9, 1974, the day Richard Nixon resigned the presidency. It's unlikely his successor, Gerald Ford, would have signed off on such an action. Ford pardoned Nixon a month later, trying to put the nation's chapter of distrust in the executive branch in the past. Continuing to commit gross breaches of protocol would've been counter to his agenda, tight Senate primary race in Florida or not.

Then there is the Sony AVC-3400 Portapak "demo."

When Ralph Renick, the news director who said, "let's give it a try," had been in Houston at the NAB show in March 1974, he no doubt saw the new portable electronic cameras intended for news-gathering: Bosch Fernseh, Edital, Phillips-Norelco, and Ikegami, to name just a few. But no Sony. They hadn't even been there.

The Sony Portapak, a single-tube color camera with a half-inch, reel-to-reel helical-scan videotape recorder, was marketed primarily to educational and business users. It had nowhere near the picture quality or physical ruggedness necessary for broadcast news.

WTVJ had invested $10,000 in a Consolidated Video Systems time-base corrector anyway - no small sum - just so they could play the video from the camera on air.

If Renick had been among the news directors in the one percent to answer in the affirmative on The Ohio State University's questionnaire on future investment in portable electronic cameras in the summer of 1973, he certainly would have gotten a better camera than the Sony AVC-3400.

Of course, they didn't buy it. It was a "demo," on loan from "some sales rep." No one even paid attention to it. Even Renick expressed a lukewarm affirmation in employing the device on a possible exclusive story.

This indicates that their ENG system, such as it was, was more of a place-holder, in case someone else in the market made a move toward live capability. That, in turn, would suggest they got it sometime after the SLA/SWAT shootout in South Central Los Angeles had alerted TV newsrooms around the country as to the possibilities of Electronic News-Gathering.

Therefore, one can surmise that the time span in which ENG hit the streets of Miami would have been sometime between May 17 and August 9, 1974.

Why would the news director of the number-one station in the 15th-largest market in the nation be willing to entertain a sales rep of a manufacturer of a mediocre educational-use one-tube camera and a half-inch, reel-to-reel, helical-scan videotape recorder - after it hadn't even showed up at the biggest broadcasting showroom of the year in Houston? Because Sony was on the verge of making a big move into broadcasting with its three-year-old U-Matic Video-Cassette System; which was about to become an integral part of Flaherty's ENG system at KMOX-TV up in St. Louis, Missouri, the country's 12th-largest market, which was scheduled to go fully electric on September 21.

St. Louis Post-Dispatch

St. Louis, Missouri, has a long, rich history when it comes to news-gathering. The city got its first newspaper, *The Missouri Gazette,* in 1808. By the mid-19th century, competition was fierce among the numerous volumes published on a daily basis. Joseph Pulitzer arrived in this media mecca in 1868 at 21 years old, with no money and no possessions. His first job was as a hostler at a mule stable. Of the experience he wrote, "The man who has not cared for 16 mules does not know what work and troubles are." That may be why, when he landed a job as a reporter for the *Westliche Post,* he didn't mind working 16-hour days, from 10 a.m. until 2 a.m., chasing down leads and working way beyond deadline – all this, while also studying for the Missouri bar exam.

In two years, he was nominated for the post of Missouri State Representative – as a Republican - in Jefferson City. Adding to his growing reputation as an ambitious young man, he also acquired part-ownership of the paper. To describe him as a person of considerable energy would be an understatement.

Born in Hungary to a wealthy family, Pulitzer was educated by private tutors and learned to ride a horse by the time he was 11. Hard times struck after his father died, however. The family became impoverished, and he attempted to enlist in one of the European armies of the time, with no luck. Eventually he met some recruiters for the United States

Union Army, engaged at that time with the Army of the Confederate States, in the conflict known as the American Civil War, and decided to emigrate to the new world.

When he arrived in Boston, he discovered that the recruiters who'd paid his passage were going to take a portion of his enlistment pay, so he bolted. He then went to New York and offered his services to military recruiters there.

He served in the calvary for eight months before Appomattox. Returning to New York, he briefly tried whaling but soon found it dull. Broke, with nowhere to go, he sold his last silk handkerchief for seventy-five cents and hopped a freight boxcar for the American West.

By the time Pulitzer turned 30, he was disillusioned with politics at the State House in Jefferson City, so he returned to St. Louis to look around for opportunities in the newspaper business. He purchased the bankrupt *St. Louis Dispatch* at public auction, then merged it with the *St. Louis Evening Post*. Thus was born the *St. Louis Post-Dispatch*.

Eventually, Pulitzer would move back to New York City and buy the *New York World*, soon getting into a circulation war with the *New York Journal*, owned by William Randolph Hearst, Patty's grandfather. The two publishing tycoons created a sensationalist style of news reporting, called "yellow journalism" to win the most readers.

Whatever the paper's philosophy, the *Post-Dispatch* was a news juggernaut. So when radio came on the scene, the publishers didn't ignore it, or lobby congress to regulate it - they got into it, way ahead of everyone else. They started experimenting with a signal in 1921 and officially went on the air in June 1922, about the time the precursors of the National Association of Broadcasters were forming.

The station's call letters were KSD; the 'S' stood for St. Louis, and the 'D' for *Dispatch*, in honor of the paper Pulitzer had saved from bankruptcy. KSD was one of the first eight stations of the NBC radio network that Sarnoff had started in 1926.

Of course, this legacy media powerhouse got into the television game quickly, going on the air in February 1947, from the first purpose-built television station constructed after World War II. The radio station's position on the AM dial was at 550, so when the TV station started sending programming out over the air waves, it got the number 5 spot on the TV dial and, like the radio station, it was an NBC affiliate as well, barony of the House of Sarnoff and equipped by the RCA labs in Camden.

NEWSROOM

CBS established a radio network in 1927. KMOX, which had been on the air a little more than a year, was one of the first 16 stations in the group. Two years later, CBS bought KMOX and made it into a 50,000-watt clear-channel station, that could be heard from coast to coast.

In the early Fifties, the network started applying for the necessary licenses to broadcast television on channel 11 in St Louis. By January of 1957, it was ready to break ground when its TV affiliate in town, KWK-TV, offered to sell its channel four license for $4,000,000. CBS took the station owners up on the offer, bought the license and got the channel position on the dial right next to KSD's. Then CBS changed its new station call letters to KMOX - and the competition began.

Sixteen years on, the ratings race between the two newsrooms was at a virtual dead heat at the 6 o'clock hour, but KSD still had the lead at 10 o'clock - 398,000 viewers against KMOX's 325,000. Then Joseph Flaherty placed the Akai VT-100, one of the cameras made in Ota City, Land of a Thousand Factories in the KMOX newsroom. The Akai, with Its one-quarter-inch helical-scan tape recorder, could go live, unlike the Sony Portapak. Once it hit the streets in St. Louis the news-gathering game soon changed, things became a lot more up tempo in the 12th largest market in the country.

On March 6, 1973, KMOX interrupted its Tuesday night movie at 9:03 p.m. to carry John Poelker's victory speech. He won the Democratic primary for the office of mayor of St. Louis. Not long after, KMOX went live again with a reaction from the losing contender, incumbent Mayor Alfonso Cervantes. Two days later, television critic John Archibald wrote in the *St. Louis Post-Dispatch*, "KMOX-TV isn't expected to have a monopoly on such coverage for long. KSD-TV has a similar camera, but is not yet ready to use it for live transmission."

But then KSD didn't go live. Instead, a couple of months later, the station unexpectedly stole the long-time 10 o'clock news anchor Max Roby from KMOX for a salary of $70,000 a year, equal to $430,000 in 2022.

A year later, KMOX placed a full-page ad in the *St. Louis Post-Dispatch*, on page ten of section C. It read: "As of February 26, 1974, KSD-TV has still not used a mini-camera for live transmission. They talk about their mini-camera equipment. But we use ours. In fact, we average a half-a-dozen reports a week, most of them live." Electronic News-Gathering had pushed the station over the hump at six o'clock; the race for viewers during the 10 o'clock news shows had become tight as well.

The lead text on the advertisement that ran in the Pulitzer-owned *Post-Dispatch* that February, in large bold letters at the bottom, were: "NEWSROOM, the shortest distance between you and the news. Where the mini-camera lives."

That summer, construction got underway on a brand-new set at KMOX, one designed for the second-generation minicam in an all-electronic newsroom. The layout was the physical embodiment of the editorial process in Electronic News-Gathering, constructed to demonstrate the commitment of the station to provide the service it was - in the words of Senator Clarence Dill at the 12th NAB convention in Cincinnati - "bound to give if they are to justify the use of the radio frequencies the government granted them."

And it was all there on TV, for everybody to see, the tools that would banish once and for all the phrase "Film at eleven" to the ash heap of history.

There were three cameras in the new newsroom. One was set up for an anchor head-and-shoulders shot, another for a guest cutaway, and a third was ready for a wide shot. In the main anchor-shot, the newsroom with its desk and type writers stretched out into the background. In the distance there were four glass booths, called "Decision Rooms," where edit decision lists, or EDLs, were prepared.

The camera for the wide shot, located to the right of the main camera, showed the newsroom from a higher angle. In the background of the wide shot, set off to one side of the newsroom, slightly higher than the surrounding desk, was the ENC console, where the newsroom's Executive News Coordinator worked.

In September of 1974, the ENC was Fred Burrows, who'd started out in the station's film department in 1955, when he'd been just 17 years old. He'd gone to the startup CBS abandoned on Channel 11 for a brief period, directing wrestling shows, high school sports shows, and a children's show hosted by Captain Eleven. He went back to KMOX in 1960 and proceeded to work his way into the newsroom, becoming a director, a producer, and an assignment desk editor. Then, during the last week of summer, 1974, as the station ditched all its film cameras and processing equipment, he took the reins of the newest beast in the race for eyeballs against the Pulitzer owned KSD, Joseph Flaherty's Electronic News Gathering system, in "Live Mode."

On the console where Burrows spent his days coordinating news acquisition there were three monitors: Channel A, Channel B, and another one equipped with a switcher, so he could look in on every other video process being executed in the newsroom, at the push of a button.

On the Channel A and B monitors, he could watch the feed from the field crews in the process of gathering the news. That's how it worked in "Live Mode." When the crew - two operators and a reporter - got to a scene, they hopped out of the truck, tuned in the Microwave Associates transmitter, and went live before they started gathering elements for their story. Burrows, back at the station behind the console, talking on one of his two phones, flipping through his Rolodex, kept an eye on what the field crews were doing. If things got interesting, like an automobile accident or a structure fire, he could flip a switch and pop the live shot up over programming, as the story was being gathered. It was that simple.

Most of the time, though, the live signal was just recorded on an International Video Corporation, or IVC, one-inch videotape recorder. A staff writer took the tape to one of the Decision Rooms, where the recorded images were displayed on a monitor that had a numerical counter showing the point in time the video was gathered.

In the late Sixties, three companies figured out how to keep time electronically on videotape, which allowed for easier editing. On October 6, 1970, at the New York Hilton, during the Society's 108th Technical Conference, Ellis Dahlin of CBS, and Charles Anderson of Ampex presented a report on their efforts for standardization of various methods of keeping time on a moving tape. The American National Standards Institute didn't approve their recommendations until April 1975 and, by that time, everyone was already using what had become known as the *SMPTE Timecode*.

In KMOX's Decision Rooms, a writer could look at the gathered video on a screen, with a lower-third graphic displaying the SMPTE timecode. Pushing a button froze the number; that point in time would be noted on the edit decision list.

After the tape was logged, it and the EDL were taken to the Datatron Editor located behind the Decision Rooms. The SMPTE timecodes on the EDL were then punched into the minicomputer as the one-inch helical-scan tape was loaded onto a player and the big, fat, transverse scan, Quad tape was loaded onto a recorder. Once the timecodes for the edits were entered into the Datatron's memory, a mere push of a button would cause the two decks to execute the commands and edit together - with the help of the time-base corrector - the desired shots and the audio into a final cut, which would then be shown in the next newscast.

The newsroom had three sets of equipment out in the field, carried around in Chevrolet vans (instead of in Fords, like Chicago's WBBM used). Other than that, the Microwave Associates transmitter, the CVS time-base corrector, the parabolic Nurad dish, and the good old Ikegami HL-33, were all the same. There was just one more tool included in this latest iteration of the system: a new portable videotape recorder, for when the crew went beyond the microwave signal's range and entered "Tape Mode." It was the Sony VO-3800.

Sony

Tokyo Tsushin Kogyo Kabushiki Kaisha, which translates to English as Tokyo Telecommunications Engineering Corporation, the company that eventually became Sony, was founded by Masaru Ibuka and Akio Morita in 1946.

Masaru Ibuka, descendent of a samurai of the late Edo period (1853 – '67), was born in Morioka, in northern Japan. His father, Nitobe Inazo, was also born there. As a youth, Nitobe Inazo showed great academic promise, and was selected to attend the second class of the newly founded American-modeled agricultural college. While there, he converted to Christianity. He continued his graduate studies in

America, where he met his wife, and also studied in Germany, before going home to Japan to become the principal at the prep school for Tokyo Imperial University, where he met Ibuka's mother, Tasuku Ibuka, one of his students.

The son was as intellectually gifted as the father, but he tended more toward industry rather than academia. While attending Tokyo's Waseda University, one of his professors, Dr. Tadaoki Yamamoto, asked the young Ibuka and another student build a giant speaker for a public address system for Meiji Jingu Stadium, Japan's first baseball field. At that time, PA systems had been around only a little more than a decade, so Ibuka was on the cutting edge of electronic mass communication from an early date.

While Ibuka was in college, some officers of the Japanese Kwangtung Army stationed in Manchuria, located along the frontier area between China and Russia and north of the Korean peninsula, went rogue. They were there guarding the rail line Japan had taken from Russia in the war of 1905. In September of 1931 they staged a false flag attack on the railroad and blamed the whole thing on the Chinese. They then proceeded to occupy the entire territory, changing Its name to Manchukuo. The Prime Minister of Japan at the time, Tsuyoshi Inukai, tried to rein in the runaway army, but was assassinated for his efforts. Then came the coup d'état of February 26, 1936, in which several moderate politicians were killed. The coup failed, but the military's control of the government tightened. After that, Japan rapidly became a police state under military control.

Upon graduation from college Ibuka took a job as a chemist in a film processing lab and would have probably spent an enjoyable life in that pursuit - except for the fact that Japan was in the process of being overwhelmed by a growing movement of ultranationalism.

The year after the coup d'etat, Japan invaded China, putting the country in a state of war that would last for the next eight years. Soon after, Ibuka was told to report to the Imperial Navy Wartime Research Committee as a civilian contractor with the Japan Precision Instrument Company to help design and test new equipment for the war effort. While serving there, he met Akio Morita, an officer in the Imperial Japanese Navy.

On the night of March 9, 1945, more than 300 B-29s dropped incendiary bombs on Tokyo, creating a huge firestorm that destroyed 16 square miles of the city, killed nearly a 100,000 people, and caused a million more people to be homeless. Five months later, the United States Army Air Force dropped two nuclear bombs: one on Hiroshima and, three days later, one on Nagasaki. On the same day the Nagasaki bomb dropped, a million Russian Soviet troops crossed into Manchukuo.

By this time, the Emperor of Japan (known in the west as Hirohito) had had enough. He convinced a few engineers from Nippon Hoso Kyokai - which roughly translates to Japan Broadcasting Corporation (generally referred to simply as the NHK) - to visit his palace bunker and record him on a phonograph as he surrendered to the Allied powers. It was necessary to smuggle the disk out of the palace to avoid certain elements in the Army, but at noon, August 15, 1945, Japan's surrender was announced over the airwaves of Japan, officially ending World War II.

The following month, Ibuka led his committee of 20 or so unemployed engineers to the center of the wreckage of Tokyo. There they set up a radio repair and improvement shop in the old switchboard room of one of the few buildings to have survived the firebombing, the Shirokiya Department Store.

The first thing this group of engineers did was make everyone's radio in Tokyo capable of receiving both long-range and short-wave radio signals.

Ever since the coup d'état, the military hadn't allowed short-wave radios, which enable reception from distant places, so the only programming that Japanese citizens could hear was from local broadcast. Ibuka and his crew installed converters that overrode the mechanism that blocked the vacuum tubes from receiving those megahertz waves, and suddenly everyone in Japan could listen to radio programs broadcast from places like Australia and Hawaii. After the devastation of the war, no one had any money, so the little band of engineers was paid in rice. With so much rice on their hands, they tried to manufacture a rice cooker, but this product did not prove a success.

Around this time, after reading about their efforts in a newspaper column, Akio Morita rejoined the committee. With funding from his father, a sake brewery owner (among other things), the group of engineers and designers founded Tokyo Tsushin Kogyo Kabushiki Kaisha, which they shortened to the catchy *Totsuko.*

By late 1946, Ibuka and Morita were searching throughout Tokyo for a suitable building to house a factory. They'd sold the company's only truck, an old Datsun, and had to travel in the city on foot, as the temperatures dropped with the approach of winter. One day they took a train south, disembarked at Shinagawa Station, on the southern edge of Tokyo's urban core, and headed west, inland, and uphill, away from the water and the drying seaweed on shores of Tokyo Bay.

They came to the district of Gotenyama, a neighborhood of hills known for its cherry blossoms during the Edo period. The area is still one of the top spots for seeing the bursting pink spring display along the Meguro River. There Ibuka and Morita discovered a building which the Nippon Carburetor Company had used as a warehouse. It was about four miles north of the Haneda Airport, (or Haneda Army base as it was known during the occupation) and directly north of what was at that time being organized as Ota City. This is where they set up the headquarters of Totsuko.

At this time, the company was converting military radar equipment into transmitters for the NHK, whose own equipment had been severely damaged in the war. Perhaps because, like everyone else, NHK was short of money, it gave Totsuko one of Nazi Germany's wire sound recorders which the Japanese Army had been using during WW II. It was the same machine the Ampex founder had taken from the defeated Nazis, patent-free, and used to develop magnetic tape in Redwood City, California. By the early Fifties, Totsuko had developed its own magnetic tape and was on its way to becoming a manufacturing concern.

U-Matic

After establishing the company with the successful rollout of audiotape, Ibuka travelled to America in search of new markets for electronics. He discovered that the Bell Telephone Company was about to license the patent for its transistor, the solid-state replacement for the vacuum tube and the greatest invention of the 20th century, to any company with $25,000. It took some time, but before long Morita was able to make the trip back and deliver the check and return with an example of the device and all the literature on it he could find. Post-war Japan was operating under a treaty that didn't allow any military development, so Totsuko's research had to focus on consumer applications for the transistor. It was the first time such applications for the device were researched. Eventually, they discovered that an additive to the doped silicone increased the power output, so they designed a small "pocket-sized" radio receiver.

It was released in the U.S. market with an American manufacturer's brand name after another American company's mini-radio had come out, but because Totsuko's transistor was better, it was louder and, therefore, far more popular.

Having themselves a hit on their hands, and free to market their product under their own name after the initial distribution, Ibuku and Morita decided to come up with a name a little catchier in English than *Totsuko*. First, they determined how many letters their brand name should have. They considered three, but Morita liked the brand name *Ford*, and so they settled on four letters. Ibuka, the guy who'd built the giant speaker for the first PA system in the oldest baseball field in the country, likely was aware that the Latin word for sound is "sonus." The inspiration to combine that with the slang for *son*, or *junior*, "sonny" (which was how members of the American Occupation Forces addressed kids in Shinagawa as they tossed them a stick of Wrigley's gum) led them to the simple and memorable *Sony*.

After its transistor radio took over the American youth market, Sony set its eyes on the greatest prize of all: television.

The company started researching cathode-ray tube technology for television sets and magnetic tape for videotape recorders. In 1960, they struck a deal with Ampex for an exchange of technology. Ampex was interested in Sony's transistor research, and Sony was interested in whatever Ampex had. The agreement between the two companies was possible because Sony was willing to stay out of the Ampex broadcast market and concentrate on educational and home-use videotape recorders instead.

The company had had good luck early on with its audio tape marketed for home use. Morita went so far as to write a brochure explaining the possibilities of audiotape for consumers. In America, audiotape was used primarily by professionals - musicians or journalist - not by the general populace. The reel-to-reel recorder design that Totsuko had developed in the early days of the company appealed to an unexpected group of committed, fascinated buyers: educators. It was a lesson Sony would not soon forget. So, several years later, when company leaders came to an agreement for technology sharing with Ampex, they weren't overly concerned by being left out of the narrow broadcast market in America in Sixties.

Sony managers and engineers decided that a consumer videotape recorder should use a cassette versus the reel-to-reel playback system to make the machine easier to operate. The job of making a videotape cassette was given to 34-year-old Nobutoshi Kihara, a postwar graduate of Waseda University, and one of the first engineers to begin to look for opportunities in the wire recorder design Totsuko had been given after the war.

It took Sony nearly a decade, but in late 1969, at the National Association of Educational Broadcasters annual convention in Washington, D.C., a Sony engineer demonstrated the design concept of its new cassette recording system for videotape, the U-Matic.

The machine was an incredible piece of engineering. The cassette was a plastic box about the size of a textbook. To load it into the machine, one simply put this familiar-shaped plastic box into a slot under the lid of an opening and pushed it down into the machine. Once fully loaded, the tape was magically freed from the plastic box and flowed copiously out in the shape of a wave, wrapping around a circular video head, which was set at the slight helical-scan recording angle. Then, suddenly, the uptake reel locked in and the tape was ready to go. The path the tape took in the machine formed a U, first by wrapping around the video head and then going back around the entire circular works to return back into the plastic box. This aspect of the design is what led Sony to call its system the U-Matic.

When the operator pushed eject, the tape unwound from its tubular path, rapidly returning into the familiar-shaped plastic box, and then popped out of the machine. The tape was now protected from the rough handling of the casual, absent-minded operator. It was practically a foolproof, inde-structible system.

The cassette tapes started being manufactured in late 1972; by January 1974, in *BM/E's* second annual issue fea-turing film vs. tape content, a writer observed: "A brand-new trend, coming to full force during the past year, is a pro-tape influence among the large advertisers from their experience with the video cassette – which means up to now the Sony U-matic system. The U-matic has become so widespread in industrial and business communications that tape is a new vernacular in broad reaches of American industry."

In the closing months of 1974, as the U-Matic was hitting the streets of St. Louis, Nobutoshi Kihara and his team of en-gineers were back in Tokyo putting the finishing touches on the latest development in videotape recording, the SL-6300, an all-in-one, 18-inch television set and compact videotape recorder in a teakwood cabinet, designed to overwhelm the home video recording market through a thing Morita had thought up called - "time shifting," in which the viewer was no longer constrained to watch a show only on the date and time that it aired.

The cassette used in this new recorder was the size of a pa-perback novel, one of those pulp fiction affairs found at the five-and-dime, and it held an hour's worth of videotape. They again named the system after the path the tape took through the machine, as well as the nickname given to the second system Kihara and his team developed for Sony, which was the second letter in the Greek alphabet: Beta, that, combined with the Latin word for "the greatest," gave the new system its famous name - Betamax.

WHAT RECESSION?

MONDAY, APRIL 7, 1975

Early adaptors

During the last quarter of 1974, more and more stations across the country had discarded the old machines and chemicals used for image gathering from the previous century and invested in the new electronic system of ENG: WCBD in Charleston, South Carolina; KRIS in Corpus Christie, Texas; KUTV in Salt Lake City, Utah; and KETV in Omaha, Nebraska, to name just a few.

Like KMOX, WCBD also went fully electric, using four of the new Akai VT-150s made in Ota City. On November 5, 1974, the day of the nationwide midterm elections, a station photographer shot a video of Mendel Jackson Davis, in his living room, watching WCBD on TV, as he was being declared the winner of the seat of the 1st Congressional District of South Carolina. The photographer then hustled back to the station and got the clip on the air 15 minutes later.

KRIS went with three VT-150s and a couple of silent-film cameras. On election night, crews went around town and got "Man on the Street," or MOS, interviews, which were turned around in ten minutes and put on the air. In January, these efforts, along with others, were recounted in the two main engineering trade magazines of the day, *Broadcast Management/Engineering* (*BM/E*) and *Broadcast Engineering*, for which Joe Roizen reported.

The third annual video tape assessment in *BM/E* no longer even included film in the equation. The cover story header crowned the victor of the ongoing competition, it read: "Special Report on Electronic Journalism." Repeated several times - in a spiral line of reverse text (whiteface type), resembling that of an old news wire machine - the phrase "WE INTERRUPT THIS ISSUE TO BRING YOU INSTANT TV NEWS" proclaimed the possibilities of a new world of live news coverage.

Inside, starting on page 34, 18 pages of coverage start with the lede: "Electronic News Gathering: It Is Off The Launching Pad, With Full Flight Ahead." The subheading read: "TV cameras such as the PCP-90 have been used for years, but news departments never really had a total system for handling news electronically. Simpler cameras, truly portable VTR's, TBC's, editing systems and light-weight microwave gear have changed all this. ENG is now taking off like a jet." This was followed by a roundup of experiences with the new technology from across the country, as well as an article about time-base correctors.

The January issue of *Broadcast Engineering* also ran a cover story on ENG, with the headline: "ELECTRONIC JOURNALISM: A new dimension in the news." The cover art included two photographs: one, a staged motorcycle accident scene, showing a photojournalist catching the action with the new eight-pound, three-ounce Sony DXC-1600 camera; the other, a behind-the-scenes look at an engineer cueing up a big, fat, reel-to-reel Quad tape onto a tape recorder. A CVS time-base corrector and a Sony VO-2850 U-Matic VTR were prominently displayed in the foreground. Joe Roizen's wife, Donna, had shot the time-base corrector and the U-Matic VTR while traveling with her husband as he consulted with station personel on video tape technology.

Inside, 13 pages were dedicated to the new paradigm in image-acquisition, beginning on page 18 with an article by Ronald N. Merrell, the magazine's director. Its headline asked the rhetorical question, "Where has EJ been all these years?" The subhead adds further context to a changing industry: "Is electronic journalism really new? Or is what we're seeing an extension of local news reporting that allows events to be covered more conveniently in real time?"

Merrell goes through an abbreviated early history of radio and TV, in particular their relationship in the sports and news arenas, arriving at the conclusion that both could now deliver content with equal immediacy. He hesitates, however, as to whether film would be completely replaced by portable video cameras, time-base correctors, and portable VTRs.

Following that piece, there's a round-up of electronic news-gathering developments around the country, running the header "Electronic journalism hits the streets." Likely written by Joe Roizen - though he doesn't get a byline, perhaps because his wife was credited with the cover photo – its style is more creative than the straight-up technical reporting elsewhere that month, omitting the tedious acronyms and number designations of the electronic system's various pieces, just focusing on success stories of those involved. The article concludes with a paragraph on the overall effect the new technology could have on the news gathering industry.

"At this writing, local electronic journalism is a growing trend. In many cases, its acceptance will be either bumped or pushed by union interest. Of course some manufacturers and stations see this trend as an invasion of the film territory. Doubtless, it will have that kind of effect in the beginning. In the long haul, it's a lot more likely that the trend will gather in people who, in the past, have not paid all that much attention to actively recording local news events. The trend, eventually, will lead to an increased interest in local news coverage."

One can imagine engineers across the U.S. - guys who'd spent their careers babysitting the huge pedestal-mounted video cameras in their air-conditioned studios, behemoths which required constant and careful adjustment - finishing up the article, then contemplating that last paragraph and the intended meaning of "people who, in the past, have not paid all that much attention to actively recording local news events." They knew whom those words implicated, and they knew what their futures held if Roizen's prediction came to pass: the replacement of the dependable 19-century machine used for news-gathering outside the studio walls with an electronic camera that would constantly require their attention going forward.

It was not beyond the realm of possibility that quite a few of the January issues of *Broadcast Engineering* were flung across a desk or two with a bit more force than necessary, accompanied perhaps by a disapproving grunt, as the busy readers turned their attention to that day's maintenance schedule for the fussy studio cameras.

Those January 1975 issues of the two magazines also marked the first appearance of full-page advertisements for Sony's new VO-3800, VideoRanger, the portable U-Matic tape recorder which had become part of KMOX's ENG system in St. Louis a little more than three months earlier. Also appearing for the first time in both publications was a full-page ad for Consolidated Video Systems' next magical black box, the CVS-600. The header on the ad announces: "Electronic Video Compression is No Big Thing!" The text continues: "It's just another little first from CVS. It lets you shrink a video picture and place it where you want." This technique, which came to be known as picture-in-picture, or PIP for short, would have a significant impact on the look of news as Electronic News-Gathering gained momentum.

Ninth Annual Winter Television Conference

One month after KMOX went fully electric, the Society of Motion Picture and Television Engineers finally got around to addressing the growing role that videotape was playing in the world of news-gathering. In the October *Journal*, the following notice appeared:

"*SMPTE Winter Television Conference, St. Francis Hotel, San Francisco, January 24-25.* Charles E. Anderson, Ampex Corp., has been appointed Program Chairman for SMPTE's Ninth Annual Winter Television Conference, it was announced by SMPTE Vice President for Television Affairs, Joseph A. Flaherty, Jr., CBS Television Network. Anderson has wasted no time in planning his program. He intends to have 24 papers on the program and so far he has commitments for 20. Anderson said the program will emphasize television news with papers from Cinema Products, Eastman Kodak Co., and CBS Television Network already in the works."

On Friday morning, January 24, 1975, Joe and Donna Roizen left their home and headed into downtown San

Francisco, to the queen of hotels on Union Square, the St. Francis, to attend the Society's Ninth Annual Winter Television Conference. It was the second winter conference to be held in the 70-year-old, 13-story brick hotel, updated four years prior with an unfortunate 32-story tower behind it. Back in January 1971, probably while the paint was still drying in the tower's newly remodeled areas, the Society had had its Fourth Annual Winter Television Conference, with the theme *Video Magnetic Recording* - 300 people attended.

That Friday in 1971, Joe Roizen had been the session chair of the morning presentations on helical-scan videotape and disc recorders. He'd also made the opening presentation on the updated French TV system, known as SECAM.

Four years later, he was back there reporting on the biggest standardization challenge to face television stations since the conversion to color nine years earlier, and in the process, trying to impart an honest reading on ongoing efforts to, in those familiar words of the Society's founder C. Francis Jenkins, "*secure best standards of equipment, quality, performance, nomenclature, and, unconsciously, perhaps, a code of ethics.*"

The two-day conference featured an assemblage of heavy-hitters from the world of image-gathering. RCA's Anthony H. Lind, inventor of the Quadruplex VTR, which used the big, fat, two-inch color television tape known as Quad, demonstrated the company's new 16mm film cartridge. Paul

Grigsby, from Kodak, introduced its new 16mm color film for news-gathering, Eastman Ektachrome Video News Film 7240, which boasted a faster processing time. Ralph Hucaby, chief engineer since 1953 at WLAC-TV, in Nashville, talked about his station's ENG experience. CBS affiliate WLAC housed the studios where the comedy/musical TV show *Hee Haw* was recorded, and so had the funds to secure one of the early Ikegami HL-33 cameras, along with the rest of the ENG kit. Hucaby was on hand to share the station's cost savings due to its adaption of the new technology. Consolidated Video Systems' William Hendershot III demonstrated the new CVS-600 and its magical video-compression capability. And a certain Joseph Rothstein, of Fairchild Semiconductor Components Group, talked about his company's new application for silicone called a charged-coupled device, or CCD. He claimed it would someday replace the vacuum tubes in video cameras, those fussy decedents of the image dissector and the iconoscope, which required constant attention and replacement. But the conference's star attractions were Joseph Flaherty of CBS and Ed DiGiulio of Cinema Products.

Flaherty led with the CBS presentation. After a brief introduction, he stated, "On September 21, 1974, all the news film cameras, film processing, viewing and editing equipment were removed from service at KMOX-TV and replaced with electronic counterparts." He continued, "In effecting this changeover, an entirely new system was devised to gather and broadcast television news." He then described the KMOX newsroom and how it was designed for "maximum efficiency in the coverage of the news from the initial story lead through to the final broadcast." He explained how the E.N.C. consul, where Fred Burrows worked, operated. He went through the process of covering stories in the field with microwave signals and the round parabola antennas and shared the editing and assembling process in the edit-decision booths and with the Datatron.

He then reported the results of all those efforts. First, he covered the increase in immediacy Electronic News Gathering provided, then the discovery that, closer to news time, when it was most needed, image-gathering increased, therefore leading to an increase in productivity overall. Finally, he got down to the most important subject on the minds of everyone there: money.

"Even though the electronic news-gathering equipment is new and therefore subject to higher capital depreciation charges, real annual operating cost savings of fifteen percent are being achieved, compared with the previous film operation," he claimed.

He pointed out cost savings by getting rid of the guy on a motorcycle who had to drive the film back to the station after it was shot, plus the guy who operated the machine that developed the film. He admitted the video editor at the Datatron was going to cost more than the film editor taping strips of cellulose acetate together, but he claimed labor for Electronic News-Gathering was only 80 percent that of film. Then he moved on to materials. KMOX had shot 1,040,000 feet of film the year before it went electric, at a cost $83,000. That, plus processing chemicals, which cost $18,000, added up to $101,000 total expenditures, compared to a mere $6,000 dollars for video tape.

All told, Flaherty claimed, "the cost of gathering, editing, and broadcasting a single news story electronically was fifty seven percent of what it would be using film." As to the "final arbiter of success" - the eyeballs on your broadcast - he pointed out that "during the first nine months ... the all-electronic newsgathering system was in operation at KMOX-TV the audience rating for the late local evening news program moved from a poor second to first place in the market."

The success of KMOX over taking KSD in the ratings race was no small matter. Most conference attendees would've been aware of the reputation of St. Louis' Pulitzer-owned powerhouse because it had just been recognized just that month as the number one news station in America by *TV-Radio Age Magazine*. Flaherty was careful not to take all the credit for the ratings success, acknowledging that "a number of factors affect these audience ratings," but he did make the point that ENG "may" have been a "significant" contributor to KMOX's success - a point not lost to those in attendance.

When Flaherty finished, Ed DiGliulio rose for his presentation, *Developing Trends in Film and Electronic News Gathering Techniques for Television.*

He began with a complaint, "First of all, I want to say that I resent appearing to be 'the man in the high button shoes,' fighting the last ditch defense for news film." "High button shoes" was a reference to 19th-century woman's boots, styled with a low heel and buttons up the side well above the ankle. Beginning in the early Roaring Twenties, with the birth of the flapper and dresses' rising hemlines, high-button boots were replaced by shoes with a higher heel and a thin strap - the pump. Yet out of fashion woman of the day continued to wear the sturdy outdated boots.

Picturing the man who'd won his Academy Award for the Silent Pellicle Reflex Conversion System five-and-a-half years earlier sporting footwear once fancied by Victorian-era woman would have certainly elicited chuckles from the audience.

He went on: "My company has been in existence for seven years, the date I left Mitchell Camera and started Cinema Products. And we were primarily in 35mm equipment until we did make our entry in 16mm TV-newsfilm. In those short seven years, we have become the largest camera manufacturer in the United States."

He was also the only film camera manufacturer to show up at the conference that day, and so it was his responsibility to remind everyone where they'd been.

"When TV news exploded suddenly in the early 50's, equipment manufacturers were pretty well caught unawares. The TV news people were desperately looking for equipment. It seemed that the little Auricon Cine Voice 100 ft. camera had a good number of features that made it suitable. It was a silent camera, it was simple and reliable. But it didn't completely fill the bill. So a number of enterprising rental equipment companies made conversions to it, to add Mitchell magazines, and add power supplies and such. F&B/ CECO, General Camera, Gorden Yoder, and a number of others, did an excellent job of doing this. And these conversions basically were the thing that we suffered with for the better part of twenty years. And I don't think that was very good performance on the technical side in serving such a vital and growing industry."

He pointed out that his company had improved the two-decades-old technical response to local news needs. "We introduced the CP-16 at the SMPTE Conference in November of 1971 in Montreal. We took a systems approach." And then he gave a nod to the new technical efforts by CBS. "I was glad to hear Mr. Flaherty relate to a total system concept. I think it's the only way one can consider these things. I think they did an admirable job at KMOX."

After that, the gloves came off.

After describing the CP-16 system he'd designed from the old Auricon base, he got into greater detail concerning some of Flaherty's claims about the cost benefits of switching to an all-electronic system. He stated that Flaherty had "presented some cost data. And of course I can't question the validity of this data. I was a bit surprised, though to see that the capital equipment cost was so nearly the same for film and video-tape, when I know that the comparable video camera and its recorder cost about 8-10 times what our film camera does." He further called into question the wisdom of making a total switch to all-electronic news-gathering in the first place, say-ing, "I was also rather amused to see the announcement in the trade press in which they describe the total investment was approximately $400,000. Projections of saving on film, film processing, and additional technicians needed for the old system show that the network should make its money back within seven years. Now I ask you, gentleman, how many of you would invest $400,000 with the expectation that you will break even in seven years? I think if it were an apartment building, I might be inclined since I don't ex-pect the technology of apartment buildings to move too far forward in seven years. But I don't know that any one of us would dare say the same for electronic news gathering."

Finally, he stated to the 400 engineers present that January day in 1975: "I think that developments and progress will be made in film. Eastman Kodak has never been known to be a shrinking violet, and Cinema Products isn't either. We're going to develop new hardware, we're going to develop new techniques, and we're not going to go 'smilingly into the sunset.' We're going to enjoy the competition.'"

In the March issue of the Society's journal, Conference Chairmen Joseph Semmelmayer wrote, "There was a lively floor debate about the validity of some of the cost reduction claims made by the electronic news gathering proponents. This debate is likely to go on for some time to come."

Roizen, whose report ran in *Broadcast Engineering*, was a bit more unequivocal. After brief bios on Flaherty and Hucaby, he wrote, "Not that the proponents of film are about to fold their tripods and silently steal away! There was a lively debate from the floor about the validity of some of the cost reduction claims and other advantages being put forward by the all electronic protagonist." After describing the film advocates arguments, he continued, "Nevertheless, it would appear that the new methods are here to stay and will continue to expand." And further, "The general consensus by representatives of various levels of television broadcast operations from network news down to the low rate card stations was that Electronic Journalism will expand to meet modern television news needs using whatever hardware is tailored for this application, even if some limitations in picture quality have to be accepted. Their position is that 16 mm news film with rapid processing already imposes a quality limitation."

Three photographs shot by Donna Roizen accompanied the article. The first showed CVS's Hal Blakeslee demonstrating its new "digital video synchronizer," the CVS-600, with this cutline: "CVS announced it has the patent on digital time base correction techniques, a fact that will concern many manufacturers." There was a picture of Joe Flaherty at lunch, sitting by Charles E. Anderson, conference program chairman, deep in conversation. It's one of the few photographs of Flaherty in which he doesn't have a broad grin on his face. The last photo shows Dr. Lester Lee, a Chinese immigrant who got his Ph.D. at Stanford University. He founded the company Recortec, one of the earliest Silicon Valley startups established by an Asian-American. He was pictured with an Ampex VR-1100 tape machine; the cutline read: "Dr. Lee delivered a paper on updating quad VTR's."

There was a good amount of image-gathering equipment displayed at the winter conference, the real equipment show was, of course, the NAB convention, scheduled to convene 10 weeks later, in Las Vegas, Nevada.

Vegas Baby ... Vegas!

It was the first time the National Association of Broadcasters would meet at the entertainment mecca in the Mojave Desert, and there was some concern among organizers and manufacturers that delegates wouldn't be able to tear themselves away from the city's offerings long enough to really give the convention their full attention. To accommodate for the late-night revelry, there were no early-bird sessions scheduled.

In the march 31 issue of *Broadcasting,* a special report on the impending 53rd meet-up explained, "Early-bird sessions might be appropriate in Chicago or Washington, but the NAB's feeling was that asking conventioners to rise with the sun in Las Vegas might be asking too much." So, nothing was slotted for conferees until 9 a.m. That's when the Electronic News-Gathering Workshop would kick off the convention's engineering conference portion, in the Convention Center's Room 18.

For attendees whose rooms faced south in the 30-storey Las Vegas Hilton, looking out of the window on the morning of Monday, April 7, 1975, the view of the convention center may have brought to mind a flying saucer that had recently descended from the heavens and landed in the middle of the desert. The huge, silver-domed, 6,000-seat arena of the Las Vegas Convention Center was a famous showplace. It had hosted the Beatles second American concert and a heavyweight championship fight between Muhammad Ali and Floyd Patterson in 1965. It was a far cry from the Sheraton Park in Washington D.C., or Chicago's Conrad Hilton, however. Surrounded by a landscape dotted with Paloverde and Yucca trees, with the mountains of the McCullough Range on the horizon, the huge, shining silver dome would have had an otherworldly appearance, and perhaps brought to mind the unknown new era of image-gathering that was becoming a reality, thrust upon the broadcast industry by some alien force that couldn't be negotiated with.

Room 18 was just off the convention center's South Hall. To get there, delegates entered the flying saucer to register, then headed south to the 90,000 square feet of exhibition space. First, they walked into the North Hall and its 90 booths. Directly to the left was Harris Broadcasting's booth, radio transmitter manufacturers. Directly to the right was the vast RCA booth. On display among the myriad of machines the Camden labs had cooked up was an odd-looking, A-frame-shaped prototype of a camera called the TK-76 Newsmaker Mini, which would be on the market by the second quarter of the next year.

Further down the center aisle over to the right, delegates would have come to the Phillips Norelco booth, makers of the PCP-90, with its new entry into the ENG market, the LDK-11. Beyond that, an aisle branched off right, toward the Eastman Kodak booth. There, attendees learned about the new 16mm film, Ektachrome 7240. To their left was Ampex, then Grass Valley and, finally, Fernseh from Germany's Upper Rhine region, with its new ENG camera, the KCN 92.

After that, the booths began to shrink in size. Marconi Electronics, on the right, featured the Mark VIII portable camera. Further down on the left was Hitachi Shibaden, with its new SK-70 camera. Facing Hitachi was Microwave

Associates, showcasing its sturdy solid-state microwave transmitters. Nearby stood a good-sized booth in which Consolidated Video Systems displayed its innovative wares.

Continuing south delegates would have passed through a large doorway, where the U.S. Army, the Army Reserve, the U.S. Air Force, and the Postal Service had set up small booths. Beyond was the South Hall.

South Hall housed another 103 booths. Delegates from newsrooms, and those concerned with newsroom operations, would have veered right toward the meeting rooms, seeking number 18. They would have then passed the booths of the U.S. Marine Corps and Television Equipment Associates, before coming to the Sony booth. There Sony had their portable VO-3800 U-matic VTR and the portable DXC-1600 camera on display. Next to Sony was the Asaca Corporation, and its ACC-3000 camera and backpack. Just beyond this was Room 18.

Perhaps, thinking they'd be early enough to get a good seat, they may have been alarmed at the number of delegates already there. If the newsroom guys were in a group, it's not beyond the realm of possibility that one of them sat down and saved some seats, while the others made a quick circuit to find the other ENG offerings in the hall.

Returning to the South Hall's central aisle, they would have found JVC, and its GS-4500 camera and PV-4500 VTR. Next to them was Editel, with its new camera, the

ENC-II. Right next to them, Ikegami had the newest Handy Lookey out of the Land of a Thousand Factories, the HL-35. To find Akai, delegates would've had to make their way to the other side of the building from Room 18, to an alcove off South Hall. This was called East Hall and connected to the south end of a concourse which ran along the eastern side of the building and was right next to a snack bar. There were another 20 booths in East Hall, among them attendees would have found Nurad and the four-foot parabolic antenna used in ENG.

Cinema Products' booth was all the way at the building's south end, along the wall of South Hall, between Dynasciences Video Products and a company called Paulmar Incorporated.

By the time the ENG workshop was ready to start, every seat in Room 18 was taken and, according to the ensuing issue of *Broadcasting*, "delegates were standing three-deep at the back of the room, completely lined the side walls and were crouched or seated on the floor in front of the stage." The panel was made up of some of the same presenters who'd spoken at the Society's Winter Conference in San Francisco, including Anthony H. Lind, of RCA, and Ralph Hucaby from WLAC in Nashville. Speaking on behalf of CBS was Thomas M. Battista, news director at KMOX, instead of Flaherty. The panel also included Albert H. Chrismark, from Meredith Corporation, Robert Mauser of NBC in New

York, and Julius Barnathan, president of ABC's Broadcast Operations & Engineering.

When Barnathan wasn't helping the Bureau of Standards develop closed-captioning for the hearing-impaired, he was overseeing the networks coverage of the quadrennial Olympics, among other things. A World War II Navy veteran, he'd gotten a master's degree in statistics at Columbia University before starting at ABC Network in 1954. On that April day, he was cementing his already-solid reputation as an outspoken and occasionally controversial leader in the broadcast industry.

"If you're not already into electronic news gathering, get your toe in the water," was his take on the current state of affairs in broadcast news. Further, he said, knowingly, "The first key to ENG is the ability to go live." The second key was that it could "save your ass late in the afternoon." He didn't think it mattered how much of the new equipment you bought, it was the "human engineering" that needed to be done - better to get the gear soon and do something with it to stay ahead of the curve. He did pause his full-throated endorsement of ENG long enough to consider the issue of standardization, bringing attention to the difference between "portable" and "mobile." *Portable* meant it could be carried. That day in 1975, he had to admit the state-of-the-art was mobile, since the high-quality equipment tipped the scales at a hefty 30 pounds.

Hucaby brought up an interesting conundrum that WLAC had encountered. Initially, the new system of news-gathering was adapted, with a stated policy: "There shall be no archiving." But then: "it dawned on us that license renewal is coming." A hasty adjustment was made. Two directives were issued: Preserve only those videos which had aired and record over everything else. KMOX's Battista, said their policy was to hold on to everything for 60 days and keep only the important stuff after that. Barnathan, in his typical fashion, opined that archiving could become "the greatest nightmare of all time," since, "it just lies around and no one will make a decision."

Next Battista played a video featuring the new KMOX newsroom. Then he made the observation, "We were the first station to go all ENG. We won't be the last."

In the next issue of *Broadcasting*, the reporter who went to the conference made this observation, "It was apparent from the remarks of the morning – and from touring the adjacent exhibition halls – that those electing to enter the field have an increasing number of options to choose among. That led Mr. Barnathan to remark about the 'confusion factor' in the business now. It was clear, however, that he wasn't recommending waiting until eventual standards emerge."

At 10:30 a.m. the newsmen left Room 18 and poured back into the exhibit halls, once again braving the gauntlet of image-gathering apparatuses as they headed back to the huge flying saucer to attend the opening general assembly and hear the opening address by NAB president Vincent T. Wasilewski.

Call Upon Our Greatest Capacities

The Management/Engineering Luncheon was scheduled to begin at noon in the Las Vegas Hilton Ballroom. Secretary of State Henry Kissinger, First Lady Betty Ford, and President Gerald Ford would be in attendance; Ford was scheduled to deliver a speech after lunch. He began:

"First, I want to congratulate the members of the National Association of Broadcasters on your courage in holding your convention here in Las Vegas. You could be the first broadcasters in history to go from a station break – to a station broke." After that icebreaker, Ford went on to talk economics. "This convention represents an opportunity for your industry to share problems, technological innovation, and trends in the broadcasting industry. Your industry has a unique challenge because of its power and influence in the nation. But like all other businesses, you are concerned about the stability of our economy, which influences your ability to survive and to serve your customers."

By the start of that year, the stock market had bottomed out and had started to climb back up again, the unemployment rate had peaked at nearly nine percent, and oil prices had come down, though not nearly as low as what they'd been before the Yom Kippur war. In March, according to the National Bureau of Economic Research, the 16-month 1974 - '75 Recession officially came to an end, though these things are hard to perceive when one is in the midst of a downturn. It would be another year before anyone knew for sure when the recession had actually ended.

After going over his plans to improve the economy - including a tax break and a cut of $17,000,000,000 in government spending, which the Democrat-controlled Congress ignored, instead adding $7,000,000,000 more in spending - he said, "Our continuing concern is over-stimulation of the economy through excessive government spending." He then went into the boiler-plate arguments from Republicans in the Congressional minority concerned with an increasing deficit. Near the end of his remarks, he said: "It is true that we have suffered setbacks at home and abroad. But it is essential that Americans retain their self-confidence and perspective. This is the time to mobilize our assets and to call upon our greatest capacities. I appeal to you to share my optimism. In my own life span, I heard the broadcast of Lindbergh's first flight across the Atlantic. And I first learned from broadcast of the need for emergency mercy flights of Vietnamese orphans. The media tells us what is happening. But it is up to us to respond. The news is only hopeless if we give up hope."

By 2:45 p.m., the engineers were back in Room 18, continuing their conference with some short presentations of abstracts for ongoing research. At 4 p.m., the acting bureau chiefs of the FCC offices concerned with television hosted their yearly hour-long panel discussion. By 6 p.m., everyone was back in their hotel rooms, getting ready for a night out on the town.

Of course, Joe Roizen stayed for the entire convention, talking to attendees and vendors, sizing up the direction the industry was taking. In his report published in the May *Broadcast Engineering*, he noted, "While attendance was supposedly lower than at previous NABs, in terms of registered delegates, it was quite obvious that those attending were from higher levels of management and that they had come to the show with the serious intent of buying something. Most vendors admitted with surprise that a great deal of their equipment sold right off the floor." Furthermore, he wrote, "The foremost impression gained from the look at the exhibits of the Las Vegas NAB was, 'What recession?'. According to all accounts, things looked good on the monitor screens as well as in the cash register."

Apparently, station managers and engineers had heeded President Ford's call to mobilize their assets and call upon their greatest capacities or, at least, followed Julius Barnathan's advice and stuck their toes in the water. It still remained to be seen, however, how all the "human engineering" was going to work out.

PICTURE IN PICTURE

THURSDAY, NOVEMBER 20, !975

Portapak II

Frank Beacham was 26 years old when he left *Florida Today* at the end of 1973. He moved from his beachside home on Cocoa Beach, with a view of Cape Canaveral, and headed north for Jacksonville and a job at WJXT-TV. In a single decade, he'd managed a radio station on weekends, covered the 1968 Democratic National Convention in Chicago, worked for a senator, a press service, and a regional newspaper. Now he was going to the very pinnacle of American investigative journalism. Of course, he didn't stay very long.

WJXT was the second TV station established in Florida. On the air six months after WTVJ was in Miami, it was part of Post-Newsweek's investigative juggernaut that Bob Woodward and Carl Bernstein, of *The Washington Post*, had just made famous in their investigation of the Watergate break-in. WJXT was that station to which former president Richard Nixon had alluded in a White House recording in

1972, threatening to complicate its licensing renewal. By the time Beacham walked in the door, the station's investigative unit, over seen by Bill Grove, news director and main anchor since 1952, known as The Walter Cronkite of Jacksonville, was one of the best in the nation.

On his first day at WJXT, Beacham received a phone call from the Post-Newsweek Stations' (now the Graham Media Group) Chief Executive Officer Katherine Graham. In his book *The Whole World Was Watching*, he recalled what she told him. "If you receive pressure not to do your job from anyone – anyone at all – I want you to call me directly."

Despite the fact he was "threatened, sued and called every name in the book" during his time at WJXT, he never made that call to Ms. Graham. Just as he had done in Neshoba County, Mississippi, when he was refused gas at a filling station, he smiled and kept moving. The abuse that was piled on him at WJXT was due to a rather high-profile investigation which had started right after he began work at the station, an investigation into no less a personage than a Florida senator.

On January 17, 1974, Larry E. Williams, former fundraiser for U.S. Senator Edward J. Gurney, Republican, was indicted by a federal grand jury for accepting $10,000 in political contributions from a home builder and contractor in exchange for setting up a low-interest loan from the Federal Housing Administration. The ensuing investigation of the senator was executed in Jacksonville at the Duval County Federal Courthouse. Beacham was thrown into this closely watched political investigation, along with reporters from *The New York Times* and *The Miami Herald*. At one point, he had to write a quick update to the story for the CBS network news. Walter Cronkite read his story on the air, verbatim. Beacham wrote about the experience: "For me at the time, this was a very big deal, Cronkite re-wrote virtually everything given him, but he didn't touch my copy."

Due to his widely seen coverage, he was offered a job at *The Miami Herald*. By the second half of 1974, the now 27-year-old had scored a gig at an established big-city newspaper, on the courthouse beat, no less. He found it not to be to his liking, however. "I detested even entering the courthouse. It was a totally phony place that I had to pretend to take seriously." Not only that, but he'd reached a point at which a reporter was no longer something he wanted to be. "I had come to the realization that working for a big-city newspaper or any other news organization was the last thing I wanted to do. I had been there, done that. I had seen the biases and claims of objectivity at all levels of the media. Some were better than others, but none were where I wanted to spend a lifetime."

In early 1975 he took some time off and went down south to Key West. One evening, he found himself sitting between two literary giants: Tennessee Williams and Truman Capote, "both drunk and drug fueled to the hilt." While he admits he doesn't remember much of what was said that night, he was apparently sufficiently inspired from this chance encounter to borrow $12,000 from family members and go out on his own. He purchased a Sony Portapak, the same camera and VTR outfit that WTVJ had used to shoot Secretary of State Henry Kissinger as he deplaned at a small executive airport the previous summer. With the new Portapak in hand, he "hung out a shingle as a 'professional' videographer."

He started out shooting depositions and "Day in the Life" videos for trial attorneys he'd met covering the Broward and Dade County courthouse beats. "Sometimes the videos worked extremely well, increasing jury rewards in cases where the recordings portrayed a particularly compelling story."

There were other times when things didn't go as well. "I'll never forget," he wrote, "traveling to Buffalo, New York from Miami in a snowstorm in the dead of winter to shoot a video deposition, only to arrive home with nothing on the tape. The video had failed and there was no way to check it while on the road. We were often literally flying by the seat of our pants."

By September 20, 1975, Beacham was in Starke, Florida, recording Freddie Pitts and Wilbert Lee as they were being released from Raiford Prison. Both men had been wrongfully convicted of murder in what was, at the time, referred to as "the saddest, most blatant miscarriage of justice in Florida's history."

The two men had been sentenced to death 12 years earlier by an all-white jury, without a trial because they'd pleaded guilty after being beaten into confessing – falsely – by police officers. A *Miami Herald* reporter, Gene Miller, had published a book recounting an investigation he'd launched, *Invitation to a Lynching*, for which he earned a second Pulitzer Prize. The book also caught the attention of then-Governor Reubin Askew, who eventually pardoned Lee and Pitts. When the gates of the prison opened and the two men walked free, Beacham was there with his Sony Portapak, recording the whole thing.

Beacham related this observation about the early days of Electronic News Gathering: "Video was so rare in those days that, despite the hit and miss technology, I did make a little money that first year. But it wasn't enough to sustain a real business."

Human Engineering in a Sub-tropical Paradise

The hit-and-miss theme was just getting started in 1975. Sometime in the summer, over at the Wometco Complex on North Miami Avenue, three new CBS ENG kits were delivered to WTVJ's loading dock. Robin Hirsch wrote about his first experiences with the new gear in his book, *The History of Image Gathering*.

"I was off on the Friday that the video tape gear arrived. When I showed up to work on Sunday, the weekend producer told me I would be shooting with this new video gear and that an intern who had been in the day before would show me how it all hooked up. That's right, an intern."

Of course, things didn't go so well.

"We got back to the station and we had audio, but no picture. All we saw was some nasty old video snow. I can still picture it in my mind and recall that sick feeling in my stomach. Unbeknownst to us the video cable from the camera control unit to the deck was a multi strand cable. Each strand connected to a separate pin and transmitted different information to the deck. Apparently the strand that delivered video had broken at its solder point but the one that told the deck to roll was still connected. Since the early decks had no warning lights to tell me that the deck was not recording video, well I was up that proverbial creek with no paddle." At that point, he grabbed his film camera and hustled back out to get some kind of imagery to put on air. "We learned from our disasters. Everyday was a new adventure . . . We also always carried a loaded film camera just in case."

Hirsch tells of recollections of the transition in his book, described to him by two other photographers on the WTVJ staff at the time, Al Sunshine and Jim Duffy.

As Sunshine explained, "The downside to the emergence of video was that it came on just at the height of the 16mm film camera development. Cameras like the CP 16A had integrated, built in audio mixers. They were also smaller, lighter, and quiet as a mouse. Suddenly, I was handed the video tape camera."

"Now I was shooting with a camera and a backpack attached to a record deck. It was like shooting while giving a piggyback ride to a small child," he lamented. "The camera was also constantly getting yanked by the guy carrying the deck who could not get used to a concept of the tether."

The issues didn't stop there. Sunshine continued, "you had to leave everything turned on if you wanted to roll. The deck also had to be left in record mode with the tape threaded up on the heads. Standing outside of a courthouse waiting for a defendant to emerge now posed serious issues. Do I leave the camera on and maybe the batteries die when I need to roll? Do I turn everything off and hope I can get it up and running before I miss the shot? It took about five seconds for the deck to thread up and the camera to warm up, would my shot be over by then? Film cameras did not have these issues, but tape cameras sure did. In the news arena this was a huge problem."

Sunshine summed up the whole conversion with this statement. "Bottom line, we had no idea what we were doing out there. The gear had just kind of shown up one day. We had no training on the nuances of videotape gear. We knew how to turn it all on and hook it up, but the rest of the time, we were just flying by the seats of our pants."

Jim Duffy had been assigned to WTVJ's Broward County Bureau in Fort Lauderdale, about 30 miles due north of Downtown Miami. "From the tech side, I think the transition years from film to video are the funniest to look back on," Duffy recalled. "I remember using that horrible Ikegami backpack that felt like it weighed eighty pounds." It actually weighed 30, as did the camera and the VO-3800 VTR. Add in the accessories – lens and batteries – and the whole kit came to a just under 100 pounds. And these guys were lugging all this around while chasing news stories in South Florida's summer heat. Of course, the weight was only the first of many other issues.

Hirsch pointed out one issue in particular. "Since this was electronic equipment, it fell under the supervision of the TV station's engineering department. They were nice guys, but kind of clueless when it came to the finer points of news coverage. For example, at our shop, the entire unit, which consisted of three separate pieces, camera, control unit, and deck, was transported in our ENG van in specially designed drawers. That's right everything had to be disassembled and loaded into foam lined compartments in the van's cargo area."

This proved troublesome for Jim Duffy. "It required so much time to pull out of its cases and hook up. When you were trying to do this on the scene of a breaking story, it could be very stressful. The story could be over by the time you got it all together."

While Duffy obviously has a good sense of humor - recalling these memories as some of the "funniest" of his career, - he admitted in Hirsch's book, "many were the days I looked wistfully at my good old CP-16 film camera. I was still in my twenties, but was already longing for the good old days." Hirsch added a litany of other problems with the new technology on top of Sunshine's and Duffy's reminisces. "Foremost in the assessment," he recalls, "was the fact that those early video images really did not look all that great."

"For the visual purist among us, the number one issue was contrast ratio, which is the ratio of the luminance between the brightest part of the frame, and the darkest. Film's ratio was around 1/256, while videotape fell in around 1/64. This meant that film had four times the range between dark and light areas of the given frame. In essence, film was rich and textured while video was flat and boring to look at."

What really gave Hirsch fits were the vacuum tubes, modern descendants of Farnsworth's image dissector and Zworykin's iconoscope. Of these temperamental devices he wrote: "Then there were the camera tubes, anybody remember those? The early video cameras used red, green, and blue plumbicon and saticon tubes to create the color image. Oh boy were those fun. They were the weirdest things ever and often seemed to go out of their way to make your life miserable. The most important rule was to be very careful where you aimed the camera. If you pointed it too long at a very bright object, like a production lamp or the sun, the tubes were subject to burn-in damage. This was even true if the camera was not turned on. Burn-ins were loads of fun. You ended up with an ugly yellow smudge in your image. The only cure for this was to put the camera on a tripod, aim it a very bright white surface, open the iris all the way, and leave it there for several hours. Somehow this cooked the burn-in away. Unfortunately, if you were out on the job, you had little choice but to keep working and shoot everything with a yellow smudge in all your shots."

Shooting all day at the southern extremities of the Sunshine State made the risk of burn-ins a constant threat. One can easily imagine Hirsch being super-cognizant of not pointing the lens directly at the sun, but then the reflection of the sun bouncing off some window of a car, or a building would sneak up and cause the ugly little yellow smudge to be in his shot for the rest of the day, a day that would not include standing around watching the newscast and basking in the glow of a job well done but, instead, a whole day dreading when your efforts would hit the air, and the look on the face of the Lion of the Miami media market when he came back on camera. It would be enough to make you dread coming to work if you knew you were going to be using the Ikegami HL-35 that day.

"And then there was 'going live.'."

The cameras may have been heavy, delicate, and temperamental beast, but there was no arguing with the game changing element of live news coverage.

On Thursday, November 20, 1975, Ronald Reagan, former governor of California, woke up in Washington, D.C., went to the National Press Club, and announced he was challenging President Gerald Ford for the Republican nomination to the presidency in the upcoming primary season. After the speech, he and his wife Nancy boarded a flight with their new Secret-Service detail and headed south to Miami to make a quick campaign stop at the Ramada Inn, right next to the international airport, before heading back up to New Hampshire.

Events in Miami were described in the *New York Times* the following day.

"In Miami the Californian's campaign, less than six hours old, was marred by an incident in which Secret Service agents, on the first day of their assignment to Mr. Reagan, wrestled a young man to the ground after he had emerged from a crowd carrying a toy pistol."

WTVJ's reporter Bob Mayer was on the scene with a film camera, but quite suddenly the story about the former California governor's long shot attempt at the highest office in the land had become a hard news story, and film coverage wasn't going to cut it anymore.

Mayer was, at that time, a little over six years into a 40-year career at WTVJ. All during that time, he would be the station's science, medical, consumer, business, and automobile reporter, all before being promoted to morning anchorman. Much of what he put on the air he kept, and today a great deal of it can be found on YouTube, under the username, *thecardsaysmoops*. On May 25, 2007, he uploaded the station's first-ever live breaking-news cut-in, giving the public up--to-minute coverage of the aftermath of Reagan's visit to Miami on that Thursday in November of 1975.

WTVJ had dropped some serious coin in its efforts to bring Electronic News-Gathering to South Florida. It was the only local affiliate in the entire United States to purchase Consolidated Video System's newest technical break through, the CVS-600, with its picture-in-picture capability. Watching Mayer's clip on YouTube, one can see the benefit the device could bring to late-breaking live coverage.

Two hours after Reagan was whisked away and the pretend assassin had been wrestled to the ground, folks who were watching Channel Four in Miami that day saw their TV screens go black, then saw the words THE LIVE EYE – white text on a black background - fade in. Underneath that slogan, the statement WTVJ SPECIAL REPORT.

A couple of seconds later, the title card dissolved to a shot of Ralph Renick. "Ronald Reagan flew into Miami midafternoon." Renick began, "after announcing in Washington, earlier today, that he is a candidate for the Republican Presidential nomination. He met here with a crowd of local supporters at the Ramada Inn off Lejeune Road, at 3941 Northwest twenty second street. As he arrived there, a man, appearing to have a gun, apparently grabbed Reagan, and seemed to wrestle him to the ground."

At this point, a black-and-white photo of Reagan speaking behind Renick's right shoulder, dissolved, replaced by a live video image of Bob Mayer, composed in a wide shot outside the Ramada, absentmindedly flipping through his notes.

Renick continued, "Channel four reporter, Bob Mayer, was at the scene in the crowd and saw what happened. And we will switch live to the scene now, with our Live Eye unit, for this report from Bob Mayer."

Then the director in the control room pushed a button, the CVS-600 switched the small picture of Mayer with the large picture of Renick, and just like that, the viewer was face-to-face with Bob Mayer, full screen. He then begins his report with the latest information on the incident: a tentative identification of the person who wielded the toy gun.

As Mayer gave his report, the photographer operating the camera carefully executed a slow zoom-in on Mayer, only to suddenly – inexplicably - stop short, on a poorly composed medium shot. Viewers at home probably could almost sense the anxious disquietude of the photographer.

Hirsch, describing what it was like behind the live camera, wrote, "For an image gatherer back then 'going live' was new, exciting, and a major adrenaline rush. I mean, shooting live news images on a breaking news story? Knowing that an entire city was watching your camera work gave the image gatherers a sense of power and responsibility that had never been there before. Image gatherers were used to shooting stories, but going live with a breaking news story was a very different experience that required a totally different mindset. You had to slow down, keep your shots steady, and stay locked into what you were doing. All the while your heart is pumping like crazy as the adrenaline rushes through your body. There was no worse fear than messing up while live in front of an audience of millions."

Film, the Basic Medium

Scenes such as this were playing out all across America that fall. According to a report in *Broadcast Management/Engineering* magazine, in a private survey of 780 stations, 195 - one in four - reported having ENG equipment. But the writer of that report was confident that "You ain't seen nuttin' yet!"

There were also indications in the magazine that by late 1975, Ed DiGiulio, president of Cinema Products, maker of the famed CP-16/A&R-16mm film cameras, had stopped enjoying the competition. The magazine's October issue marked the first time in 32 months in which Cinema Products had not bought a single advertisement within its pages.

Beginning in February of 1973, after *BM/E*'s inaugural January issue comparing film and videotape, Cinema Products had at least one ad, usually a full page, in every issue from then on. In the second half of 1973, with the development of the entire CP-16 system, which included an auxiliary sound mixer, an external VU meter, a light kit, and even a tripod, the company was running three or four ads in every issue.

The July 1974 *BM/E* arrived on station engineers' desk 45 days after Ikegami's HL-33 from Ota City, Land of a Thousand Factories, had captured the shootout at East 54th and Compton Avenue live. Within its pages DiGiulio published "An Open Letter to the TV News Industry," in which he pointed out, "Our CP-16s are the first truly professional 16mm sound cameras designed *specifically* to meet the demanding requirements of TV-newsfilm operations."

A year later, he published another Open Letter, *"Going ENG all the way is an idea whose time has not yet come."* He concluded his letter with this advice: "If you must be the first kid on your block with total ENG, be my guest. But if you want to manage a rational news operation, I urge you to consider 16mm newsfilm as the mainstay of your news gathering operation."

Two months later, Cinema Products disappeared from the pages of the magazine.

Eastman Kodak, on the other hand, had increased its advertising dollars in BM/E considerably.

In 1973, the company had purchased only a single two-page ad in the magazine, in the May issue's special insert concerning cable, which featured Judith Schwan, Kodak's superintendent of emulsion research. In a 150-word statement, she described some of the advances the company had made, including creating a new projector that could fast-forward and fast-reverse, all while allowing the viewer to watch the image.

The next year, Kodak bought a campaign of six ads in the magazine. Each advertisement promoted its new 8mm film system, a Kodak Supermatic 200 Sound Camera and the Supermatic 8 Processor, which was able to develop a 50-foot roll of the diminutive film in under 14 minutes.

Then, early in 1975, Kodak ramped up its game, targeting its efforts directly toward local newsrooms. Beginning in March, Kodak placed the same full-page ad in every issue (except June and August), which was headlined "At KY-3-TV, THE BRAND OF REPORTING AND THE BRAND OF FILM HAVE A LOT IN COMMON." Below this was a group photo of the station's newsroom staff, all of whom hold one of their arms up, extending three fingers on their hands. The ad text continued: "When the people in this picture wave three fingers in the air, what they're saying is, 'We're number one' at Springfield, Missouri, Channel 3. Thanks to hard-nosed reporting and hard-hitting promotion, KYTV is the undisputed broadcast king in the Queen City of the Ozarks. By a margin of 3 to 1."

Amongst the group holding up three fingers was Virgil Ward, legendary host of the syndicated TV program *Championship Fishing*. The ad copy read, "You can catch their weekly fishing show on 87 markets in the U.S. and Canada. And when Virgil packs his rod and reel, he includes a reel of Eastman film."

Ward probably took more than one reel of film when he went out on the water. It's a pretty safe assumption that they burned through film like crazy producing that show, which may explain why they were featured in the promotional campaign to begin with.

By October, Kodak had refined its ad campaign with a new slogan: "*Film. The basic medium.*" The ad that introduced this slogan, which ran on page 26 and 27, included a 300-word essay that pressed the importance of image quality in newsgathering. It read: "As any pro will tell you," the text read, "it's not so much what you shoot with, but what you shoot at, that makes for a newsworthy item. But as any viewer will tell you, if it doesn't look 'interesting' on the home screen, an item may be ignored, regardless of its content. So when we say film is the basic medium, we think it supports what's basic to good reporting. Film's fine image quality lets it function as the backbone of quality reporting. And its versatility helps you get the depth that every major story needs."

Two months later, on page 27 of the last issue of *Broadcast Management/Engineering* of 1975, a new station was featured in Kodak's *Basic Medium* campaign, Oklahoma City's WKY-TV.

The headline on the ad read, "Kodak salutes the NPPA 'Newsfilm Station of the Year.'" Below that was a photo of WKY's three main anchors: Ernie Schultz, noon; Jack Ogle, 6 p.m.; and George Tomek, 10 p.m. The men, gathered around assignment editor Gene Allen, stare intently at something on his desk. Beneath the photo were two columns of text, each with its own headline. The first headline was "This is the heart of WKY-TV," referring to the photo above. The second column's headline was "And this is the backbone." That headline referred to an image below, of a news photographer shouldering a CP-16/A camera, pointing it at the viewer. Unlike the three office guys in the top picture, the photographer wasn't wearing a tie and he had long hair and a moustache. The cutline of the photo of the backbone of the WKY's newsroom photo read: "Darrell Barton, Chief Photographer."

Darrell Wayne Barton was born in 1942 in Crossett, Arkansas, a town of less than 5,000 people, situated a little more than seven miles north of the state's border with Louisiana and 50 miles west of the Mississippi River, right on the edge of the Arkansas Delta region. One of his early childhood memories was of driving his family's horse-drawn vegetable wagon into town. When he was in eighth grade, a *Time-Life* photographer came to his school to speak about his vocation. Young Darrell was bitten by the photojournalism bug. It wasn't long afterward he sold his first photograph. Three years later, he told his father he wanted to be a professional photographer. His father replied that photography made a good hobby but it was not something he should pursue as a career.

After graduating from high school, he took a job with a photography studio, taking school pictures, wedding photos, and, of course, baby pictures. Eventually, he joined the U.S. Marine Corps, intending to be a military photographer, but the recruiter misrepresented enlistment details and he ended up in Vietnam as combat infantryman instead.

Upon completing his enlistment, he went to college at Wichita State, in Kansas. While there he worked on the staff of *The Sunflower*, the student-run campus newspaper. One of his early assignments was to photograph someone boarding a bus. Later he recalled, "The buses were on strike and no one was riding. I saw this cute blond at a McDonald's and asked her to stand by the bus and act like she was getting on. Best picture I ever took and I've been married to her for 39 years."

Eventually he landed a job at Wichita's ABC affiliate, KAKE-TV, and worked there for two years. Then, in the Spring of 1969, he joined WKY, which was the NBC affiliate in Oklahoma City, which at that time had a nationwide reputation as a great photography shop, having just won Newsfilm Station of the Year in '68. Within a year, Barton was promoted to chief photographer; by the end of 1974, he'd been awarded the National Press Photographers Association's "Newsfilm Cameraman of the Year" honors.

The year-long contest required a photographer to enter several stories representing different aspects of news-gathering. One story's subject had to be breaking news, another a feature, yet another a sports story. It required a demonstration of excellence in shooting news in a broad spectrum of situations and storytelling styles. Prior to Barton's winning the award, it had been mostly the territory of network freelancers or cameramen in top 10 markets. Barton had been the first winner from a medium-market station. At that time, Oklahoma City was ranked number 43 in market size, according to Barton – though according to the1974 *Broadcast Yearbook* it was ranked 39.

In 1975 he'd helped WKY win its second Newsfilm Station of the Year award. In April of 1976, *BM/E* published an article on the station's approach to news in the ever-changing environment of film versus tape.

"'Lets face it, in a market like this . . . we aren't likely to have too many big stories,' Barton says. 'But we make the most of what we have. That includes shooting a higher than average ratio of film per story, including as many different angles as possible.'"

His shooting style on a story about a quilting bee and his style on another piece on a blood drive were described thusly: "He spent considerable time speaking to the people involved. He found out why they were really there, what they were doing, and who they were. When he was ready to film, he treated both stories as mini-documentaries. There were few standup interviews. Instead, Barton took full advantage of the portability of his CP-16/A. There were at least 15 scenes filmed for each story. Barton ranged physically from sitting on the floor to standing on tables, looking for interesting visual angles, while recording wild sound on film with a shotgun microphone."

It was, among other things, this plethora of angles which made the newsroom managers at WKY hesitant to jump on the ENG bandwagon. They did have a kit, however, which included the camera from the Upper Rhine region, the Bosch Fernseh KCN, as well as the Sony VO 3800. But Ernie Shultz, the station's noon anchor, was quoted as saying, "As a daily working tool, it isn't nearly as portable as our film cameras. Instead of getting 10 or 15 angles on a story, we usually end up with four or five. This changes the pace of the story on the air, makes it slower."

Not only that, but there was the difference in the look of the two mediums. The article continued: "Since the bulk of each news program is film, one can not indiscriminately switch to ENG without a noticeable colorimetry shift."

So, the station's newsroom managers and promotion managers decided "not to ballyhoo the 'mini-cam' capability out of proportion. 'I think some stations have made a big mistake by coming on too strong, too fast, with the instant news potential of ENG in their promos,' Schultz says. 'It confuses everyone and creates expectations which are impossible to live up to.'"

A Digital Camera in Rochester

That December, in 1975, when Kodak first used Darrell Barton and his CP-16 to illustrate the backbone of the WKY news operation in its *Basic Medium* ad campaign, deep inside the research labs at the 120-acre Kodak Park in Rochester, New York, a 25-year-old Steven J. Sasson was finishing up his research on the functionality of Fairchild Semiconductor's charged coupled device that Joseph Rothstein had talked about at the Society's Ninth Annual Winter Television Conference. In his lab that month, Sasson photographed a woman named Joy, using the first digital camera. The toaster-sized camera was able to save the image captured by the silicon replacement for the dreaded vacuum tubes digitally onto an audio cassette tape. When this audio cassette tape was played back, it could load the image onto a television screen.

When he demonstrated the film-free camera and television viewing to his higher-ups, they were not impressed. "Who would want to look at their pictures on a TV screen?"

Perhaps out of curiosity they'd inquired as to just how long it would take before the digital technique would equal Kodak's 110 film. That was the company's product that had the lowest image quality.

Sasson referred to the decade-old observation Gordon Moore made when he was at Fairchild Semiconductor, which he'd published in *Electronics* magazine on April 19, 1965, in the article, *Cramming more components onto integrated circuits*. Moore had predicted that the number of transistors on a microchip would double every year. Based on that theory, which had become known in the previous decade as *Moore's Law*, Sasson figured it would take 15 years to arrive at the two million pixels necessary to compete against 110 film.

After he reported this projection back to the bosses, they told him to keep his industry-changing invention to himself. There would be no presentation at a SMPTE Technical Conference for the original toaster-sized digital camera. No paper published in any technical journal. No efforts at future standardization. None of the *unselfish exchange of views* that Jenkin's, back in 1916, had so celebrated. Instead, the breakthrough camera of the era would be tucked inside some closet in some storage room somewhere on the 120-acre Rochester Park campus while research into digital memory storage continued.

In hindsight, it may not have been the best strategy for Kodak to follow.

RCA TK-76

JANUARY 23, 1976

Ta Da ...

At 5 p.m. on Monday, September 29, 1975, the hardware display at the Society of Motion Picture and Television Engineers' 117th Technical Conference & Equipment Exhibit opened with great fanfare, including a ceremonial ribbon cutting, at Los Angeles' Century City Hotel. It was the largest such show the Society had ever hosted, with 110 exhibitors. More than 1,200 people were registered to attend; many more motion-picture industry types came through just to check out the new gear that week. There was a significant amount of interest for a hardware show - it was the Society's first gathering held on United States soil since the gun battle between the LAPD S.W.A.T. team and the SLA, and a lot had happened since then.

The 1974 115th Spring Conference, after the New York City Fall conference - the one where Flaherty had introduced the Ikegami HL-33, had been held April 21 - 26 at Century

City as well, a mere 11 miles away from where the intense firefight would go live nationwide 22 days later.

The 116th Conference had been held in October 1974 in Toronto. In the February 1975 *American Cinematographer,* Anton Wilson wrote, "The equipment show at the recent 116th SMPTE Technical Conference and Equipment Exhibit in Toronto was relatively small compared with those of the shows held in New York and Los Angeles. Not only was the show small in size, but there were few earthshaking new products."

When spring rolled around again, for the first time in the Society's history, no conference was held at all.

Back in July 1974, at the Society's annual Board of Governors meeting, a resolution had been passed, which read: "*Resolved that beginning in 1975 the Society hold one major Conference per year in the fall, the 1975 Conference to be held in Los Angeles and the 1976 Conference to be held in New York.*" This curtailing of Society gatherings was no doubt due to the energy crisis; it led to a larger than-usual show in the autumn of 1975.

"Noteworthy" at the 117th equipment exhibit, according to a report which appeared in the Society's November *Journal,* "was the increase in the amount of video equipment shown (as compared to even two years ago)." Joseph Roizen was there, of course, he observed: "A tour of the three halls that housed the equipment exhibits showed the increasing penetration of video equipment into what was an almost exclusively film hardware show a few years ago." He also pointed out that "the emphasis in the video exhibits was on Electronic News Gathering."

The electronic camera-makers who were on hand included Asaka, International Video Corporation, RCA, Sony, and Toshiba. Notable for their absence were Akai, Bosch-Fernseh, Phillips Norelco, and Ikegami – though Ikegami cameras were on display at the Frezzolini Electronics booth, demonstrating a new line of "lightweight power packs" for the HL-33 & 35 - but all the manufacturers with whom Joe Flaherty had worked with skipped the show.

Flaherty was there nonetheless, giving the opening presentation Thursday morning to the *News Gathering for Television* session, the Society's inaugural conference session to focus on Electronic News Gathering.

According to the *Journal* report, "Ed DiGiulio, Session and Topic Chairman, introduced Mr. Flaherty of CBS as 'The Guru of Electronic Newsgathering.'" In his presentation, Flaherty speculated, "By the end of 1975, 132 independent TV stations would be using ENG. All of CBS's owned-and-operated stations use ENG. Currently, 33 CBS affiliates have at least one system and by the end of the year this number will be increased to 52 stations." As it turned out, his estimates concerning the spread of ENG were low. He did admit that "CBS was still a big user of film and will continue to be so." As to what the final mix between film and video might be, he was unwilling to venture a guess.

DiGiulio, for his part, displayed two new breakthrough pieces of equipment. "Of special interest," stated the *Journal* report, "were the additions Cinema Products had made to its Cinevid system one of them being an electronic viewfinder described as a 'video-assist' system. In operation, a lightweight video camera of very small dimensions picks up a 400-line video image directly from the CP-16R reflex ground glass. This image can be transmitted to monitors or can be recorded on video tape to provide 'instant' dailies." Less remarked upon was the new camera support device DiGiulio had developed, in partnership with cinematographer Garrett Brown, called a Steadicam.

Roizen reported on the broad scope of the RCA line of products. "The RCA exhibit played both sides of the fence, with the production version of their ENG camera, the TK-76, and their fast sequence film cartridge scanner, the TCP 1624, they could handle either medium." The Society's *Journal* expanded on his assessment. "RCA Corp. exhibited, besides its film projection equipment, a lightweight TK-76 portable color TV camera, which needs no backpack and is as rugged and easy to operate as a film camera. It has 'big camera' automatic operating features for producing quality color pictures, and uses 16 mm cine-type lenses."

To the Hollywood industry crowd wandering the floors of the three halls, the little video camera, colored in the same signature blue hue as the rest of the RCA line of broadcast equipment, would have likely appeared as something of an oddity. It was reported by Herb A. Lightman, in the December *American Cinematographer*, "The Equipment Exhibition, although much larger than ever before, presented few if any major new items which had not already been featured."

Lightman had been in London in June for *FILM-75*, the fourth biennial International Technology Conference and Exhibition sponsored by the British Kinematograph, Sound and Television Society, which was the Steadicam's coming out party. According to Lightman's write-up in the September *American Cinematographer*, from watching "raw footage shot by Haskell Wexler, ASC for a Keds (shoe) commercial, in which very energetic teenagers run in fast random movements ... with the camera 'floating' alongside them ... (i)t became obvious that this development is no mere gimmick, but is, instead, a major advance that could have a very significant impact on future film-making."

That the 117th Conference was the setting for the first U.S. demonstration of the new device didn't warrant much excitement, according to Lightman. There was no mention whatsoever of RCA's new video camera.

In reality, it's unlikely that most of the camera's target customers made the trip to Los Angeles that week. Lodging a medium-market TV station's chief engineer at the aluminum-sheathed Century City Hotel for one night to go to a single morning's session on Electronic News Gathering and then take a quick peek at RCA's new camera - still under development for manufacture and not due to hit the streets for another 10 months - before hopping a flight home was not something most cost-conscious General Managers back East and in the Midwest would have entertained. The absence of this segment of the industry weakened any word-of-mouth excitement which could have highlighted the camera's possibilities, making the first public viewing of RCA's third-generation video camera rather less than earthshaking.

10th Annual Winter Television Conference

The three image-acquisition equipment shows in 1975 - San Francisco's Winter Conference, the NAB convention in Las Vegas, and the Society's Los Angeles' Technical Conference - took place on or near the West Coast. A full year was a long stretch to not hold equipment exhibitions in the Eastern Time Zone, but that situation was about to be remedied. In the Society's November 1975 *Journal*, Frederick Remley, head of University of Michigan's Television Center and the organizer of the Society's first Winter Television Conference, announced: "... SMPTE returns to the place where the first one was held, Detroit. The meeting is set for January 23 and 24 at the Sheraton-Southfield Hotel."

Of course, the conference, which was to be focused *on Television Newsgathering and Digital Video*, wasn't returning exactly to where it had first been held, the austere and intimidating Horace H Rackham Building.

Much had changed in Detroit in the 10 years since 300 engineers had braved a major blizzard to congregate at the Rackham to learn about color television broadcasting. Six months later, the worst riot to take place on American soil since the New York City Draft Riots more than a century earlier, erupted about a mile-and-a-half to the west of Rackham. The immediate aftermath of the bloodiest incident of the "Long, hot summer of 1967" was a sharp increase in white flight to the suburbs. Detroit schools lost nearly three-quarters of their white students in the next decade. At the same time, there was a marked uptick in gun sales and crime. In 1967, there were 232 homicides in Detroit; by 1974, that number had soared to 751.

So, the Society decided to hold the 1976 gathering 10 miles northwest of the Rackham, up the John C. Lodge Freeway, just across Eight Mile Road, the border between Black Detroit to the south and the white suburbs to the north, in what had become the greater metropolitan area's broadcast media corridor.

Along a four-mile stretch of the Lodge Freeway in Southfield, just north of Detroit city limits, four broadcast concerns had established studios in the previous 16 years.

WXYZ -TV, Detroit's ABC affiliate, had opened its studios on Ten Mile Road in 1959, west of the freeway. WKBD-TV, primarily a sports station, opened its studios on Eleven Mile Road in 1965. WJBK – TV, the area's CBS affiliate, opened its studios on Nine Mile Road, east of the freeway, in 1970. That same year, the Specs Howard School of Broadcast Arts – a private career school offering curricula in broadcast media arts – began operations off Eight Mile Road, by the freeway's west side.

In 1973, the 17-storey high, 400-room Southfield-Sheraton Hotel was thrown up on the south side of Nine Mile Road, across from WJBK. An advertisement in the November 1977 issue of *The Detroit Jewish News* described the accommodations. "Guest rooms at the Sheraton-Southfield Hotel are handsome, modern and beautifully appointed, including rich wood paneling and color TV. There's 'Yesterday's,' our famous entertainment and dancing spot, plus a delightful restaurant."

The day before the conference, the temperature in Detroit barely made it into the low 30s. By the time the sun set at 5:30 p.m., the mercury was quickly dropping toward the teens. One can imagine the equipment manufacturers' crews, unloading their wares to set them up for display, their breath forming icy clouds around them as they struggled across the parking lot with the heavy crates, cursing the frigid air, while being careful not to damage the delicate electronics inside.

Nine of the 23 exhibitors, stepping around frozen patches on the ground to get into the hotel that evening, had cameras to display. The exhibit was staged in Yesterday's large ballroom. It must have seemed bizarre to set the gear up in such a polished, refined space while outside, the frosty winter gripped the earth.

Ballroom dancing was a popular Detroit pastime. Two ballrooms near downtown, the Grande and the Vanity, had been popular spots from the Twenties into the Fifties. Changing taste and Detroit's general decline by the late Sixties caused the transition from dance emporiums to venues for garage bands like the Stooges and MC-5. By the seventies, there was a resurgence of interest in ballroom dancing among Baby Boomers, and Yesterday's at the Shereton-Southfield was a safe venue for a night of dancing. There was also a growing dance trend called *disco*, which may have made its appearance in the ballroom in late 1975. But on the Thursday, Friday, and Saturday in late January 1976, when the Society's Winter Television Conference moved in, right in the middle of one of the most significant standardization challenges since the introduction of color, the ballroom was transformed into the first state-side trade-show space for local television broadcasters east of the Mississippi for over a year.

As the equipment displays were fine-tuned for their debuts, sales representatives for the various manufacturers were across the street at WJBK, hosting a wine-and-cheese get together for the broadcasters.

The stakes were high for everyone there. The new paradigm in news-gathering was still in flux, uncertainty was the rule of the day, and the players were on edge. All they had to do was look south across Eight Mile Road, at the city of Detroit, to see the carnage uncertain economic times can wreak on an industry. Automobile manufacturers were the hardest hit by the Arab oil embargo and the ensuing recession. There was a new phrase in the country's lexicon: Sticker Shock, that queasy feeling hitting Americans when they went to the car lot and looked at the price tags stuck in the windows of new cars. Then there was the giant shift in what those buyers were looking to buy. The days of the big, gas-guzzling sedans with huge engines were long gone. The muscle car was a thing of the past - the last Chevrolet Chevelle, the final big block, high-cubic-inch, super-torque-producing monster, had rolled off the assembly line the year before. Small, fuel-efficient Ford Pintos had been one of the best-selling cars in the country for the last two years and – ominously - for the first time, Japanese automobile manufacturers were making major inroads into America's domestic car market.

At the pre-conference gathering at WJBK on Thursday night, the two groups - broadcasters and manufacturers - sipped merlot and nibbled on aged gouda as they stared each other down, trying to divine which hardware system had the most promising, profitable future. For the broadcasters, choosing the wrong course of action could be detrimental to their employers' bottom line, not to mention their very livelihood. For the manufacturers, inclusion in the system, whatever system was chosen, was the ultimate goal. Missing the bus on that choice could leave one without a livelihood as well.

What Has ENG Done for Us

The conference was divided into two sections: one featuring ENG, which would take up all day on Friday; the other focusing on digital video, scheduled for Saturday. Bright and early Friday morning, 700 broadcasters and manufacturers amassed in a meeting room for a full day of paper presentations and discussions - to hopefully, in the words of the Society's founder, C. Francis Jenkins, *"secure best standards of equipment, quality, performance, nomenclature, and, unconsciously, perhaps, a code of ethics."* Fortunately for posterity, all the presentations and discussions on Friday were published by the Society in a 164-page special issue. What follows here attempts to shed some light on the high-stakes decisions everyone in attendance that Friday were facing as they attempted to choose a course of action for the future of news-gathering in an instant – or at least at the speed of light – electronic environment.

Joe Flaherty welcomed all in attendance and then introduced the first speaker, Raymond J. Smith, director of technical operations, at WKYC – TV, NBC's Cleveland affiliate. His presentation was peppered with hard-learned truths concerning covering the news with the new electronic equipment. "There should be a minimum of things which need to be assembled, patched, or whatever. It should be almost impossible to make a mistake," he warned. "The important thing to remember is that the E.J. crew (Electronic Journalism crew, NBC's preferred term for ENG) will be trying to equal or better the performance of a film crew. If your unit must be austere, that still does not mean it cannot be easy to use and well built. If it will be more elaborate, keep in mind that for a fast breaking story, Murphy's Law says it will be manned by the least qualified people on your staff. Don't let an over designed engineering dream cause so much confusion that a good story is missed."

Next up was Hugo Bondy, chief engineer at Atlanta's WAGA – TV. The 67-year-old Bondy had held that position at WAGA for more than two decades. He'd also hosted the third Winter Television Conference in Atlanta back in 1969. It would be safe to assume everyone in attendance would have paid very close attention to what he had to say.

WAGA was a CBS affiliate and, as such, had gotten Flaherty's kit, the Ikegami and the Sony VO-3800, along with most everything else, excepting Consolidated Video

System's Time Base Corrector, they'd chosen to go with the Ampex model instead. WAGA's microwave receiver, instead of being on a tall building downtown, was mounted on their tower located at their studios at 1551 Briarcliff Road, four and half miles northeast of Georgia's state capitol building.

"Perhaps this report should be subtitled; 'How to learn from others' mistakes and make some of your own.'," Bondy began. After describing the setup of their Dodge B Series Maxivan, he turned to the array of four Nurad receiving horns 950 feet up on the 1,100-foot-tall transmission tower. He explained that that was "the last elevator stop on our triangular Stainless tower." Then he described the editing system they'd set up in the studios. Finally, he got down to the numbers.

"What has ENG done for us besides giving us a better means of getting in the News? Let's take December, 1975. During December the News Department 'shot' 518 stories, 364 film – 154 ENG or 30% ENG. Of the latter 87 were taped and carried back to the studio, 67 were microwaved back to ENG Control. Thirty of these were taped and microwaved from the scene. This is because it was physically impossible to feed the van direct from the camera and our window microwave was not then in operation. Thirty-seven of the stories were microwaved 'live.' In 90% of the latter cases where 'live' coverage was provided the story simply would not have been aired had we not had this capability."

"As to the reduction of film. . .one of the hoped-for results of this exercise: December, 1974 saw the processing of 122,400 feet of film against 85,300 in December, 1975 – a 30 percent reduction. However, in toto, the number of stories handled both via ENG and film increased by 18% over the preceding year despite the retirement of one of our nine film units. It would seem that a single ENG unit can be better than 2 times as effective as a film unit."

Having demonstrated the cost savings and the increased production from using the new gear; he addressed the soundness of the gear itself.

"Here I must put in some good words concerning the Ikegami HL33 camera now superseded by the HL35. This is equipment about which we have nothing but good to report. It must be the most rugged and stable item that we've acquired within recent years. It had been necessary to re-register this camera but four times since we acquired it in February, 1975. It was not necessary to re-register it following a bad wreck in October. The Ampex TBC800, (their time-based corrector) after some initial start-up problems, has proved to be a reliable work horse."

"Now. . .as to the weaknesses: They're all spelled Sony."

He then went on a veritable engineer's rant, listing the shortcomings of the U-Matic machinery, including a low signal to noise ratio which caused jitter in the picture, a lack of video and audio output controls on the VO-2850 - the recording and playback deck back at the studio. The final "irritant," he griped, was an inability to see the SMPTE timecode when rewinding and fast-forwarding.

"Surely Sony will iron out these problems in due time but, for us, the time is now." He fumed.

He concluded with some thoughts for the future. "Will ENG ever replace news film? Ever is a long time and I'm not that much of a seer but I am not holding my breath yet. Film footage will, undoubtably, shrink. A year ago I would have said 40%. Now? Who knows perhaps that it will drop to 20%."

Whether film dropping to a fifth of total production in the newsroom gave pause to anyone there is not recorded. There was apparently some push-back on his claim that an ENG kit could be twice as productive as a film kit. It required the addition of an explanatory footnote when his presentation was published in the special issue. So, his claims did engender some dialogue among those present. Perhaps some asked each other the question: "If only one in five stories are actually being shot on film at some future date, what would be the point of keeping the film cameras around?" One would be hard-pressed to make an argument for maintaining the expensive film chain necessary for the old way of doing things - a system which cost more and delivered less, but perhaps looked a little prettier.

Then the equipment manufacturers began their presentations.

What Are You News Directors Doing?

Nick H. Nishi rose to speak on behalf of Ikegami Tsushinki, the company from Ota City, Japan, the land of a thousand factories, makers of the camera that had started the whole revolution. The 38 year old Nishi was born in Okayama Japan, about 300 miles east of Tokyo. He had graduated from Kanagawa University in Yokohama, and gotten a job in Ota City, about eight miles from the campus, in 1963. After more than a decade with the company, during which time he'd "played a key role in the research and development of Ikegami's Broadcast Products," he'd become the vice president of Ikegami Electronics, U.S.A.

His presentation was brief and to the point.

"The Ikegami HL series of hand-held color cameras is the most widely used camera of this type in the world today," he announced. "More than 300 sets of these have been sold and they are being used by US broadcasters, including all three networks."

After describing the specifications of the HL 33, the 33A1, and the 35, each of which had an increasing F-stop of sensitivity, he stated, "Mini-camera use is in the process of changing as more and more stations acquire them. Back in the days of Black and White TV, small cameras were generally thought to be useful only at Political Conventions, and were then shelved once the conventions were over. However, today, because of the increased interest in ENG coverage and the Mini-camera versatility for sports and remote pickups, the Mini-camera has become an important tool for the progressive broadcaster."

He concluded, "The future possibilities for Mini-cameras in the Television Broadcast Industry are virtually unlimited. High quality Mini-cameras becoming standard equipment at most television stations will be the trend of the future."

With that, he yielded the floor.

Then, from the House of Sarnoff, the descendant of American Marconi, the Radio Corporation of America, the veritable RCA, came Anthony H. Lind. The man who was responsible for the Quadruplex, who was then the manager of New Products Engineering and Studio and Control Equipment at the labs in Camden, presented the latest innovation from the engineers who brought live video into space, the TK-76.

Lind began, "Since September ..." [and the Society's 117th Conference] "... the product design has been completed and the camera is now in its first production cycle."

He then listed some of the physical attributes that RCA thought a camera used for gathering news ought to have.

"After extensive studies, including careful analysis of several packaging configurations plus construction of mock-up camera systems representing these configurations, the single package approach was chosen as the most efficient approach."

Further, he continued, the engineers in Camden had decided that: "The camera design should be such that the camera is balanced on the cameraman's shoulder, thereby reducing potential back strain when the camera must be held for extended periods of time. The camera should have a well-positioned and sturdy carrying handle on top for convenience in transporting it in the field." Also, it had been decided that: "The total camera package, including a lens and viewfinder, should not exceed twenty pounds in weight."

Lind then claimed, "The product design TK-76 achieves all of these goals."

One of the ways the smaller weight and size was achieved was through: "The use of new types of integrated circuits." Lind explained that "new printed circuit techniques, and some unique circuit designs have substantially reduced the physical size of the circuit boards while maintaining high performance."

The presentation ended with the first-ever demonstration of a production model. With that, the modern broadcast video camera entered Plato's *Realm of Forms.*

Then it was Sony's turn.

David K. MacDonald stood to make the case for the U-Matic. At 36 years old, he'd hired on as regional sales manager at Sony only four years earlier, in Detroit. He'd advanced rapidly to the position of general manager of Sony Corporation of America's Broadcast Division. A graduate of

Boston University, he had done some post-graduate work at Harvard University.

He began, perhaps as a retort to Bondy's exasperated plea that 'now' was the time to fix the issues with tape recorders, by bringing attention to the fact that broadcast news interest had not historically done business with Sony. "Industrial and educational users associated with helical scan recording techniques are familiar with the extremely rapid rate manufacturers have been able to develop new products to meet non-broadcast applications."

"Broadcasters on the other hand have not seen a similar high velocity technology," he declared. "To be sure, there have been improvements in broadcast television but I would contend that they have evolved in what could be best described as a 'normal' pace. If my colleagues from Ampex and RCA take issue with this assertion, I would think they would admit that the rate of technological advancement in the broadcast industry comes nowhere near the revolutionary pace experienced by a simple elementary school teacher who has been 'in' to video for the last decade."

How the broadcasters in the room - general managers, chief engineers, and news directors, folks accustomed to the idea that they were at the cutting edge of communication technology - felt at being compared in a negative light to video-savvy elementary school teachers is unknown. Perhaps in keeping with the spirit of C. Francis Jenkins' counsel, "*It is an unselfish exchange of views which will make our gatherings interesting, and the discussions of individual investigation valuable,"* those present stayed silent.

"One very significant reason that broadcast technology has not moved as fast as its industrial counterpart," MacDonald explained, "has been the long standing establishment of a quad standard." But then he pointed out that the time-base corrector had changed all that, making ENG possible, ending - before anyone really realized it - Quad's reign. Because of this inclusion of a new format into the high-volume business model of broadcast news, he claimed, "by the end of calendar 1975, almost four hundred stations in the United States were engaged in some degree of electronic news gathering."

"Of the total number of stations using ENG, 88% were using a capsulated U-Matic format as a VTR. The rush to experiment in ENG was so wide spread that Sony was never able to increase production to meet the demand and we remain in a severe backorder position today."

He wanted to reassure everyone, however, that Sony was on top of it, "I expect a major acceleration of research and development over the next few years and we expect that NAB 76 will be an indicator that a more aggressive pursuit of the broadcast business is in the making."

Then the conference broke for lunch.

Leading off after the break was Ed DiGiulio, the last manufacturer of 16 mm film cameras in America, making the final case for the film chain in television news.

"The whole question of film versus tape in television news gathering operation, in the last analysis," he stated early in his remarks, "has got to get down to a question of quality versus cost and the cost-effectiveness of one system versus another. After talking to many news directors, equipment manufacturers, cameramen, etc., over the past year or more, I am more than ever convinced that *a balanced mix of video and film cameras* is the smart way, in terms of cost and quality, for the modern news gathering operation to go."

"I realize I am standing up here 'spitting into the wind,' trying to bring common sense and rationality into an issue that is becoming increasingly charged with emotion. We have become inundated with a barrage of hype and hyperbole on the marvels of minicams. Cameramen have told me that they have been stopped on the street by people who asked them if the CP-16 they were carrying was a minicam. They replied, 'yes, it was,' and the bystander walked away contented."

"To paraphrase Marshall McLuhan, 'The medium is becoming the message.' What are you news directors doing? Are you selling news or are you selling hardware?"

DiGiulio wasn't discounting a change in trends though, saying "Lest you think this is just brave talk from a badly battered film camera manufacturer, I would add that I have been advised by Eastman Kodak that their sales of news film in 1975 were appreciably up from 1974."

Besides, he had other irons in the fire.

"The most exciting project we are currently working on, however, which is very close to fruition, is a camera stabilizing technique which is equally valid for film and video cameras. We currently have a working prototype 35mm film version, which has been used with outstanding success on two major feature films that have just completed principal photography. The first, shot in New York, is *Marathon Man*, on which the director of photography was Conrad Hall. The second was the film based on the life of Woodie Guthrie, called *Bound For Glory*. The director of photography on that show was Haskell Wexler."

"We are currently working in close cooperation with RCA to adapt this stabilizing system to the TK76 camera. If all goes according to schedule, we plan to assemble a prototype rig in the next few weeks, with the intention of having some exciting videotape footage that RCA can demonstrate at the forthcoming NAB convention."

A Stedicam for ENG ... the idea of such a combination may have caused more than one news director in the room to swoon at the universe of possibilities.

The rest of the afternoon's session speakers included a two-way radio maker, an antenna maker, Microwave Associates' John Fielek, who reported on his company's rugged little solid-state transmitter, and NBC's Robert Mausler, who shared how the network employed the Sony line of equipment in its news plant, saying: "The cassette feature of this equipment has proved to be particularly suitable for the highly mobile fast-moving use that Electronic Journalism demands."

After the second session, everyone left for dinner, passing through the equipment show in Yesterday's ornate ballroom.

A Whole New Breed of Journalist

After their meal attendees reassembled in the meeting room for the evening program, a "Rap Session" which would include, as printed in November's *Journal*, "a station news director, chief engineer, an electronic cameraman, station manager and engineer."

As it happened, the electronic cameraman didn't make the cut to be on the panel that Friday night, due to the fact a few network guys showed up.

The panel commenced with nine members. Henry Owen, chief engineer across the road at WJBK, chaired the panel. Also hailing from local environs were John Tallerico, news director at WILX – TV, located in Lansing, Michigan, about an hour drive to the west, and Charles Kotcher, chief engineer at WXYZ, the ABC affiliate up on Ten Mile Road.

Along with Raymond Smith and Hugo Bondy, who'd come in from out of state, Charles Meyer, supervisor of engineering at WBBM – TV in Chicago made the trip.

Members on the panel from the network level were Thomas Battista, who'd been news director at KMOX when the station had gone fully electric 15 months ago, who now was CBS-TV Stations Division's executive vice president, plus another CBS network representative, Raymond D. Schneider, director of special projects, engineering and development.

Representing the NBC network, scion of the House of Sarnoff, and equipped by the RCA labs in Camden, was James Kitchell, NBC News Services general manager. The 48-year-old was a legend in the news business. He had been, for a time, lead producer of the famed news duo of Chet Huntley and David Brinkley, and was the newsman who negotiated with Major General Donald N. Yates to allow live coverage of NASA's space launches beginning in 1957. It can be assumed the news cameraman who'd originally been slated for the panel stepped aside graciously to let Kitchell take his spot.

The first question after Henry Owen brought the 'rap session' to order was, "Could the panel comment on their image of the ultimate Electronic News gathering Operation?"

Ray Schneider opined that at some future date, a camera would be capable of sending an image and sound through radio frequency directly, without the need for a separate transmitter, time-base corrector, or even a truck. James Kitchell envisioned a world where someone could go to the bottom of the Grand Canyon, open a brief case from which an umbrella popped out and start transmitting to a domestic satellite. Thomas Battista figured tape would be replaced with a disc system in the near future. Hugo Bondy, in his straight-from-the-hip method of delivery, said, "It sounds very good. But let's get down to earth . . . A gentleman back here asked a question and didn't go far enough. He should have asked, who can see into the mind of the user, if anybody can do that . . . " He trailed off, his musings unable to be heard clearly.

It was up to Raymond Smith to sum up the reality everyone was facing. "Somebody wiser than us once made a statement that went something like this: 'Anything the mind can conceive and believe the mind can achieve.' In response to that, the innate greed, if you will, of the news people or program people will force developments which we can't possibly imagine in this particular area. It will keep going. And the response will come from the big manufacturers, who must respond in order to stay in business."

Not long after, Kitchell added, "Ray Smith and I have had friendly conversations about this: There is a serious problem in our business, in the television news business, on the part of news people, in understanding the technological changes we're going through. Certainly the engineering representatives and news people who are here should take the message back that their people should learn more about this field. I find within our organization, in our stations, and at the network level, that really the people don't understand it."

"I think there is no question the future is there, the whole means of covering stories - - we're developing a whole new breed of journalist, a whole new breed of reporters. It used to be very easy for a reporter to go and shoot film and come back and screen it and write his script and so forth. Now we have the capability of doing stories live, and he's got to be able to report it live. He says it now, and that's it. And it's a totally different type of journalist who is being developed."

Eventually the discussion turned to more technical issues. An audience member spoke up. "I'd like to ask one member of the panel who is an engineer and one member of the panel who is a newsman . . . what would be the three most important parameters for an electronic news camera?"

Charles Meyer said, "Well, I guess we're looking for a camera that's highly portable, sensitive and dependable."

Charles Kotcher, from up the road at WXYZ, shared that, "It's a matter of weight; and the improvement is still in the area of portability."

Ray Schneider opined, "In order of priority, I put reliability on top. You may be willing to tolerate a camera that is a little too big and you may be willing to pay more money than you think you would like to pay for it, you may be willing to accept that quality may not be quite as good as you want – but the day you go out with that camera for the first time and it doesn't work, and you know that over the years your film camera has been reliable, that blows the whole deal as far as I'm concerned."

Bondy, the gruff veteran, concurred, "I think the primary consideration has to be reliability."

There was a long discussion concerning archiving. No one on the panel knew how long tape would last. An audience member stood up and said, "I'm Peter Hansen from Denmark . . . the storage possibility – storage capability of videotape – I think – I daresay that we have recently aired 15-year-old two-inch quadruplex tape made on first generation Ampex recorders. And they showed out quite nicely. I hesitate to say if they have deteriorated."

About an hour into the 90-minute discussion someone asked, "Mr. Schneider, would you suggest that if a station goes all ENG it would need more than one editor?"

Schneider responded, "Well, I can answer that by saying in St. Louis we have one editor."

That would've been the Datatron mini-computer located behind the edit decision rooms on the KMOX newsroom set.

By this point, MacDonald would have been getting antsy. Sony was about to make a big play for the edit control mini-computer in its new ENG line-up. In the upcoming February issue of *BM/E*, Sony had bought two full pages of advertising space, side by side, promoting its new total system, which included the editor, and announced its debut on

March 21, the first day of the NAB convention in Chicago. His job depended on moving a significant number of those units, but Sony had been taking it on the chin all evening during the panel discussion.

About 30 minutes into the discussion, someone asked, "I'd like to address Mr. Tallerico. I understand, from what you said, that you are using Sony cameras and tape machines. I'd like to know what type of reliability you are experiencing with that type of equipment, and how much increased maintenance is it taking to keep these running over a film system?"

Tallerico replied, "In three months, we now have one unit that has been out a week. Other than that, when I had my CP-16s, within the first month I had one go down. We got it repaired, luckily within a day, but this was the first major problem. And I foresee future problems, in that, as I had problems in the past with my little Sony tape recorders, my little audio cassette recorders, it's getting parts for them. And I certainly hope that Sony will increase the parts. We have the technical capability of repairing the machines and the service people to do so. It's not how quickly we can repair these units, it's getting the parts."

Then Henry Owen asked, "Is there anyone on the panel that might have any numbers that they might have gathered on the reliability of the system?"

Probably in unison, the entire room turned to Bondy, on the far-left end of the table.

"Sony's already mad at me so I may as well give you this one. The Sony went into it's operation for our news department personnel who in their usual haphazard methods, wrecked two of their 2850's. One of them was out of commission for three months, the reason being this: There is a little plastic Teflon gear that raises the cassette up into position so you can remove it. There wasn't one in the United Sates. Someone finally remembered that someone in New York had gone to Japan and come back with three of these things. They found them in the guy's desk while he was on vacation. Now, that's a heck of a way to do a business."

That was only one of several instances in which Sony's service record was called into question. Now someone had asked how many editors were needed to be operationally safe in the all electronic method of news-gathering, and was told one would do, because "in St. Louis we have one."

And it was a Datatron Vidicue, made in America.

"What do you do if your editor fails?"

Schneider replied, "You repair it."

MacDonald knew that if everyone was worried about parts being delivered from Japan, no one was going to buy his machine, and Sony would be a smaller part of the system. He had to do something quick.

"I have to make some response on behalf of SONY Corporation since we've been attacked so badly in this session," he declared from the audience.

"We have had for over six months two hot lines, one in Compton, California; one in Long Island City, N.Y., manned by Engineers who can pull parts as needed. The hot line is limited only to broadcast use. I just talked to two fellows that didn't know the hotlines existed. We send that information out by bulletin to every chief engineer and every general manager listed in the 1974 Television Fact Book."

Tallerico pushed back. "We know how to repair the machines ... but once again, I must say the parts are our problem."

MacDonald replied, "But the hotline, as you know is open ten hours a day, and the broadcaster has a standard five hundred dollar parts credit line with SONY Corporation. Every broadcast station in the United States automatically gets five hundred dollars worth of parts credit . You can pick up the telephone, call the hotline and for any part that deals with a 3800 or a 2850 or DXC-1600 and also the ECN-50 microphone, and order these parts directly."

Someone in the audience said, "Now, obviously, I am still without a camera for a week and a half ..."

To which MacDonald responded, "I suggest you try a test. You get a hot line number; pick out any part number and see if you can't get that part within 48 hours."

Another audience member spoke up. "I'd like to know what the telephone number is. For the last parts I needed, they had to go directly – we had to place an overseas call to

Tokyo, and we got it that way – to Japan Airlines, then to California, and California to Detroit."

The discussion then turned to issues concerning labor union jurisdiction.

Half an hour later, Owen began to wrap things up. "We'll take one more question," he announced.

"I'd be very interested in the comments of the panel and people in the audience, in regard to time base correctors," someone said, continuing, "Can it be that time-base correctors are all we need them to be – we haven't had a single comment all night?"

Owen replied, "Do you have a particular question about time-base correctors, because we could spend another two hours …"

Schneider responded anyway. "When they're in the plant, and kept there, they are quite reliable. When carried out, you should be ready to cope with problems. New and better models are becoming available every year."

With that, the first true standardization conference on Electronic News-Gathering concluded. For participants heading home, there was plenty to think about. It was as if a whole new country had opened up to the broadcasters who'd been there. Just one example of the mind-blowing possibilities had been pointed out in the first half-hour of the panel discussion, when someone asked, "I'd like to get back to the news question for a moment, if I might. Considering the projection of the developments of the ENG technology, do any of you gentlemen foresee a development of an all-news television station in the near future?"

Henry Owen paraphrased the question for the rest of the crowd. "The question has been raised as to whether the members of the panel, in their infinite wisdom and crystal balls, foresee that an all-news station is practicable or likely? – I guess analogous to the all-news radio stations we now enjoy."

James Kitchell's answer was quick and unequivocal, "Yes."

ENG'S TRIUMPH

SUNDAY, MARCH 21, 1976

WEDNESDAY, SEPTEMBER 22, 1976

AND FRIDAY, JANUARY 28,1977

Lake Shore Drive

The National Association of Broadcasters convened its 54th annual convention 56 days later in Chicago. It was the 25th time since 1923, the year that the NAB had incorporated at the Drake Hotel downtown on Michigan Avenue, that the city had hosted the gathering. Washington D.C. had only hosted them six times, the second most of any other city. So, it wouldn't have been farfetched to call the city of Chicago the association's home. But the meeting in late March of 1976 would be the last time delegates would meet in the city where the NAB's first president, E. F. McDonald, challenged the Commerce Department's control over radio broadcasters.

Starting in 1936, whenever the NAB held its annual convention in Chicago, attendees gathered in the enormous

253

Stevens Hotel, two miles south of the Drake. The structure, built in 1927, in the fading style of Beaux-Arts - the grandiose amalgam of Neoclassicism, Renaissance and Baroque, that was formulated by the engineers and designers in the early nineteenth century at the Ecole des Beaux-Arts in Paris - was celebrated as the largest hotel in the world when it opened. The 29-storey brick behemoth still occupies an entire city block along Michigan Avenue, right across the street from Grant Park, and 2,000 feet from the famed Buckingham Fountain. After World War II, the hotel was purchased by the Hilton Corporation and renamed for its president, Conrad Hilton.

In 1972, seven months prior to Joe Flaherty's demonstration at the Society's 112th conference, the NAB celebrated its 50th year at that hotel, and the equipment show was the biggest that had ever been staged by the association, with 141 exhibitors commanding all the space the hotel offered in four separate halls.

Four years later, after the ENG revolution, the manufacturers who were requesting space had increased by 30 percent. The growing companies were also requesting larger areas for their ever-expanding lines of electronic equipment. The Conrad Hilton was not equipped for the 200-plus exhibits so the convention was moved a mile-and-a-half south, to the city's massive convention center, McCormick Place, the largest center of its kind in North America.

Chicago's convention center had been built in the late Fifties, south of Soldier Field and the Field Museum of Natural History, right on the Lake Michigan shoreline. A little more than six years after it opened, the original building was destroyed by fire. Not long after, a new structure was commissioned by the city fathers. Its designer, Gene Summers, had spent most of his career as special assistant to the famous architect Ludwig Mies van der Rohe, founder of The Second Chicago School of Architecture.

Ludwig Mies van der Rohe was born in Aachan, Germany, west of the Lower Rhine River. When he was 36, he submitted a design of a glass-sheathed skyscraper in a competition for the first skyscraper to be built in Berlin. The unprecedented idea of a glass tower cemented his reputation as a leading modernist architect. By the time he was in his forties, he was head of the architecture department at Bauhaus, a renowned school of design, architecture and applied arts; he eventually became the director of the entire school. Unfortunately, he was living in a Germany under the yoke of the Nazi regime – and the Third Reich abhorred anything modern. The Nazis were intolerant of many things, particularly things international and otherwise beyond the scope of their taste, which tended to the martial wrapped up in a racist theory of National Identity, and they tended to react with intense violence to everything else. By the time Mies decided to leave his home and emigrate to America he was teaching classes in an abandoned telephone factory after he and his students had been physically removed from their original campus location.

After a short stint working on a vacation home for a rich advertising executive in Wyoming, Mies got an offer to head the Architecture Department at the newly established Illinois Institute of Technology, where, in addition to teaching, he designed the campus master plan and all the buildings. Soon he was designing tall steel towers with glass curtain walls which were built all over the country. His apogee was New York City's Seagram Building, where he convinced skeptical financiers to leave a half-block of Manhattan real estate empty, to front a 38-storey glass-and-steel tower. The effect of the design was so overwhelming that rental fees in the building that commanded the rest of the block more than made up for the lost revenue due to the empty space. Overseeing the construction of the Seagram Building in New York while Mies remained in Chicago was 29-year-old Gene Summers.

Mies was really into an idea he called *fluid space* or *universal space*, in which the border between the outside and the inside of a building was blurred. That's why he used panes of glass in steel columns as exterior walls. One of his designs incorporated a large empty space walled in entirely by glass. This building had a cantilevered roof sticking out on all four sides to block direct sunlight during the warmest part of the day. Inside the glass-enclosed space, mobile walls could be employed to create temporary workspaces for those inside who could then get the sensation of being outside by looking in any direction opposite a wall. He tried to get the design built twice: once in Cuba, as the headquarters for Bacardi rums, and again in Schweinfurt, Germany, a city fewer than 200 miles from his birthplace.

Finally, near the end of his life, Mies was commissioned by the German government – officials wanted its famed son to design a building to stand wherever he pleased in the city of Berlin. He was entirely unaware of what they were going to do with it, and probably didn't care - he just wanted to build a four-sided glass building with a large, cantilevered roof and no inside walls. As it turned out, the building became the New National Gallery, a space for displaying the modern art the Nazi's had despised so much.

That was the last building Mies worked on before he died. By the time it was finished, Gene Summers had been placed as head of design with the politically connected C.F. Murphy and Associates architecture firm in Chicago. Not long after that, the firm was commissioned by the city to design a replacement for the convention center that had burned down. Summers took the form his mentor had worked on for all those years and super-sized it. The result, a massive, low-sitting shrine to Ludwig Mies van der Rohe, was described by the *Chicago Tribune* architecture critic Blair Kamin as "a bravura exercise in architectural modernism."

It must have been a surreal sight for the 52-year-old Joe Roizen, riding south in the hotel courtesy van on Sunday morning, March 21, 1976, at a brisk 55 miles per hour, cruising down Lake Shore Drive, passing Soldier Field on the left, looking ahead to see the steel black roof of McCormick Place come into view.

It had only been 20 years earlier that videotape had been unveiled for the first time to unexpecting broadcasters at the Conrad Hilton on the eve of the 34th Annual NAB Convention in 1956. By late March of 1976, the various recording types, width sizes, and containers for holding tape had exploded, forcing the NAB to move its annual equipment show to one of the largest trade show venues in the world.

A few seconds after passing the stadium, Roizen would have crossed over East 18th Drive; from that height he'd have the best vantage point to get a good look at the building. There was no grand sign reading "McCormick Place," no discernable entrance with crowds coming and going - just a slim, sparsely populated viaduct crossing Lake Shore Drive from a commuter train station on the west side of the highway. As he approached the viaduct a few seconds later, Roizen would have gotten a good look at the structure's massive roof, jutting out 75 feet beyond the dark glass exterior into thin air, with no apparent supports, seemingly defying gravity. Maybe, as he passed the building, he thought about the engineering accomplishment of overcoming an impossible physical barrier. And, maybe, Roizen felt a certain sense of satisfaction that the new era in electronic image acquisition was dawning that day inside such a quintessential demonstration of modern possibility.

But how does one get inside? He may have also wondered, as he continued south at 55 miles an hour for another mile down Lake Shore Drive before exiting the freeway and doubling back.

Now appearing on his right was a strip of green space between him and the lake, stretching to the horizon. There were hardly any parking spaces in sight. Up ahead, set on its 20-foot-tall brick plinth, the glass box and its impossibly huge roof were quickly coming into view. Then, suddenly, he was whisked into the plinth itself, and brought to one of six "gates" - a bank of glass doors - and deposited, from all appearances, in an underground tunnel, at his final destination.

Once inside, it was at least a 200-foot trek to the exhibit hall entrance. Upon entering the 95,000-square-foot room, with a forest of columns holding up the 14-foot high ceiling, he would have been met with a cornucopia of the latest in electronic broadcasting equipment.

All was not well in the huge exhibit hall, however.

Labor Union Ennui

Roizen referred to the mood parenthetically in his review, which was the lead story in the May issue of *Broadcast*

Engineering. After a brief introduction, in which he wrote, "the old timers could fall into VTR nostalgia and the exhibitors had 'SOLD' signs on most of their displays," he observed in his second paragraph: "There was plenty of reason for all the euphoria (in spite of the set-up problems) among the exhibitors."

The weekly trade magazine *Broadcasting* fills in the details. "There was only one dark aspect; difficulties with the trade unions in getting booths set up. That trouble and the resulting extra cost to exhibitors, led several to suggest it may be the last time the NAB comes to Chicago."

The article goes on to report. "Small companies were even more irked by 'nonsense' attributed to the trade unions, especially the International Brotherhood of Electrical Workers union, when to move a machine already on wheels or plug in a unit required waiting for the services of the appropriate trade people."

"The problems appeared fairly universal to the exhibit floor, extending to both the large and small companies."

The day before was the first time temperatures in Chicago had risen above 70 degrees that year. Plus, the sun had come out that Saturday morning as the electricians headed into work. Most likely, they were not pleased at the prospect of putting this behemoth trade show together, involving really complicated, delicate electronics, inside the vast wasteland that was McCormick Place, on such a beautiful day. Besides, the last convention center had burned to the ground because someone had mishandled the electric circuity during a trade show. Who wanted that hassle coming down on them? So, perhaps, the electrical trade union's recalcitrance at facing off with assembling the working parts of what, up to that time, was the biggest and boldest foray yet by manufacturers in an ongoing standardization war between 19th-century machinery and 20th-century digital hardware was understandable.

Fortunately, there was little that could slow down the ENG revolution. As Roizen described it, "Surprises abounded in ENG cameras, new VTRs, editing gear, signal processing: factory fresh or refurbished, it was all there to be scrutinized, tested, compared and committed for so that the reels of progress could roll again in high gear."

The next day, at the Monday Television-Engineering Luncheon, Roizen experienced an especially proud moment. "Addressing the special luncheon," Roizen related, "[was] Douglas Edwards," the first *CBS Evening News* anchor, "who was the first newscaster to be recorded and delayed by Ampex VR-1000 machines at Television City in Hollywood. [He] reviewed his and other programs that switched from kinescopes to magnetic tape. His remarks were interspersed with short VTR segments that represented advances in recording technology." One video clip shown was "from the Nixon/Kruschev Kitchen Debate in Moscow (1959)." He reported this fact in passing, neglecting to mention in the article who was at the controls of the camera that day.

Frank Beacham was also there, attending his first NAB convention and returning to the city where he'd first seen the Sony Portapak eight years before at the Democratic National Convention. He approached the NAB convention in the same way he'd approached the radio station in South Carolina when he was in high school, and the same way he'd approached Senator Kennedy's office in Washington, D.C., after he'd evaded service in the U.S. Coast Guard - directly.

Of course, just like in Las Vegas, the RCA display – the biggest display at the convention that year - was to the right as one entered the hall. They'd rolled in an 18-foot-long 'TV minivan' to show their commitment to the new practice of "Electronic Journalism," as they called it. Then they plugged in the TK-76 and simulated live shots in a studio adjacent to the van. They also took the camera and roamed McCormick Place, going upstairs, into the big hall, with 50-foot high ceilings and glass walls on three sides, showing a flower show being held at the same time. It was a fortunate circumstance, Mies van der Rohe's fascination with fluid space, for the TK-76 had plenty of indirect sunlight to work with - diffused though it was throughout most of the show by cloudy skies - but the picture, nevertheless, would have been far superior to the usual trade show exercise.

The 27-year-old Frank Beacham took one look at the set-up at RCA's area and walked over to the financing tent across the aisle, against the south wall of the hall. There he announced to an "RCA representative" that he "wanted to finance a TK-76 camera package."

"I was stunned," he recalled, "that no one laughed!"

He went on, "I told RCA my background as a film cameraman and that I wanted to work freelance for the major television networks with the new gear as they made the transition from film to video. RCA paid close attention and actually took me seriously. They asked how much money I could place as a down payment on the purchase. I told them all I had was $7,500. In an instant, they said we had a deal. I wrote RCA a check for $7,500 and had bought close to $100,000 worth of broadcast gear. And yes, I was fully aware that I had forever signed away my soul."

Such was the impact of the last NAB convention to be held in the city of its birth.

RCA sold 175 of its new third-generation cameras in three days. Sony, whose large booth was a couple hundred more feet into the hall and a little east of the main aisle, sold 175 VTRs to go with the cameras and, in all likelihood, even more than that. A couple hundred feet north, on the west side of the main aisle, Ikegami had a good-sized booth with its new HL-77 camera on display, a third-generation one-piece, just like the TK-76 that would be on the market, as its name suggested, the next year.

According to Roizen, at least 14 manufacturers had some kind of electronic portable camera on display at that show, and they were selling like hotcakes. NAB '76 would go down in history with industry insiders as the show that launched the era of Electronic News Gathering and banished forever the old news term "Film at eleven."

The Crystal Place Suite

Six months later, Roizen boarded a plane and made another one of his many Atlantic crossings to London and the Fifth Biennial International Broadcasting Convention, better known as IBC. More than 3,000 delegates from more than 50 nations arrived to participate in the convention held every other year at the Grosvenor House Hotel. The hotel had opened two years after Chicago's Conrad Hilton, and like that venerable institution, it too was ill-equipped for the demands a new paradigm in image-acquisition made on convention facilities. Roizen observed, "The ornately chandeliered 'Great Room', as the exhibit hall in the Grosvenor House Hotel is called, was filled to capacity and was simply not great enough. Consequently, many exhibitors chose to put their exhibits at other locations and lure potential customers over in shuttle buses or taxis."

One such group of exhibitors - the Americans and their new ENG system – had set up camp at the London Hilton.

The 28-storey London Hilton Hotel, at 22 Park Lane, was within sight of the Statue of Achilles at the southeast corner of Hyde Park and just to the northeast of Buckingham Palace. Built in 1963, it was the first skyscraper hotel in London. A couple of years after opening, Food and Beverage Director Lim Ewe Hin decided to capitalize on the success of *Goldfinger*, the third James Bond film, and established the 007 Night Spot. He collected a bunch of props from Pinewood Studios and hired actor Harold Sakata, who played Oddjob, the super-villain Goldfinger's menacing chauffeur. Sakata escorted patrons from the lobby elevator up to the bar on the second floor. Folks who were said to have stopped in were Ronald Reagan, Telly Savalas, Raquel Welch and Diana Rigg.

A little more than a decade after the bar opened, Joseph Flaherty, John Fielek, of Microwave Associates (makers of the rugged solid-state transmitter that had been designed for the nose cones of combat jet aircraft), Frederik Johannes Van Roessel of Phillips Norelco (makers of the first production line of Flaherty's first generation PCP-90 minicam), and Masahiko Morizono, who'd headed Sony's video-product division since 1972, playing a major role in developing equipment for broadcast use, all accepted the IBC's invitation to put together a display and hold a technical session on the new system of news-gathering at the convention. To their dismay, they were the only ones who showed up, so the exhibit was cancelled and they each ended up showing their wares in their respective hotel suites.

But the technical session went on as planned.

On Wednesday, September 22, 1976, Flaherty and the above-mentioned equipment manufacturers sat down in the hotel's wedding suite with Alan Protheroe, of BBC News, and E. R. Rout, head of BBC's designs department and panel moderator, for a discussion on the new American method of news-gathering.

The Crystal Palace Suite is on the hotel's third floor, facing Park Lane. The sole window looks out onto Hyde Park and the Statue of Achilles. It's a large room, 60 by 30 feet, with only two entrances - a small one for service on a side wall, and a wider one for wedding party guest, in a far corner of the room, away from the window, opposite from the service egress. Although it served admirably as a wedding venue, the space did not lend itself well to a panel discussion about breakthrough technology in a quickly growing global industry.

Roizen described the scene in a report published in the January *Broadcast Engineering*.

"The lucky ones got there early and staked out their seats in the Crystal Palace Suite of the London Hilton. The not so lucky ones were spread out on the floor, in the aisles and on the window sills. The most unfortunate found themselves on the outside balcony overlooking the 007 bar, waiting to get into the packed conference chamber either at the session break or to replace any departing members. There was not much doubt that ENG was a hot topic and the panel were in for a lively discussion."

After introducing the panelists, Roizen described how "the moderator injected a little opening levity by introducing each panel member with a mildly humorous title while asking him to stand up and be recognized. Flaherty was introduced as the Godfather of ENG and he demurred this title by claiming to be more like a midwife. Sony's representative, Morrie Morizono, was labelled 'Mr. U-Matic' and was asked to stand. He brought the house down with the deadpan statement, 'But I am standing!' before he actually got up."

After the introductions, panel moderator E.R. Rout, of the BBC, made an opening statement which, as Roizen reported, described the "dichotomous views" concerning ENG held by broadcasters in the United Kingdom. Roizen helpfully informed the reader, parenthetically, that "(news departments are for-engineering against)".

Then there was a "slightly audible commotion outside the door" after which "Julius Barnathan, Engineering Vice President of ABC, was admitted to the room."

Roizen described the outspoken and at times controversial broadcast engineer's interruption of the session thusly:

"Barnathan was obviously distressed at the fact that his network had not been officially invited to participate in the

ENG session, even though as he put it, they had just been through the bloodbath of two Olympiads at Innsbruck and Montreal. Taking the microphone, he made his own opening statement in which he berated the IBC organizers for not anticipating the size of the audience (several hundred people were turned away) and for not having a suitable hall in which to hold the session. He claimed the 16mm news films he had seen on European TV were often so bad in quality that he thanked God for ENG."

"With this controversial beginning, the ENG session was off and running," wrote Roizen. From his description, it seemed it was very busy.

"There was lively audience participation both before and after the coffee break and the subjects of vehicle size, complexity of equipment, recording on site versus direct links, lighting and sound for ENG operations were thoroughly aired. It was evident that U.K. television news departments were pushing their reluctant technical colleagues to at least experiment with portable, light weight ENG gear."

Since so many people had been denied access to the session, a quickly scheduled repeat session was planned for the next day to meet the unanticipated demand.

And with that, Electronic News Gathering had arrived in Europe.

Roizen's review of the IBC appeared in the January 1977 issue of *Broadcast Engineering*, the magazine's third January roundup of ENG trends since 1975. The issue included two other articles about ENG. One was written by Ron Whittaker; its headline was "ENG: The News Will Never Be The Same Again." It reported the challenges WJXT in Jacksonville, Florida had gone through in its adaptation of the new electronic tools of news-gathering. The other article ran the headline "It's The News Package That Sells, Not Just The Equipment."

That one was written by William D. Gordon, the chief photographer for WFMY-TV, the CBS affiliate in the Greensboro/Winston Salem/High Point metropolitan region in North Carolina, known as the Piedmont Triad. Gordon made the argument that the 21-county, 100-mile-radius reporting area made film the best option for filling the "14-minute news hole." He made the same argument Darrell Barton had made one year before: "If we were in a metropolitan area where there were a lot of spot news stories occurring in a concentrated area, ENG equipment might be more important to us. However, in the Piedmont region, if something's happening close to newscast, the major limiting factor in covering it and getting it on the air is travel time, not the speed of processing." He concludes his article with this observation: "From the way we select stories to the way we film and edit them, we are expressing WFMY-TV's news philosophy. How we work says a good deal about who we are and what we want to be. To prove 'we were there' isn't enough."

These two articles, along with Roizen's review of the IBC in London, totaled 12 pages concerning local broadcast news image-gathering in that issue alone.

Meanwhile, at *Broadcast Management/Engineering*, in that publication's fifth January round-up, editors had pumped up electronic coverage to 27 pages, including articles like "News-ENG extends the reporter's day," "Commercials-Mini cam and 3/4 in. tape score in producing commercials," "Documentaries-ENG equipment revives documentary production," and "Drama-Drama shows next to be done by ENG-type equipment?"

The headline starting the magazine's special report was "ENG Sweeps the Newsroom; Invades New Areas of Teleproduction." The subhead explains: "With the news operations of most stations irrevocably changed, electronic field production equipment has begun to take on new territory and former strongholds of other media."

Namely, *film*.

11th Annual Winter Television Conference

On January 20, 1977, Jimmy Carter was sworn in as the Nation's 39th president.

One week later, and four years after the Society's little-noticed and barely-attended conference just before Richard Nixon's inauguration, at Key Biscayne 's Sonesta Beach Hotel, well over 1,000 attendees descended on the St. Francis Hotel in San Francisco's Union Square for the 11th Annual SMPTE Winter Television Conference. The theme of the Friday session was *Beyond ENG*, Saturday's session was themed *Digital Video*, as it had been in Detroit one year earlier.

Roizen, program chair for Saturday's digital session, described Friday's opening presentation in the March 1977 issue of *Broadcast Engineering*.

"Perhaps the most impressive demonstration by Flaherty was in the domain of the application of one-inch helical VTR's to originate program production of sitcom-type weekly shows now shot on film. CBS experimented with the currently popular Bob Newhart and Phyllis shows which are done on 35mm movie cameras. For this experiment the setup included Thomson-CSF 1515 triaxial studio cameras and Thomson Labs Microcams."

"Consecutive sequences of the same images made by each of the three camera setups were replayed from Sony BVH 1000 recorders and there was virtually no visible differences on the color monitor screens between the three different originations."

Unfortunately, not that many of the Thomson CSF Microcams ever were manufactured.

Thomson CSF was a venerable French conglomerate founded in 1893, an offshoot of the Texas company Thomson-Houston Electric Company, prior to its merger with Edison General Electric Company, to form General

Electric (GE). The multinational entity based in Paris was into many things, including telephones in the Middle East and defense contracts at home, as well as building video cameras. It had lately picked up the manufacturing arm of CBS Laboratories, so now it had the Flaherty system, but the Microcam was still a two-piece, and no one wanted that anymore. Instead, the third generation TK-76 one piece was the way to go, so the camera never really caught on.

But its picture was spot-on, beating out the 35mm image captured by the old Mitchell BNCs at Television City in Hollywood. And of course, Sony's new helical-scan, one-inch tape was the state-of-the-art at that time. Flaherty's second demonstration proved more fruitful than his first at Century City and accelerated the pace of adaptation, but other folks on that Friday were still not sure.

The last presenter for the Friday sessions before the evening panel discussion was Scott Gibbs, a photographer at KPIX-TV, the San Francisco CBS affiliate. His presentation was described in the Society's March *Journal*: "Scott Gibbs … recounted the miseries and trauma of an untrained team suddenly thrust into an ENG environment." Roizen, in his report, was more pointed if a little less dramatic in his description of the photographer's address. "Scott Gibbs, an experienced film producer, was given the job of setting up his station's ENG equipment and he found he could do it adequately, but wasn't fully convinced of its superiority over his old medium."

And with that, the last muffled out cry of resistance was recorded for the record.

Joe Roizen led off Saturday's sessions with a summary of what digital technology had brought to the realm of image gathering.

"Digital conversion and large capacity, solid state memories which can store a field or a frame of TV information have created a variety of very useful digital products that time base stabilize, synchronize and standards translate television signals for a wide variety of purposes."

What started out as Consolidated Video Systems' black box that could store the information from a magnetized strip of plastic long enough to overcome timing issues between two tape machines had created a plethora of other uses.

These included the transmission of images of Jupiter back to Earth from the Pioneer 10 space probe in 1973 to images transmitted from helicopters at the Montreal Olympics the previous July. He also showed images from the BBC he'd gotten in September when he was covering the IBC, which showed the "Magazine of the Air" technique of inserting text digitally into the picture which "at the touch of a small keyboard on the home receiver, presented the home viewer with alphanumeric (or graphic) news headlines, weather, stock quotations, theater listings, horoscope readings, or the recipe of the day." He predicted that the tool of digital memory was so useful to image broadcasting that, "TV studios and production houses will be so digitized, the only analog devices left will be the people telling the computers what to do." Finally, he likened the state-of-the-art in digital technology that late January day in 1977, one week into the Carter presidency, as "the tip of an iceberg with the bulk of its future still shrouded below the surface."

As it so happened, there was a group of people 40 miles to the south, down Interstate 280, in the Santa Clara Valley, the incubator of start-ups, beginning to plumb those depths that very week. Folks at 20863 Stevens Creek Boulevard were fewer than five miles from where Consolidated Video Systems was designing its digital memory boxes, or time-base correctors. They were just 10 miles south of the Stanford campus and the famed Hewlett-Packard garage. The company, incorporated only five months earlier, was moving into its first real office space after a year of working from the proverbial Silicon Valley garage. One of the company's founders, a certain Steve Wozniac, had reluctantly just quit his job at Hewlett Packard so he could work full time at the new start-up.

Wozniac, or "The Woz" as friends called him, was working nonstop at that time, putting the final touches on his new design for a digital memory box meant for the home consumer market, known as a personal home computer. His computer was called an Apple 2, and it would be one of what *Byte* magazine called "The 1977 Trinity."

It wasn't the first home computer introduced - that was the Commodore PET (Personal Electronic Transactor) unveiled earlier that month. Nor did it sell the most - that honor went to Radio Shack's TRS-80, which that very week was also in its final design stages in Fort Worth, Texas. But it was the one in the Trinity debuting that year which did the most to ignite the imagination as to the possibility of one's own digital memory box attached to a TV screen. This phenomenon was due in a large part to Wozniac's partner in the new company, Steve Jobs.

It would be Jobs' vision and tenacity that would put the tools of Electronic News-Gathering in the palm of humanity's hands three decades hence, in the form of a wireless phone equipped with a capacitive touchscreen and a silicon chip camera.

DIGITAL HDTV

MONDAY, MARCH 23, !992

The Dreams and Hallucinations of the Future

Four years later, on January 20, 1981, Ronald Reagan was sworn in as the 40th President of the United States. It was morning in America. The previous four years of the Carter presidency had not been much better for the United States than Nixon's second term. It was so bad, in fact, that a new measurement for the nation's health entered the lexicon, "The misery Index." But for local news operations times were good, with large profits rolling in, newscast becoming longer and public interest in news expanding.

Seventeen days after Reagan took the Oath of Office, the Society of Motion Picture and Television Engineers held its 15th Television Conference - the "Winter" appellation had been dropped three years earlier. The event was back at the historic St Francis Hotel in San Francisco, 20 miles to the north of Ampex's sprawling operations in Redwood City, and 800 people attended.

One of them was a leading light in the feature film industry, Francis Ford Coppola. His photograph appears twice in the Society's April *Journal*. In the first one, he's seen looking through a camera viewfinder as an Asian gentleman stands attentively nearby. The picture's cutline explains: "... the renowned Director and Producer, studies the picture quality attainable with the NHK high-definition color camera, while Dr. Fujio of NHK looks on." The second photo is of Coppola and Fujio, as well as Joseph Polonsky, technical director of Microcam-makers Thomson-CSF, and the Godfather of ENG, Joseph Flaherty.

The four of them were captured together for posterity standing next to the new NHK high-definition camera. In the picture, Flaherty looks positively giddy, as does Polonsky. Fujio is glancing nervously at the camera, monitoring its functions, and Coppola looks at the photographer directly, hands clasped behind his back, a grave look on his face, as if in deference to the audacity of the technology on display.

Coppola had been an early advocate of the electronic means of image-gathering, recording Marlon Brando as he auditioned for the lead in the film *The Godfather*, on black-and-white helical scan videotape in 1970. As a presenter for the Best Director Academy Award in April of 1979, he'd famously gone off-script to passionately pontificate on the future of film. "Cinema as we know it is going to radically change," he had raved that evening, like some Native

American seer, "in three years it will be electronic. It will be digital, it will bounce off satellites, and it will create the dreams and hallucinations of the future, of the world." A year later, he was in Wisconsin with Edmund Gerald Brown, working the presidential primary, the same place where 20 years before Pennebaker and crew had introduced America to cinema-verite. Only this time, Coppola had gone all in with ENG. He'd put on a live broadcast to drum up enthusiasm for Brown and grab more votes. It did not go well; the event came to be known as "Apocalypse Brown." On that early February day at the conference in the St. Francis, he was about to begin production on his first box-office flop, *One from the Heart*. During production, he used Ed DiGiulio's video-assist system for instant dailies.

The reason he looked so serious in the *Journal* photo was because the camera and monitor on display next to him had achieved what had once been unthinkable: the four-minute mile of image-acquisition - video that could be projected.

Analog HD

Back in October 1972, *American Cinematographer* magazine published a special issue on "Videotape and Film," in preparation for the Society's 112th Technical Conference, at which Flaherty gave his first demonstration. In that issue, Wilton Holm, Society president and panel moderator at the Friday afternoon discussion, had published an article with the title "The Great Film-Tape Debate," where he wrote the following.

"I suggest that some of the current claims be viewed a bit skeptically, I refer specifically to the alleged claim that, by starting with a 525 or 625-line tape and employing such well-known tricks as compressing the CRT raster and employing a bit of edge enhancement and noise reduction, a better color print can be produced than one made from a 35mm color-film original ... In other words, a 525 or 625-line video recording, as a result of alleged electronic magic, cannot acquire greater definition than a 35mm film which has definition equivalent to 1200 to 1400 lines."

That meant any image acquisition intended for projection needed at least twice as many lines before it could match the quality of film.

Of course, Flaherty wasn't looking to project the images coming out of the Bosch-Fernseh video camera. He was just intending to take over some of the TV production, like prime-time network programming and commercials. He knew what NHK was up to, though.

Immediately after Japan finished hosting the 1964 Summer Olympics - the first to be broadcast by satellite - NHK turned to researching television at its new headquarters near the Olympic Village. The goal of the research was to "unlock the fundamental mechanism of video and sound interaction with the five human senses," in an effort to create a "sensation of reality," or a *telepresence*, as the NHK engineers called it.

What they came up with as an ideal standard was a rectangle a bit wider than what's known as the golden ratio and a picture made up of 75 lines fewer than film's low-end definition of 1,200 lines. At 1,125 lines, it was beyond the ability of the unaided human eye to ascertain the difference between the two.

That meant that the final barrier Wilton Holm had mounted to ensure film's status as the preferred medium for image acquisition intended for projection had been toppled.

The four men, posing for posterity beside to the next big breakthrough technology for image acquisition, having experienced eight years of explosive growth in motion picture technology, may have figured it would be a short time (around a decade) before the new system would be standardized and feature films meant for theatrical projection could be shot on it. As it turned out, though, it would be 20 years before Coppola's protégé, George Lucas, would shoot the fifth instalment of his *Star Wars* franchise with the Sony HDW-F900, chopped by Panavision to use the prime lenses and camera support systems common in feature film production.

In the intervening two decades, a standardization process emerged in a different manner than the preceding ENG rollout or the post-World War II television rollout. It seemed more akin to the development process of Farnsworth's Image Dissector and Zworykin's Iconoscope, or the way color was kicked down the road in the Fifties and Sixties: a slow, stilted, unsteady affair of interminable length.

One problem was that no one was especially keen to adopt an entirely Japanese-made system. As it also was with the car makers, America's two main TV manufacturers, RCA and Zenith, were not having an easy time in the Eighties due to competition from Japanese manufacturers. And it wasn't just American appliances at risk from foreign competition, as Senator Al Gore (D-TN), pointed out when Flaherty demonstrated the NHK system at the United States Capitol Building. The country's semiconductor industry was also vulnerable. So, the entire standardization process for high-definition television began life under a cloud of Protectionism.

By the 25th Television Conference in February 1991 in Detroit at the Renaissance Center's Westin Hotel, along the banks of the Detroit River, HDTV was practically dead in the water. Ken Shaw, of Ampex, gave the presentation *Format Choices for the Future*. He began with the issue that had been on everyone's mind during the entirety of the Eighties: "All the talk and speculation about HDTV and advanced TV has many worried that equipment bought today could be obsolete tomorrow. And since no one knows what form advanced television will take, or when, making a decision is all the more difficult. The fact is, the widespread implementation of this 'future' television is far enough away that anyone purchasing 525- or 625-line equipment today is going to have paid off that investment long before there is a demand to switch to HDTV, Wider Aspect Ratio, or whatever."

That exasperated "whatever" probably summed up the attitude of most broadcast engineers when it came to high-definition television. After all, they had other things on their minds that winter.

Camcorder

At the NAB Convention after the Society's 1981 conference, three concept models for fully integrated one-piece cameras and videotape recorders were introduced: the RCA Hawkeye, the Sony BVW-1, and the Panasonic AU/AK-100. The Sony rig used the Betamax cassette that had been released for the home market in 1975 with an upgraded tape inside. The RCA and Panasonic cameras used the 'Video Home System,' or VHS, cassette.

Developed by JVC after Sony's U-Matic had been established as the universal system for three-quarter-inch tape, and in tandem with Sony's Betamax in the early Seventies, VHS hit the American marketplace in August of 1977, in the form of the RCA VBT200 video cassette recorder, or VCR. The great consumer videotape format war of the late Seventies and early Eighties is beyond the scope of this book, but it should just be noted that when the NAB convened in April of 1981, the battle was fully involved, and VHS had a slight edge.

The Hawkeye hit the streets in October of 1982 at local news operations in Chicago, Philadelphia, Boston and Detroit. As for the Panasonic AU/AK-100? No word was heard of it again after the NAB convention, presumably Panasonic turned its attention to the home recording market to avoid competing with RCA that year.

The Sony BVW-1 arrived not long after the Hawkeye.

The camera that was stamped with the serial number "3" as it rolled off the assembly line in Japan was put on an airplane and flown to Miami, Florida, and placed in the hands of Frank Beacham. One of the first things he shot with it was the National Football League's AFC Championship Game on January 23, 1983, between the Miami Dolphins and the New York Jets.

For the previous seven years, Beacham and his company Video Matrix had been shooting for network news departments as they switched from film to video. He'd spent Christmas 1977 in Egypt, covering peace talks between Anwar Sadat and Menachem Begin. In his book, *The Whole World Was Watching,* he described challenges he faced in the city of Ismailia on the west bank of the Suez Canal, where the Suez Canal Authority was headquartered, and where the Muslim Brotherhood was founded.

"Once at the location, all the television networks had to find facilities to get on the air. ABC, in desperation, rented an old chicken truck from a farmer and painted it blue on the outside, covering the rest with ABC stickers. Inside, I would work with the edit equipment from my company. The edit controller was the world's first Sony RM-440, delivered only the day before we left for Egypt. The VTRs were set-up on tables normally used to slaughter chickens."

Christmas in a chicken truck in the middle of the desert - such were the conditions of early international ENG coverage.

By 1983, the networks had, for all intents and purposes, finished the transition to ENG. For Frank Beacham, "the handwriting for the future was on the wall. We had done very well over a seven year transition, but the miles and danger were taking a toll. We all wanted a change."

Enter the Sony Betacam, and Robin Douglas Leach.

Leach was born in 1941 in London; by the time he was 18 years old he'd become the youngest "Page One" reporter at the *Daily Mail*. Soon after that, he'd immigrated to the United States and, by the early Eighties, he'd broken into television, doing segments on *AM Los Angeles* with broadcast legend Regis Philbin, and on *Entertainment Tonight*. It was while working on the latter in Miami that he met Beacham.

Beacham recalled what happened next: "In Miami, I had pitched a Betacam production workflow to Robin Leach, who was then working for our client, Entertainment Tonight. Leach was looking to bring his costs down to $100,000 per episode for a new low-budget TV show he wanted to do. Everyone else in the early 1980s had turned him down, telling him it was impossible to do television production at such low cost."

"'Could the Betacam work?' Leach asked me. 'Maybe,' I responded,"

Sometime in in 1983, Beacham gathered his equipment and some of the crew who freelanced with him, including 33-year-old Robin Hirsch, who'd resigned from WTVJ and gone independent a few years before, and headed west. They set up shop in the heart of Hollywood, getting space in Columbia Pictures' former studios on the corner of Sunset Boulevard and North Gower Street, a little over a mile from the Roosevelt Hotel on Hollywood Boulevard. Then the crew got to work bringing electronic production to the film capital of the world.

The show *Lifestyles of the Rich and Famous* was an incredible success, surprising many, including Beacham. Some of this success was due to the small shooting package that was possible with the Sony Betacam. Because of the camera's mobility, the photographers could get into places earlier cameras couldn't. Since the crew could burn tape with no concern for cost, they achieved more spontaneous and intimate moments for the viewer. Robin Hirsch describes the production working environment in his book, *The History of Image Gathering.*

"I loved working on Lifestyles of the Rich and Famous. Because we shot interviews and b-roll with major motion picture and TV stars, it really forced me to up my game, especially in the lighting department. We also shot their homes, and they were even more picky about how that footage looked than they were with their own appearance."

"We did long sweeping pans, and achingly slow zooms of the interiors and exteriors of their homes. Then we shot the stars in short, movie like, scenes around the house. We shot them in their home office, picking roses in the garden, or reading a script by the swimming pool. Everything about these shots had to be perfect. I learned early on that actors know the difference. They can sense when the lighting is good and they are very protective of their image."

And it wasn't just the stars themselves judging his work.

"Celebrities also always had their publicist on the shoot. They were charged with the task of image protection. The publicist took their job very seriously as it justified their existence. Though most were nice, some were very picky. They would sit there with their faces buried in our field monitors critiquing every aspect of my work as a means of justifying their existence. So how did I survive?"

"Every image gatherer has their bag of tricks. In my bag I carried heavy diffusion for the lights, bounce cards for the fill, home made dimmers, 25w bulbs for the practicals, and lots of black wrap. C-stands, flags, cutters, sand bags and all that grippage of Hollywood, were not realistic in our fast moving world of production."

Electronic News Gathering had arrived in the homes of the Hollywood elite.

To do the show with the new one-half-inch souped-up Betamax cassette tape, Sony built Beacham's company an edit suite that allowed for editing up to a one-inch C-type reel-to-reel tape, developed by Ampex and Sony back in 1976, and presented in a white paper at the 11th Winter Television Conference in 1977. It became the standard, replacing the big, fat, two-inch Quad tape later that year. After the success of *Lifestyles of the Rich and Famous,* plus the money saved on production, the new system of image-gathering, in Beacham's words, "took off like wildfire, soon operating almost 24-hours a day nonstop. It performed flawlessly and copycat rooms spread throughout Los Angeles within the year."

There was plenty of work available then. Cable TV had grown considerably since Bill Daniels had spoken at the Eighth Annual Winter Television Conference in Denver in 1974. RCA launched its communications satellite, Satcom 1, just one month before Detroit's Winter Conference, where the TK-76 debuted. HBO, The Disney Channel, AMC, The Weather Channel, CNN, and ESPN all began nation-wide transmission with that satellite in the ensuing years. In early January 1981, a few weeks before the 15th Television Conference, where HDTV was introduced, C-Span began broadcasting live gavel-to-gavel coverage of Congressional hearings. Seven months later, Music Television, or MTV, went live to parts of New Jersey, launching a whole new industry of music video production.

In 1983, when Beacham's low-cost edit suite, based on the small paperback-size Betamax cassette - and the truly portable one-piece camera - hit Los Angeles, the irresistible combination immediately started picking up a greater and greater share of the ever-increasing motion picture production market.

Then came the NAB convention in 1986 in Dallas, and the triumph of Sony.

Betacam SP

RCA had stopped production of the Hawkeye in 1984, the same year it released the CCD-1 camera. It was the first video news camera ever made using the solid-state charged couple device that had been introduced at the 9th Winter Television Conference by Joseph Rothstein of Fairchild Semiconductor. The CCD replaced the old vacuum tubes that, in the words of Robin Hirsh, "seemed to go out of their to make your life miserable."

Only three dozen models were shipped in the next 18 months. On October 3, 1985, RCA quit the game, sold its

Broadcast Systems division, and turned off the lights at the labs in Camden.

Panasonic suddenly got back in the broadcast game at this point, with a souped-up half-inch VHS cassette, called M-II. But it was barely hanging on in the world of broadcast news. On Thursday, April 3, 1986, Ampex announced it had entered a licensing agreement with Sony to manufacture the Betacam videotape recorder and the half-inch tape cassette. The two companies accounted for 80 to 90 percent of the broadcast tape recording market in the U.S.. Sony had already established manufacturing agreements with Thompson-CSF in France and Germany's Bosch Fernseh, making the Betacam cassette almost the sole half inch tape being used for broadcast applications in the world.

Then, at the Dallas NAB convention, Sony introduced its CCD camera, the BVW-105, and an even more souped-up tape for its Betamax cassette. The new system was dubbed *Beta SP* - the SP stood for *Superior Performance*.

Five years on, at the 25th Television Conference in Detroit, in his presentation on format choices for the future, Ken Shaw (who'd put the transition to HDTV way off into the future), said this about Sony's system: "Betacam SP has proven its durability in the field, while providing excellent first generation video quality. Betacam SP is the format of choice for field acquisition. It is lightweight, small, and draws minimal power."

He added: "Betacam SP is supported by multiple manufacturers who offer a broad range of products. Over 80-thousand Betacam units have been sold worldwide. Betacam SP, therefore, is the format to beat."

That same day, more than 6,000 miles away, on the shore of the Red Sea, in the small town of Ras al-Khafji, Saudi Arabia, network television reporters were bringing the world up to date on the aftermath of the first ground battle of the Gulf War, and the de facto standard of the time, Sony's Betacam SP, captured most of the images.

The camera system also shot most of the commercials, music videos, live sports coverage, and nearly everything else that was on television by the early Nineties, except about 85 percent of prime-time entertainment programming.

This piece of the production pie was one of the last three areas where film production was still widely used: in the dramas, crime procedurals, and situation comedies on America's TVs every night, as well as in the production and distribution of major motion pictures intended for projection in movie theaters around the world, and, of course, in still photography.

Essentially, film was still used for the same stuff it had been used for back in October of 1972, when Flaherty had given his first demonstration. In the ensuing two decades, during the ENG and digital revolutions, the growth of film was nearly static, and by the early Nineties, the question of film's future in the realm of still photography had begun to be debated more often and more intensely.

Moore's Revenge

On October 14, 1884, George Eastman received his patent for Photographic Film. By substituting flexible celluloid for plates of glass in the photographic workflow of the day, he extended to the casual user the pursuit of image gathering. The resulting consumable, a chemical covered brown strip (which eventually had perforations down both sides) from which a final product of a print was obtained, proved to be a money-maker. Eastman's company, Kodak, could sell cameras at a deep discount and make up any loss with the cost of processing the celluloid strip and creating the resulting paper print. Nearly a century later, by the time NHK's high-definition television system was introduced at the St. Francis, the company's annual sales were nearly $10 billion and over 60,000 workers were employed at Kodak Park in Rochester.

One of those workers was Steve Sasson. He'd been issued a patent for his digital camera at the end of 1978 and was busy in his lab continuing to perfect his device. He still hadn't presented his findings or design parameters to the Society of Motion Picture and Television Engineers, or any other professional organization. Shuttered away somewhere on the 120-acre campus, surrounded by an entire world that depended on the disposable celluloid strip for its decadent life-style, Sasson didn't have a lot of supporters to bounce ideas off of. So, it is not surprising that, in spite of its head start in digital imaging, Kodak didn't have a chance in the new market once the computer revolution really kicked into high gear.

In April of 1981 the Xerox Star personal computer came out. It was the first computer to use a *bitmapped* display; basically a picture-in-picture scheme called a *graphical user interface*, which included things like icons, folders, and documents, and could be manipulated by a manually operated device attached to the computer via a cable, known as a mouse. The Star did not sell well, and not long after Xerox traded the mouse and the screen icons to Apple Computer for 100,000 shares of its company stock.

Then, in August of that year, Sony introduced its CCD-equipped still camera, the Mavica. The name was derived from *Magnetic Video Camera*. It was never mass produced and sold to the public, but the rudimentary pieces for taking a still picture and immediately loading it onto a TV screen were now a publicly known concept. But moving it around, adjusting the color, and sending it to someone else wasn't possible yet. But with Moore's Law of ever-increasing computing power in full effect, all that was required to bring these two inventions together were instructions for the machine - called code - to add, at an ever-increasing rate, to the detail, the color, and the portability of the imagery carried by the ones and zeros of the binary digital language.

A million hackers heeded the call.

By 1986 there was so much code written that the Joint Photographic Experts Group (JPEG) formed to come up with a standard so BMPs, GIFs, TIFFs, PNGs, and all the other systems of code could get along. The next year, a Ph.D. student at the University of Michigan started working on what would become Photoshop on his Apple Macintosh Plus. At the NAB convention in Las Vegas in 1988, a company called Apollo Computer showed a prototype of its Avid/1 Media Composer on an Apple Macintosh II. Two months later, in Ottawa, Canada, the Moving Picture Experts Group (MPEG) held its inaugural meeting.

Kodak had been busy writing code, too. In 1989, the company made its run at keeping film relevant in the ever-changing market of still photography by introducing the Photo CD system. Film-processing labs were sold scanners and photographers were sold Photo CD players for storing and uploading images onto a computer. The next year, right on Sassoon's schedule, Kodak introduced the first professional single-lens reflex digital camera, the DCS-100 at Photokina in Cologne, Germany. It was basically a Nikon F3, equipped with a CCD and cabled into a small desktop computer slung over the photographer's shoulder. Just as with the early efforts of ENG, portability was questionable, but the results were immediate.

Unfortunately, things didn't go the way the venerable company hoped they would. In 1992, the JPEG File interchange Format (JFIF) was given to the world. Now there were other ways to get the pictures of your kids in the computer to share. Four years later, there were 25 solid-state electric cameras on the market, all using the Joint Photographic Experts Group's File Interchange Format and costing less than a thousand bucks a piece. Eastman's consumable plastic strip was beginning to look more and more redundant in a modern electronic world.

Digital HD

At the same time Kodak was coming out with its electronic still camera, things had taken a turn in the efforts toward high-definition television.

Throughout the Eighties, America had watched with trepidation as Japan and Europe had poured millions of their respective currencies into research of the next generation of television viewing and delivery technology. In the United States, meanwhile, two Republican Administrations, first Ronald Reagan's, then George Bush Senior's, had avoided pursuing TV research using tax dollars, instead relying on industrial competition to invent a system so the United States could compete with the rest of the world. The deadline for this competition was June of 1990, when final entries into the FCC's advisory committee on advanced television services, chaired by Joseph Flaherty, were due. In a surprise last-minute entry, a small company's even smaller division threw the whole industry into uncertainty.

The division had begun life in the late Sixties as the company Linkabit. It had done work for NASA in early low-power digital transmission of deep-space imagery, such as the first pictures of Jupiter from the Pioneer 10 space probe in 1975. Later, the small company created a digital video encryption process. It was then sold to Microwave Associates, makers of the rugged solid-state microwave transmitters used in ENG vans. Linkabit then became a division of the growing company, which now called itself MA/COM, to emphasize its communication line of products over its radar for military jet aircraft. While there, the division wrote the code for HBO's signal encryption for set-top satellite receivers, outsmarting the pesky wildcat dish pirates who watched the premium channel for free. The codec was called Videocipher.

In 1987, the division was acquired by General Instrument, moved from Burlington, Massachusetts, out to San Diego, California, and renamed Videocipher, after its successful codec. From this vantage point on the Pacific Rim, they watched the NHK system of HDTV go operational in Japan while continuing to pick up steam in America. Meanwhile, domestic companies couldn't seem to figure out a better way to produce high-definition television. As the deadline for pitches to the FCC closed in, the folks at Videocipher, including an MIT-educated engineer named Woo Paik, became nervous that NHK's 10-year-old spectrum-sucking HD transmission requirements, which had been regarded as the best game in town, was going to bump their little encryption codec out of the final system. So, Paik spent a week at home, writing code. He came up with a completely digital system for high-definition television, then went to the head of General Instruments - Donald Rumsfeld - and proposed they pay the $130,000 entrance fee and enter the contest for the final system.

And just like that, the United States of America was back in game, with a commanding lead no less, in the development of high-definition television.

General Instrument demonstrated a working system of DigiCipher's digital HDTV transmission in Washington D.C. on Monday, March 23, 1992. According to a description in the next week's *Broadcasting*, the demonstration was an almost religious experience.

"Singing something akin to the gospel music refrain, 'Can I get a witness?' General Instrument Corp. took its all-digital high-definition TV show to Capitol Hill last week"

"High powered government witnesses, including FCC Chairmen Alfred Sikes, answered the call and were treated to a 12-minute, 2kw, all-digital transmission of 1,050-line video, delivered from noncommercial WETA-TV Washington's suburban Maryland transmitter, through 6 MHz of spectrum, to a standard broadcast TV antenna mounted on the U.S. Capitol building roof 10 miles away."

"When it was over, leading lights were careful to distance themselves from any single proponent, but were quick to express their enthusiasm for what they deemed a milestone."

It would seem the zero-sum game approach to technology development had paid dividends, but the game was about to change.

On January 20, 1993, Bill Clinton was sworn in as the 42nd President of the United States. His vice president, Al Gore, the senator from Tennessee who'd brought up the importance of domestic chip manufacturing to Flaherty when he'd brought the NHK system up to Capitol hill, was his lead on technical issues facing the country. The Clinton administration took an active role in research and development, putting tax dollars toward research in areas deemed important to the national economy. While there was no direct involvement in advanced television research, some influence in the manner of that research can be perceived.

A month after Clinton took the oath of office, the remaining companies trying to design an HDTV system made their presentations to the FCC's Advisory Committee on Advanced Television Service. NHK had dropped out by this time, and the contenders still hanging in had all gone with digital systems. Unfortunately for the committee, all the systems were much the same or, in other words, as it was explained in the March 3 issue of *Broadcasting*, the first issue bearing the title *Broadcasting & Cable*, "analysis of the first round tests found that no single system tested high enough on all technical and economic criteria to be considered a winner or tested low enough to be considered a clear loser."

In order to come up with a solution, the advisory committee recommended that the different system designers work together to come up with the best standard for high-definition television. This idea was put into action formally two months later, and the group that became known as the "Grand Alliance" began their work. Not everyone was pleased with this outcome.

In his memoir *Known and Unknown*, Donald Rumsfeld wrote, "Once again Washington intruded. The Federal Communication Commission (FCC) effectively forced General Instrument and our partner, the Massachusetts Institute of Technology, to combine with Zenith, AT&T, Thompson, Phillips, RCA, and NBC to form what was called the Grand Alliance for digital high-definition television. The theory was that we would collaborate on fashioning an American standard for HDTV and share in the royalties. Apart from the damage that decision by the FCC did to GI's leading position-since GI was the company that had developed all-digital HDTV- the government's unhelpful involvement also contributed to the delay of the technology's introduction in America for close to a decade."

In the end, the FCC voted the final standard into existence on December 27, 1996. It was then decided that the broadcast industry would be allowed one decade to execute the switch-over. This was extended a couple of times, but by 2009, HDTV was available to every home in the United States.

A Spring Conference at Century City

In October of 1996, while the finishing touches were being put on the new HD standard, the Society held its 138th Technical Conference and World Media Expo at the Los Angeles Convention Center, just southwest of downtown L.A. It was also the Society's 80th anniversary and nearly 1,000 people were there to celebrate. A workshop preceded the conference, called *HDTV '96*; at the conference itself, 45 papers about HDTV were presented. So overwhelming was the focus on the new digital method of image acquisition that in the next month's *Journal*, the News section featured this: "SMPTE has announced that it will be holding its First Annual Spring Film Conference and Exhibition in Los Angeles, March 20 to 22, 1997." The formal announcement in the next *Journal* began, "The SMPTE focuses on television in February and then turns its attention to film in March." The theme of the inaugural Spring Film Conference was *Film: Still the Master in a Digital World*.

On February 6, 1997, 650 people gathered at Manhattan's Crown Plaza to attend the Society's 31st Television

Conference, (by then it was known as the "Advanced Motion Imaging Conference"). The theme of that year's gathering was *The Age of Compression: Nonlinear Editing, Digital Broadcasting, and Other Wonders.* In addition to presentations like *Unconnected Islands for Video Editing is a Thing of the Past* and *NLE System Design Using Mathematically Lossless Motion – JPEG,* the conference offered a special event on Thursday evening, February 6: A field trip to Lincoln Center's Sony Theater to see the new IMAX film *L5: First City in Space.*

Six weeks later, the members of the Hollywood Section of the Society - the very first section, organized way back in 1928 – again gathered at the Century Plaza Hotel for the Inaugural Spring Film Conference and Exhibition. According to the report in the June *Journal,* "200 people attended 'The Nature of Film,' the all-day seminar held on the first day of the conference." The next day, Friday, 500 attendees entered the aluminum-sheathed, crescent-shaped symbol of the old analog world's idea of modernity to take in the first of four technical sessions: production, laboratory issues, post production, and distribution/exhibition. The first session, chaired by Ed Digiulio, included the panel discussion "Cinematographers and Digital Artist: Friend or Foes?" The discussion, as the *Journal* report described, "... [was] focused on how the tools being used today are changing and impacting the way we look at production and design techniques." One of the new possibilities for users of the digital tools brought up during the panel discussion was to "allow the cinematographer to do a handheld documentary-type camera movement to create special effects."

Friday afternoon's keynote address was given by a film industry pioneer, Petro Vlahos. He was the man who perfected the blue-screen technique.

Blue screen, green screen or, as broadcaster's call it, chroma key (essentially picture-in-picture), the technique of layering visual elements in a frame, was first used in *The Thief of Bagdad* back in 1940. It wasn't totally ideal though. If the cinematographer tried to show smoke in the picture, the background showed through. The same thing happened right at the edges of moving objects within the frame; the motion created a blurred image, creating a sort of halo effect. Vlahos solved this issue.

He described how he did it during preproduction of the film *Ben Hur*, in which there was to be shown a sequence of hand-to-hand combat at sea, to be shot in 70mm film on a set at MGM studios, which would require the use of the 15-year-old blue screen technique. He worked on the problem at his office on the 15th floor of the Taft building, at the corner of Hollywood and Vine, less than a mile east of the Roosevelt Hotel. His office faced north, with a "perfect" view of the Hollywood sign.

"For the next six months," Vlahos recalled, "I sat back in my chair, feet propped up, and stared at that sign."

"Month after month," he went on, "I would mentally generate mattes and observe the results, which were always unsatisfactory. I no longer needed to use the blackboard. It was now imprinted in my mind."

Whatever he did, however, he always came to the same conclusion. "When ever there was any cross screen motion.," he observed, "the edge of the subject would blur and be semitransparent. One would see the blur of a rapidly moving hand and also see the through the blurred hand to the blue backing bchind it. After six months I concluded that no satisfactory matte could ever be made to cover the blue separation in the area of a blurred subject, because the backing and the subject occupied the same area."

So he came up with another way to develop the film. "Being limited to the green and red separation, one could print the green separation twice, once with green light and once with blue light. Just how bad could this be?"

It took him another week of figuring out a processing workflow for the film. Then he took his results to MGM for a test.

"We went out onto the blue stage where Glenn Ford was making a western. 'Glenn, come on over and sit on this stool, we want to make a test. And by the way, light up a cigar and blow some smoke.'"

One can imagine the 500 attendees from the venerable old Hollywood Section of the Society, listening to the

80-year-old industry pioneer describe his mental process for creating one of the most-used special effects of the day, waxing nostalgic for the former days of analog when problems were solved through reflection and physical manipulation, versus punching out endless lines of code on a computer. Perhaps they found themselves rejuvenated when they returned to their studios, sets, and labs the next Monday, more secure in the knowledge of their century-old format's mastery in image acquisition in an ever-growing digital world.

Alas, it was not to endure. Film, and the analog world it inhabited, would all but vanish in just 14 years.

CONCLUSION

JANUARY 1, 2009

Digital 3-D

Sometime in 1996, George Lucas and his producer Richard McCallum visited the Sony Corporation in Japan to get a look at its prototype high-definition camera. They liked what they saw and asked Sony if it could alter the camera so it would capture an image 24 times a second, as opposed to the 30 times a second that was the standard frame rate for video.

Sony answered in the affirmative and the technicians at the plant in Atsugi Japan, located on the western edge of Kanto Plain, halfway between Tokyo and Mount Fuji, built the HDW-F900 24P CineAlta camera. Lucas and McCallum shopped it around Hollywood in search of someone who could make a prime lens for it, but no one was willing to take on the project. So the first part of the *Star Wars* prequals was shot on Arriflex cameras using Eastman EXR 50D Color Negative Film 5245 for daylight shots and Kodak Vision

320T Color Negative Film 5277 for indoor stuff. They then sent it out to 3,000 theaters across the country in May of 1999 on Kodak Vision Premier Color Print Film 2393.

By the time *The Phantom Menace* hit the megaplexes, Panavision had bitten the bullet and designed a prime lens of the type used in feature film production for the Sony camera, along with a beefed-up lens mount and some modifications on the top and bottom to allow for the use of film production accessories; follow focus units, Steadicam plates, and the geared tripod heads used on professional dollies. With that, the Sony HDW-F900 was "panavised" and ready to begin image acquisition for the fifth instalment of the Star Wars franchise, *Attack of the Clones*, in June of 2000.

On Monday night, April 6, 1998, at the NAB convention in Las Vegas, Joseph Flaherty was presented with the Digital Television Pioneer Award by the weekly magazine *Broadcasting & Cable*. Don West, the magazine's editor, called the Godfather of ENG the "Father of HDTV" as he bestowed the honor. Flaherty was 68 years old that April, and had been at CBS for 41 years, the last 15 of which he'd spent shepherding into existence the biggest leap forward in image transmission since Philo T. Farnsworth had demonstrated electronic television back in 1927. And that was the second major transition Flaherty had overseen. It's a good thing he had a sense of humor. Sly lines, always delivered with a grin, like, "This is the worse HDTV you'll ever see," kept things light during the endless scrimmages over technical standards. In 2002, 30 years after his film-versus-tape challenge at the Society's 112th Technical Conference, *Attack of the Clones* premiered in theaters. That same year, the one-time U.S. Army enlistee was elevated to the rank of Officer in the French Legion of Honor by French President Jacques Chirac.

A month before *Attack of the Clones* hit the big screen, Thompson CSF, the French company that had made the Microcam, unveiled its new Grass Valley Viper FilmStream camera at the 80th Annual NAB convention in Las Vegas. The new camera recorded an uncompressed image onto a disc. Michael Mann, who'd experimented with the Sony high-definition camera for night shoots for his film *Ali*, decided to use it on his L.A. thriller *Collateral*. The movie was shot almost entirely at night, with soft diffused lights connected to dimmers to back down the illumination even more, so the camera could capture the after-dark scenery of downtown Los Angeles. The film demonstrated the electronic camera's low-light sensitivity and pointed the way ahead for using the new technology in future productions.

At the same time Tom Cruise and Jamie Foxx were delivering their performances for the first non-affects-driven production intended for wide theatrical release and recorded with an electronic workflow, almost a thousand miles off Costa Rica's west coast, James Cameron, the director responsible for the films *Terminator*, *The Abyss*, and *Titanic*, was two-and-a-half miles beneath the ocean's surface with his crew and several scientist in Russian submersibles equipped with eight Sony HDW F900s perfecting digital three-dimensional (3-D) image acquisition.

Along the East Pacific Rise, hydrothermal vents, underwater volcanos which spew vast amounts of sulfur - what the ancients referred to as brimstone - in great black plumes, create a zone that's boiling hot and deadly for most life on Earth but is, surprisingly, teeming with creatures large and small. The life forms which inhabit this inhospitable world Cameron likened to something descended from another planet, calling the 3D IMAX movie he made *Aliens of the Deep*. It was the third underwater production he'd shot using the Sony high-definition camera. In 2001, he'd used it to shoot the actual RMS Titanic ocean liner in 3D for the documentary *Ghost of the Abyss*, and in 2002 he shot the documentary *Expedition: Bismarck* in 2-D for the Discovery Channel. During these productions, he'd worked on the stereoscopic method of three-dimensional photography and projection. The movies had to be shown in IMAX theaters because they were the only moviehouses equipped with the projectors that could put out the 1,150 digitally produced lines on the screen. By the time Cameron's third underwater movie premiered on January 28, 2005, however, economics were starting to shift, and suddenly the new 3-D method was in demand.

For the next 12 months, the price on one of the new digital monitors for home viewing dropped by half. One out of every five TV sets sold in America in 2006 was a new thin widescreen plasma, or LED. Hooked up to a Dolby Surround Sound home theater system and a Digital Video Disc (DVD) player, there was no reason to drive to a sticky-floored movie theater at the local mall any longer. Why schlep the whole family to the theater when they could have the same theatrical experience in the comfort of their home in their pajamas? So just as theater owners did in the Fifties when home television sets had threatened movie theaters throughout the country then, the megaplexes went for 3D.

Disney was the first company to jump into the new digital projection. In March of 2005, CEO Michael Eisner (in negotiations with Steve Jobs over the future relationship between Disney and Pixar) decided to project the studio's next animated feature in the new stereoscopic 3-D on a select group of 100 screens. After all was said and done, the movie *Chicken Little* ended up opening on only 84 screens in 3-D - but still it tied with *The Lion King* as the largest box-office draw on an opening weekend for a Disney animated feature. Suddenly the new digital 3-D theater projection boom was on. Three years later, there were 5,000 screens equipped for digital projection. As the new projectors were moved in, the old film projectors were unceremoniously moved out.

Meanwhile, image acquisition for theatrical release continued its electronic trend.

Two months before *Collateral* hit theaters, Panavision Genesis was introduced at the Cinegear show on Universal Studios' backlot. This camera was equipped with a CCD chip the same size as the film frame used in most film cameras. Productions for *Superman Returns*, Adam Sandler's *Click*, and *Apocalypto* all used the camera in 2005 and 2006. At the NAB convention in 2006, the Red One camera was announced. By early 2007, two of the first models were sent out to New Zealand and used in Peter Jackson's *Crossing the Line*, a 14-minute short about World War I, with all the trappings of a big-budget action movie, including aerials, crane, boom, vehicle-mounted, triopod and Steadicam shots. When the finished production was screened at the 2007 NAB Convention, it caused a considerable sensation.

That convention featured another introduction: Arri brought forth its Arriflex-416 16 mm film camera, the last film camera that company would develop. In 2005, Arri had introduced its first digital camera, the experimental D-20. An updated version, the D-21, debuted three years later. Both were available for rent only, in order to not have to compete with film camera sales.

In late 2009, at the International Broadcasting Convention in Amsterdam, the company introduced the Arri Alexa. It was Initially intended just for high-definition television shows, commercials, and perhaps a few theatrical releases, but soon it caught on and, in less than a decade, was being used on 80 percent of the image acquisition intended for wide theatrical release. Two years later, in September of 2011, both Arri and Panavision quietly stopped manufacturing film cameras. Two months after that, Roger Ebert, film critic for the *Chicago Sun Times*, published an article in his blog with the headline "The sudden death of film." In it he stated, "The victory of video was quick and merciless."

Back in June of 2009, Kodak had stopped manufacturing Kodachrome for still photography, and Paul Simon's song became a relic.

Video on the other hand was just getting started.

Complementary metal-oxide-semiconductor

At approximately 2 a.m. on Thursday, January 1, 2009, Bay Area Rapid Transit police officers were dispatched to the Fruitvale transit station, in Oakland, California, in response to a call that a fight had broken out among about 20 passengers onboard the lead car of a train heading south from downtown San Francisco after the New Year's Eve celebrations there. At 2:07 a.m., officers arrived on the platform and started pulling passengers off the train. The vehemence of the response by the first officers on the scene elicited vocal protest from on lookers; a few of them pulled out their

Motorola RAZR2 V9 cell phones, flipped open the screen and keypad, and started recording video.

The video phone was an idea that had been kicking around ever since Alexander Graham Bell developed the telephone, way back in 1876. At the 1900 Paris Exposition Universelle, where the Russian artillery officer Konstantin Perskiy had coined the term television, a postcard predicting video conferencing by the year 2000 was handed out to attendees. In 1927, Bell Labs had designed a prototype of such a machine using the mechanical method of TV, the Nipkow disk. By the time the 1964 World's Fair opened in Queens, New York, it had a working model. Nine years later, however, with only 453 units in operation, Bell Telephone (which was called AT&T by that time) discontinued its efforts to produce videophones due to a lack of interest, declaring the technology a "concept looking for a market."

Not much was done after that. In 1992, "web" cameras were a new device which everyone could plug into their desktop computers. These cameras used another kind of silicon chip, the Complementary metal-oxide-semiconductor (CMOS) to acquire light. Unlike the CCD, which was the primary source of video capture, CMOS chips didn't use much power. The entire CCD must be on to capture a frame of video; a CMOS chip, on the other hand, is only on one pixel at a time. You could power that through a Universal

Serial Bus (USB) port. By 1996, the cameras were being built into the computers at the factories.

It was the Japanese who first put the CMOS chip into a mobile phone. The VP-210 VisualPhone by Kyocera Corporation was released in May 1999 and Sharp's J-SHo4 by came out on November 1, 2000. Neither device caught on in the U.S. Most Americans were happy just taking photos with their phones.

Then, in January of 2007, Steve Jobs presented the iPhone to the world. While it didn't have video capability, it was a threat to the other American cell-phone manufacturer, Motorola. So Motorola threw video conferencing into its new RAZR phone, launching it a quick nine months later. In addition to video conferencing with someone else who had the same model of RAZR phone you had, you could record the call and replay it later. If you were really interested in all its bells and whistles, you could point it at something and record a video to playback later as well.

A little over a year later, in the early hours of 2009, Tommy Cross, Margarita Carazo, Daniel Lui and Karina Vargas aimed their CMOS-equipped RAZR phones through the windows of a train they were on, which was idling on an adjacent siding from where BART police officers were attempting to remove passengers involved in a fight from a train - and pushed record.

At around 2:15 a.m., BART officers Johannes Mehserle and Tony Pirone were attempting to take a 22-year-old African-American man, Oscar Grant, into custody, charging him with resisting a police officer. Pirone had his knee on Grant's neck and was yelling obscenities at him while Mehserle was trying to place restraints on Grant's wrist. Unsuccessful at this, Mehserle stood up and, mistaking it for his taser, drew his sidearm and shot the prone Grant in the back. The bullet went through Grant, hit the concrete and ricocheted back into Grant, puncturing his lung. He died seven hours later.

The videos that the four onlookers recorded with their cell phones were uploaded onto various platforms on the World Wide Web. In one week, those videos had been downloaded more than 450,000 times from KTVU-TV's website, and were averaging a thousand views and hour on the four-year-old video platform called YouTube. The resulting public outrage stemming from the shooting led to protest and riots; the videos began to bring awareness to the treatment of African-American males by overzealous law-enforcement officers. And it was also the first time cell-phone video would be admitted as evidence in a court case against law enforcement. It wouldn't be the last.

Electronic News Gathering had arrived in the palm of all who possessed a phone equipped with a CMOS chip, and the world would never be the same again.

Today, as this is being written, one can pick up a phone or a tablet, open an application called Tiktok and watch a video that has recently been captured with a CMOS equipped drone overlooking a tank battle in Ukraine while a citizen journalist stands in front of the video - or appears in a box in the corner of the video - and explains the significance of the image as it plays.

In this latest affront to humanity left over from our Neolithic past, Russia's 19th Century style invasion of the young nation of Ukraine finds the embedded journalist of the past being replaced by armchair tacticians - hackers with time and a cause pouring over hours of imagery - delivering three minute or shorter chunks of observation and analysis (though at this writing that time has been expanded by Tiktok to 10 minutes). The picture and picture capabilities of Consolidated Video System's CVS-600, now available on every phone on the planet, will allow anyone access to an edit suite unavailable to all but professionals a mere 20 years ago. The impact of this imagery on the world, on the multitude of platforms beyond Tiktok, has brought about an unforeseen unification in world thought, a near universal condemnation of the perpetrator of the conflict. Such is the power of media and electronic news-gathering today.

Where will it go from here? The virtual reality headset, ten years old at this writing, seems the next direction the technology will take. Perhaps someday one will be able to don a headset and join a news reporter live who is equipped with a 360-degree 3D camera and get their news as if standing at the scene next to the reporter. Or, maybe, at a certain time of the day in the near future, one will don the headset and catch up on the daily activities of a photojournalist, following along, as they go about their routine of image acquisition, verité style, with little interjection by the person with the camera. But this is, at best, conjecture. If anything has been demonstrated in this volume it is that prognostication in the realm of image-acquisition, manipulation, and exhibition - in a free market - is a fool's errand. Certainly not one the author cares to pursue. But there are others with the temerity to really contemplate the future, and perhaps something can be gleaned from their prophesies.

Noosphere

Pierre Teilhard de Chardin was born in 1881 in a Chateau in the Auvergne-Rhone-Alps region of France, about 23 miles south of Vichy. His father served as a regional librarian and his mother was the great grandniece of Voltaire. Of his youth he wrote, "Auvergne moulded me. Auvergne served me both as a museum of natural history and as wildlife preserve. Sacenat (the name of the chateau) in Auvergne gave me my first taste of the joys of discovery. To Auvergne I owe my most precious possessions: a collection of pebbles and rocks still to be found there, where I lived."

He would not have much occasion throughout his life to visit his childhood home though. At 18 years of age, he entered the Jesuit novitiate, the junior college for future Jesuit Missionaries, and began his studies to be a naturalist. Nine years later, he was teaching Physics at the College de la Sainte Famille in Cairo. Four years after that, we find him at the scholastic level in the Society of Jesus - a "brother" or a "Jesuit in formation" - and studying on the southern coast of England, where he picked up an interest in evolution and paleontology. Starting in 1912, he began work on his PhD at the French National Museum of Natural History. The First World War interrupted his studies - he served as a stretcher bearer on the Western Front with the North African Zouaves - but by 1922 he'd earned his doctorate. He then went on a year long trip to China to help with the exploratory research the Jesuit's had been carrying out in China's western frontier.

When he returned to Paris in late 1924, he discovered that he was in hot water with the Church elders. Seems that as he was finishing up his thesis in 1922, he was teaching the students in his geology classes at the Catholic Institute of Paris the Theory of Evolution. This called into question his belief in original Sin. He spent the next year in Paris while his case went through the church bureaucracy. In his spare time, he attended lectures at the Sorbonne. There he met Vladimir Vernadsky and Edouard Le Roy.

Vernadsky was a brilliant Russian scientist, famous in his home country but virtually unknown in the west until the 1980's. Today, he is known as: "A principal architect of our contemporary ecological vision of the biosphere." Eduard Suess may have coined the term biosphere back in 1875, but he didn't have time to go into the thinnest and lightest sphere - focusing instead on the gargantuan bands of rock below us and the vast layers of the atmosphere above us. It was Vernadsky who provided the concept of an ecosystem to the sphere humanity inhabits. He was, in fact, that very year working on in his seminal volume - *The Biosphere* - which would introduce his ideas to the public and become a prime text of the modern environmental movement.

From Vernadsky Pierre Teilhard de Chardin and Edouard Le Roy learned the concept of a sphere beyond the biosphere yet intrinsically bound to it through human endeavor. It was a sphere in which the biosphere and humanity could evolve together and achieve sustainability by preserving and reconstructing the biosphere.

It is thought le Roy coined the term noosphere, Noo being the ancient Greek word for "mind" or "reason," to indicate mankind's thought wrapping the world in a protective sphere, in the process protecting it from harm. At any rate he started using the term in his lectures at the College of France in 1927.

By that time Vernadsky was back in St Petersburg, Russia, publishing his book, and Teilhard was back in China, having basically been banished from France, relieved of his teaching duties, disallowed from publishing his own research, and sent out to the farthest reaches of the planet. For the next 15 years he explored the Far East, Mongolia, Manchuria, the Gobi Desert, and assisted in ongoing excavations of the Peking Man site, all the while working out his theories of mankind's role in the universe in a book entitled *The Phenomenon of Man*, which he completed in 1940.

Teilhard spent the rest of his life attempting, unsuccessfully, to publish the book. It was only upon his death in 1955 that it was released to a wide audience. In its pages, Teilhard describes the five stages of evolution: geogenesis (beginning of Earth), Biogenesis (beginning of life), anthropogenesis (beginning of humanity), noogenesis (the emergence of mind), and finally the Christogenesis (genesis of the "total Christ"). Of the process of noogenesis he wrote the following: "The recognition and isolation of a new era in evolution, the era of noogenesis, obliges us to distinguish correlatively a support proportionate to the operation - that is to say, yet another membrane in the majestic assembly of telluric layers." Of this membrane he wrote, "Much more coherent and just as extensive as any preceding layer, it is really a new layer, the 'thinking layer', which, since its germination at the end of the Tertiary period, has spread over and above the world of plants and animals. In other words, outside and above the biosphere there is the noosphere."

It is natural to wonder what inspired Teilhard to add a global membrane, a thinking layer, to the existing layers of the Earth's atmosphere, e.g., the troposphere, stratosphere, mesosphere, etc. Perhaps the answer can be found in Paris in 1925, the year he was awaiting the final ruling of the Jesuit Fathers over his teaching of evolution to his students in his geology classes three years before. In April of that year the International Exhibition of Modern Decorative and Industrial Arts opened. The Art Deco movement, with its insistence of form following function and a celebration of the possibilities of technology, was born at that exhibition. Also, not to be overlooked, 1925 was the first full year of the state-run Radio Paris, which transmitted from the 36-year-old Eiffel Tower. It is not beyond the realm of possibility that between taking in classes at the Sorbonne concerning the evolution of the planet, Teilhard was also taking in the genesis of the modern radio age and digesting its possible impact on humanity's future evolution.

But whatever his inspiration, the fulfillment of part of his prophesy is undeniable. Near the end of *The Phenomenon of Man* Teilhard wrote the following:

"Noogenesis rises upwards in us and through us unceasingly. We have pointed to the principal characteristics of that movement: the closer association of the grains of thought;

the synthesis of individuals and of nations or races; the need of an autonomous and supreme personal focus to bind elementary personalities together, without deforming them, in an atmosphere of active sympathy. And, once again: all this results from the combined action of two curvatures - the roundness of the earth and the cosmic convergence of mind - in conformity with the law of complexity and consciousness.

Now when sufficient elements have sufficiently agglomerated, this essentially convergent movement will attain such intensity and such quality that mankind, taken as a whole, will be obliged - as happened to the individual forces of instinct - to reflect upon itself at a single point; that is to say, in this case, to abandon its organo-planetary foothold so as to shift its center on to the transcendent center of its increasing concentration. This will be the end and fulfilment of the spirit of the earth.

The end of the world: the wholesale internal introversion upon itself of the noosphere, which has simultaneously reached the uttermost limit of its complexity and its centrality.

The end of the world: the overthrow of equilibrium, detaching the mind, fulfilled at last, from its material matrix, so that it will henceforth rest all its weight on God-Omega."

It is, of course, anyone's guess if the Omega point will ever come to pass. But some of what Teilhard predicted back in the Thirties has already happened. The "synthesis of individuals and of nations or races;" and the "atmosphere of active sympathy" have both become regular features of life in the early 21st century where access to a free internet is available. Another prediction in the passage above can also be counted on to be true going forward as well, and that is the ever-increasing degree of complexity, which he calls a law. Anyone who has been paying attention over the last three decades can attest to this reality.

It is this complexity engineers, and those of us who are involuntary engineers, must keep an eye on, hence the reason for this volume. For if the tools of the ever more complex noosphere are to be available to a large portion of humanity, ease of use will be a priority. And that requires standardization. It therefore will behoove us to keep the words of C. Francis Jenkins in mind, *"It is our duty, therefore, as engineers, to wisely direct this standardization, to secure best standards of equipment, quality, performance, nomenclature, and, unconsciously, perhaps, a code of ethics."* It will not be easy, it never has been, but the end result of our work will lift up humanity as a whole and make for a better world.

BIBLIOGRAPHY

"31st SMPTE Advanced Motion Imaging Conference," *SMPTE Journal*, vol. 105, no. 11, Nov., pp. 718-719, 1997.

"66th Semiannual Convention Society of Motion Picture Engineers," *Journal of the Society of Motion Picture Engineers*, vol. 53, no. 3, Sept., 301-303, 1949.

"A booth-by-booth guide to the equipment exhibits," *Broadcasting*, vol. 88, no. 13, March 31, pp. 44-46, 1975.

ABC7, "May 17, 1974 coverage of SLA shooting - ABC7," *YouTube*, ABC7, Feb. 17, https://www.youtube.com/watch?v=qZLN1UHliRE, 2019.

"Advance Program," *Journal of the SMPTE*, vol. 67, no. 3, March, pp. 178-199, 1958.

"Advance Program," *Journal of the SMPTE*, vol. 67, no. 9, Sept., pp. 611-628, 1958.

"Advance Program," *Journal of the SMPTE*, vol. 69, no. 3, March, pp. 184-190, 1960.

"Advance Program," *Journal of the SMPTE*, vol. 74, no. 9, Sept., pp. 808-823, 1965.

"Advance Program," *Journal of the SMPTE*, vol.75, no. 3, March, pp. 230-246, 1966.

"Advance Program," *Journal of the SMPTE*, vol. 75, no. 9, Sept., pp. 884-904, 1966.

"Advance Program," Journal of the SMPTE, vol. 81, no. 3, March, pp. 207-210, 1972.

"Advance Program," *Journal of the SMPTE*, vol. 81, no. 9, Sept., pp. 706-708, 1972.

Abramson, Albert, *The History of Television, 1880 to 1941.* McFarland & Company, Inc, 1987.

Abramson, Albert, *The History of Television, 1942 to 2000.* McFarland & Company, Inc., 2003.

Abramson, Albert, *Zworykin, Pioneer of Television.* Urbana, Il., University of Illinois Press, 1985.

Alveras, Al, "Capitol Theater," *cinematreasures.org*, comments, May 17, 2012, [Online}. Available: cinematreasures.org/theaters/16391.

"Are Local Stations Ready for Color?" *Broadcast Management/ Engineering*, vol. 1, no. 6, June, pp. 31, 1965.

"At KY-3-TV, The Brand of Reporting and the Brand of Film have a lot in Common," *Broadcast Management/ Engineering*, vol. 11 no. 3, March, pp. 99, 1975.

Battista, Thomas A., Flaherty, Joeseph A., "The All-Electronic Newsgathering Station," *Journal of the SMPTE*, vol. 84, no. 12, Dec., pp. 958-962, 1975.

Bazin, L. J., Clarke, J. J., Lind, A. H., "A Single Package Portable Color Camera for ENG," *Television Newsgathering: 10th Annual SMPTE Winter Television Conference*, 1976, 44-54.

Beatty, Frank J., "NAB To Highlight Free Expression," *Broadcasting*, Oct. 14, pp. 17, 1946.

Beacham, Frank, *The whole World Was Watching*, St. Petersburg, FL, BookLocker.com, 2018.

"Beyond ENG and Digital Video to Highlight SMPTE Winter TV Conference in San Francisco," *SMPTE Journal*, vol. 85, no. 12, Dec., pp. 977-979, 1976.

Bondy, Hugo A., "WAGA and ENG," *Television Newsgathering: 10th Annual SMPTE Winter Television Conference*, 1976, pp. 11-20.

Brown, Les, "Press Freedom for Cable TV is Urged in Whitehead Report," *The New York Times*, vol. 123, no. 42,362, January 17, pp. 1, 1974.

Busby, E. Stanley jr., "Report on the SMPTE Winter Television Conference," *SMPTE Journal*, vol. 86, no. 3, March, pp. 158-161, 1977.

Caron, James D., "1973 Winter Television Conference: January 19-20, Key Biscayne, Florida," *Journal of the SMPTE*, vol. 81, no. 12, Dec., pp. 932, 1972.

Cianci, Philip J., *High Definition Television*, Jefferson, NC: McFarland & Company, Inc., Publishers, 2012.

"Closed Circuit," *Broadcasting*, vol. 86, no. 10, March 11, pp. 3, 1974.

"Color Mobile Unit Serves Unique Needs of WSMW-TV," *RCA Broadcast News*, vol. 146, no. 6, June, pp. 13-17, 1971.

"Color Television Broadcasting Conference and Workshop Detroit-January 27-28," *Journal of the SMPTE*, vol. 75, no. 12, Dec., pp. 1230, 1966.

Di Giulio, Edmund M., "Going ENG all the way is an idea whose time has not yet come," *Broadcast Management/Engineering*, vol. 11, no. 7, July, pp. 19, 1975.

Di Giulio, Edmund M., "I'll reflex your BNC for $6,000," *American Cinematographer*, vol. 51, no. 1, January, pp. 61, 1970.

Di Giulio, Edmund M., "Mitchell BNC Camera Required," *American Cinematographer*, vol. 47, no. 1, Jan. pp. 80, 1968.

Di Giulio, Edmund M., "Television News Gathering-A Balanced Approach," *Television Newsgathering: 10th Annual SMPTE Winter Television Conference*, 1976, 79-84.

Di Giulio, Edmund M., "Today's 16mm Cameras Are Designed for Television News Gathering," *Broadcast Management/Engineering*, vol. 11, no. 4, April, pp. 32-34, 1975.

Di Giulio, Edmund M., "TV-newsfilm got the short end of the stick until we got into the act . . .," *Broadcast Management/Engineering*, vol. 10, no. 7, July, pp. 19, 1974.

Ebert, Roger, "The sudden death of film," *RogerEbert.com*, Nov. 2, 2011, https://www.rogerebert.com/roger-ebert/the-sudden-death-of-film.

"Electronic Journalism," *Broadcast Engineering*, vol. 17, no. 1, Jan., cover, 1975.

"Electronic Journalism hits the streets," *Broadcast Engineering*, vol. 17, no. 1, Jan., pp. 24-27, 1975.

"Electronic News Gathering: It's Off the Launching Pad, With Full Speed Ahead," *Broadcast Management/Engineering*, vol. 11, no. 1, Jan., pp. 34-50, 1975.

"ENG Sweeps the Newsroom; Invades New Areas of Teleproduction," *Broadcast Management/Engineering*, vol. 13, no. 1, Jan., pp. 39, 1977.

Engbretson, Gerald C., "Production and Post Production in the Eighties," *SMPTE Journal*, vol. 90, no. 4, April, pp. 296-324, 1981.

Estrin, James, "Kodak's First Digital Moment," *The New York Times - Lens*, April 12, 2015. https://archive.nytimes.com/lens.blogs.nytimes.com/2015/08/12/kodaks-first-digital-moment/

"Exhibit Directory," *Journal of the SMPTE*, vol. 80, no. 9, Sept., pp. 756-759, 1971.

Farhi, Paul, "Going Live," *American Journalism Review*, vol. 24, no. 9, Nov., pp. 28-32, 2002.

"Film, The basic medium." *Broadcast Management/ Engineering*, vol. 11, no. 10, October, pp. 26-27, 1975.

Goldsmith, Dr. Alfred N., "Image Transmission by Radio Waves," *Proceedings of the IRE*, vol. 17, no. 9, Sept., pp. 1536-1539, 1929.

Goldsmith, Dr. Alfred N., "Luncheon Address: Annual Meeting of the IRE," *Proceedings of the IRE*, vol. 16, no. 3, March, pp. 252-254, 1928.

Gordon, William D., "It's the News Package that Sells, not just the Equipment," *Broadcast Engineering*, vol. 19, no. 1, Jan., pp. 32-36, 1977.

"E days at Nab: A happy meld of equipment and euphoria," *Broadcasting*, April 2, pp. 80-86, 1973.

Flaherty, Joseph A., A case of 'Father follows in son's footsteps," *armypictorialcenter.com*, July 23, 2004, [Online}. Available: www.armypictorialcenter.com/joseph_a_Flaherty._jr_.htm.

Flaherty, Joseph A., "Luncheon Address: 'Isn't This Where We Came In?'" *SMPTE Journal*, vol. 97, no. 4, April, pp. 333-335, 1988.

Flaherty, Joseph A, "Television News Gathering," *Journal of the SMPTE*, vol. 83, no. 9, Aug., pp. 645-648, 1974.

Flaherty, Joseph A., "Trends in Television Recording," *Journal of the SMPTE*, vol 79, no. 7, July, pp. 579-584, 1970.

Flaherty, Joseph A., Taylor, Kenneth I., "New Television Production Techniques," *Journal of the SMPTE*, vol. 80, no. 8, Aug., pp. 605-613, 1971.

"Flaherty sets hi-def goal," *Broadcasting & Cable*, April 8, pp. 54, 1998.

Ford, Gerald R., "4/7/75 - National Association of Broadcasters, Las Vegas, Nevada," *President's Speeches and Statements*, Box 7, Gerald R. Ford Presidential Library, 1975

Gilpin, Lewie V., "RCA Seeks Television Unity to Avoid More False Starts," *Broadcasting*, vol. 20, no. 11, March, pg. 16, 1941.

Harless, James D., Collins, Erik L., *Work Roles, News Gathering Equipment, and Newscast in Current U.S. Television News Departments*, Paper presented to the Annual Meeting of the Association for Education in Journalism (57th, San Diego, August 18-21, 1974).

Holm, Wilton R., "Symposium Report: Taking Motion Pictures on Film or on Videotape," *Journal of the SMPTE*, vol. 82, no. 10, Oct., pp. 846-851, 1973.

Hirsch, Robin E., *The History of Image Gathering*, Westlake Village, CA: Brickwall Publishing, 2016.

Hirsch, Samuel, "Curtain Call for Henry," *Dartmouth Alumni Magazine*, April, pp. 26-27, 1972.

Jenkins, C. Francis, "Chairman's Address," *Transactions of the Society of Motion Picture Engineers*, vol. 1, no. 2, Oct., pp. 22-23, 1916.

Izzo, John, "SMPTE's Spring Film Conference & Exhibit Welcomed by Hollywood's Film Community," *SMPTE Journal*, vol. 106, no. 6, June, pp. 406-409, 1997.

Jenkins, C. Francis, "Radio Photographs, Radio Movies, and Radio Vision," *Transactions of the Society of Motion Picture Engineers*, vol. 7, no. 16, May, pp. 78-89, 1923.

Jones, Gary W., "Report on the Dallas Winter Television Conference," *Journal of the SMPTE*, vol. 81, no. 6, June, pp. 478-479, 1972.

Kaufman, Ross, "WCVB goes with Electronic Journalism," *Broadcast Engineering*, vol. no. 3, March, pp. 45-49, 1974.

King, Thomas E., "A Report on the 112th Technical Conference," *Journal of the SMPTE*, vol. 82, no. 2, Feb., pp. 110-111, 1973.

"Kodak salutes the NPPA 'Newsfilm Station of the Year'," *Broadcast Management/Engineering*, vol. 11, no. 12, Dec., pp. 27, 1975.

Lambert, Peter, "By HDTV's Early Light," *Broadcasting*, March 30, pp. 10, 1992.

"Largest-Ever NAB Convention Witnesses Turning Point in Technology and Regulation," *Broadcast Management/ Engineering*, vol. 9, no. 5, May, pp. 26, 1973.

Lightman, Herb A., "Film 75 in London," *American Cinematographer*, vol. 56, no. 9, Sept., pp. 1078, 1975.

Lightman, Herb A., "The 117th Technical Conference and Equipmant Exhibit," *American Cinematographer*, vol. 56, no. 12, Dec., pp. 1406 -1409, 1976.

Lind, Anthony H., "Engineering Color Video Tape Recording," *RCA Engineer*, vol. 3, no. 4, Feb.-March, pp. 22-33, 1958

"Little Ampex Steals Show from Electronics Giants," *Broadcasting*, vol. 50, no. 17, pp. 31, April 23, 1956.

MacDonald, David K., "New Developments in Electronic News Gathering Equipment," *Television Newsgathering: 10th Annual SMPTE Winter Television Conference*, 1976, 68-73.

Makhrovskiy, Oleg V., "Konstantin Perskiy - Russian electrical engineer," *2010 Second Region 8 IEEE Conference on the History of Communications*, Nov., https://ieeexplore. ieee.org/document/5735290, 2010.

"Many NAB Exhibitors; AMP Sounds Sentiment," *Broadcasting*, vol. 9, no. 2, July 15, pp. 14, 1935.

Maurer, John A., "Commercial Motion Picture Production with 16-MM Equipment," *Journal of the Society of Motion Picture Engineers*, vol. 35, no. 11, Nov. pp. 437-465, 1940.

Mausler, Robert, "Electronic Journalism Editing at NBC," *Television Newsgathering: 10th Annual SMPTE Winter Television Conference*, 1976, pp. 114-122.

Mayer, Bob, "WTVJ/Miami-1975-1st Live Shot (Ralph Renick - Bob Mayer)," *YouTube*, May 25, https://www.youtube.com/watch?v=_qJfpSQ8jjY, 2007.

Merrell, Ron, "Where has EJ been all these years?" *Broadcast Engineering*, vol. 17, no. 1, Jan. pp. 18-23, 1975

Moore, Gordon E., "Cramming more components onto integrated circuits," *Electronics*, vol. 38, no. 8, April 19, pp. 114, 1965.

Moroney, Aileen, "31st SMPTE Advanced Motion Imaging Conference," *SMPTE Journal*, vol. 105, no. 12, Dec., pp. 774-775, 1996.

Moroney, Aileen, "The First Annual Spring Film Conference and Exhibition," *SMPTE Journal*, vol. 105, no. 12, Dec., pp. 778, 1996.

Morris, Alan, "A Challenge in the News . . . ENG and the new breed," *Broadcast Engineering*, vol. 17, no. 7, July, pp. 32-42, 1975.

"Much for the sellers, much for the buyers at the exhibits," *Broadcasting*, March 29, pp. 63-66, 1976.

"NAB 50," *Broadcasting*, April 3, pp. 64, 1972.

"NAB acts as audience for newsmen and Nixon," *Broadcasting*, vol. 86, no. 12, March 25, pp. 22, 1974.

"NAB heads for Las Vegas to work, yes, work," *Broadcasting*, vol. 88, no. 13, March 31, pp. 23, 1975.

Nemeyer, Sheldon, "Technical Notes: Adaptations of Newsfilming Camera Systems," *Journal of the SMPTE*, vol. 80, no.5 May, pp. 412-413, 1971.

"Newsroom," *St. Louis Post-Dispatch*, Feb. 28, pp. 10C, 1974.

"Nixon will lead small parade of politicians at NAB's 52d," *Broadcasting*, vol. 86, no. 10, March 11, pp. 46-47, 1974.

Nishi, Nick H., "Mini-Cameras," *Television Newsgathering: 10th Annual SMPTE Winter Television Conference*, 1976, pp. 35-43.

O'Connor, John J., "C.B.S. Wins Network Race on Kissinger Briefing," *The New York Times*, vol. 123, no. 41,915, October 27, pp. 82, 1972.

"On Tap in Los Angeles," *Broadcasting*, April 28, pp. 54, 1958.

"One Conference a Year," *Journal of the SMPTE*, vol. 83, no. 9, Sept., pp. 750, 1974.

"Our New Quarters," *Bulletin no. 5, Academy of Motion Pictures Arts and Sciences*, Nov., pp. 1, 1927

"Pacific Coast Section, Society of Motion Picture Engineers, Minutes of Meeting," *Journal of the Society of Motion Picture Engineers*, vol. 14, no. 4, April, pp. 464-466, 1930.

"Pay-off for NBC color next fall?" *Broadcasting*, March 1, pp. 32, 1965.

"President Hoover's Message to the Broadcasters," *Broadcasting*, vol. 1, no. 2, November 1, pp. 4, 1931.

"Program," *Journal of the SMPTE*, vol. 79, no. 9 Sept., pp. 818-846, 1970.

"Program of NAB Convention," *Broadcasting*, Oct. 21, pp. 3, 1946.

"Program of the Hollywood Convention," *Journal of the SMPTE*, vol. 35 no. 12, Dec., pp. 627-631, 1940.

"Radio Age Begins Fifth Year," *Radio Age*, vol. 5, no. 4, April, pp. 7, 1926.

Radio Broadcasting, August, pp. 271, 1924.

"RCA Victor News," *Broadcasting*, vol. 7, no. 6, September 15, back cover, 1934.

Remley, Frederick M., "Get-Together Luncheon Address," *SMPTE Journal*, vol. 100, no. 4, April, pp. 304-306, 1991.

Remley, Frederick M., SMPTE Winter TV Conference, 23-24 January, to Focus on Television Newsgathering and Digital Video," *Journal of the SMPTE*, vol. no. 11, Nov., pp. 889-890, 1975.

"Report of SMPE Progress Committee," *Journal of the Society of Motion Picture Engineers*, vol. 52, no. 5, May, pp. 580-596, 1949.

Roizen, Joe, "Electronic Journalism Steals the Show," *Broadcast Engineering*, vol. 16, no. 5, May, pp. 44-49, 1974.

Roizen, Joe, "ENG Forges Ahead at the IBC Convention," *Broadcast Engineering*, vol. 19, no. 1, Jan., pp. 44-50, 1977.

Roizen, Joe, "NAB Convention Highlights," *Broadcast Engineering*, vol. 17, no. 5, May, pp. 24-35, 1975.

Roizen, Joe, "NAB Video Review," *Broadcast Engineering*, vol. 18, no. 5, May, pp. 20-27, 1976.

Roizen, Joe, "SMPTE Fall Conference Report," *Broadcast Engineering*, vol. no. 11, Nov. pp. 54-62, !975.

Roizen, Joe, "SMPTE forum for electronic journalism," *Broadcast Engineering*, vol. 17, no. 3, March, pp. 48-53, 1975.

Roizen, Joe, "SMPTE Handles the Hot Issues," *Broadcast Engineering*, vol. 19, no. 3, March, pp. 124-138, 1977.

Roizen, Joe, "The Sensuous Test Pattern," *Broadcast Engineering*, vol. 15, no. 6, June, pp. 44-46, 1973.

Rosenbaum, David E., "Threats by Nixon Reported on Tape Heard by Inquiry," *The New York Times*, vol. 123, no. 42,481, pp. 1 and 26, 1974.

Rumsfeld, Donald, *Known and Unknown*, London, U.K., Penguin Books Ltd., 2011.

Ryder, Loren L., "Report of the President," *Journal of the Society of Motion Picture Engineers*, vol. 49, no. 1, July, pp. 1-3, 1947.

Schuneman, R. Smith, "Visual Aspects of Television News: Communicator, Message, Equipment," *Journalism Quarterly*, vol. 43, no. 2, June, pp. 281-286, 1966.

Scobey, Fred J., "Report on the 117th Technical Conference," *Journal of the SMPTE*, vol. 84, no. 11, Nov. 841-860, 1975.

"Section Meetings," *Journal of the SMPTE*, vol. 76, no. 4, April, pp.402, 1967.

Semmelmayer, Joseph, "SMPTE Winter TV Conference A Success; TV News & Digital TV Among Highlights," *Journal of the SMPTE*, vol. 84, no. 3, March, pp. 194, 1975.

Shaw, Ken, "Format Choices for the Future," *A Television Continuum 1976 to 2017: 25th Annual SMPTE Television*, 1991, pp. 210-218.

Smith, Raymond J., "Assembling an Electronic News Gathering System," *Television Newsgathering: 10th Annual SMPTE Winter Television Conference*, 1976, pp. 1-10.

"SMPTE Winter Television Conference Atlanta, GA," *Journal of the SMPTE*, vol. 78, no. 9, Sept., pp. 750, 1969.

"SMPTE Winter Television Conference - Call for Papers," *Journal of the SMPTE*, vol. 77, no. 6, June, 648, 1968.

"SMPTE Winter Television Conference St. Francis Hotel, San Francisco, January 24-25," *Journal of the SMPTE*, vol. 85, no. 10, Oct., pp. 858-859, 1974.

"So Far It's All Go For Electronic News Gathering," *Broadcast Management/Engineering*, Jan., vol. 12, no. 1, pp. 48-56, 1976.

Sony, "Sony History," Sony.com, https:www.sony.com/en/SonyInfo/CorporateInfo/History/Sony/History

Sponable, Earl I., "Report of the President," *Journal of the SMPTE*, vol. 54, no.1, Jan., pp. 3-7, 1950.

Stow, Rupert L., Owen, Henry R., Goldberg, Abraham A., "Report on the Tenth Annual SMPTE Winter Television Conference: Detroit, 23-24 January 1976," *SMPTE Journal*, vol. 85, no. 2, Feb., pp. 101-103, 1976.

Stull, William, A.S.C., "Auricon Sound Camera Makes Bow," *American Cinematographer*, vol. 23, no. 4, April, 165 - 176, 1942.

Sukow, Randy, "Could HDTV's answer be a 'grand alliance'?," *Broadcast & Cable*, March 1, pp. 54, 1993.

Taishoff, Sol, "Roosevelt Gives Broadcasters Confidence," *Broadcasting*, vol. 7, no. 7, October 1, pp. 7-10, 1934.

"Tape and Film: The Fight Goes On," *Broadcast Management/Engineering*, vol. 10, no. 1, Jan. pp. 28-33, 1974.

"Tape or Film? How To Take Aim," *Broadcast Management/Engineering*, vol. 9, no. 1, Jan., cover, 1973.

"Technicians Hold Important Meeting," *Bulletin no. 5, Academy of Motion Pictures Arts and Sciences*, Nov., pp. 2, 1927.

Teilhard de Chardin, Pierre, *The Phenomenon of Man*, New York, NY: Harper Perennial, 2008.

"Television Motif Marks New York Fair," *Broadcasting*, vol. 16, no. 9, May, pp. 20-21, 1939.

The American Presidency Project, "Question-and-Answer Session at the Annual Convention of the National Association of Broadcasters, Houston, Texas," *https:// www.presidency.ucsb.edu/documents/question-and-answer-session-the-annual-convention-the-national-association-broadcasters*, pp. 15, 1974.

"The era of ENG has arrived in TV journalism," *Broadcasting*, vol. 88, no. 15, April 14, pp. 62-63, 1975.

"The First Annual Spring Film Conference and Exhibition," *SMPTE Journal*, vol. 105, no. 11, Nov., pp. 724, 1996.

"The KTVY News Crew: Experts At Stimulating Local Interest," *Broadcast Management/Engineering*, vol. 12, no. 4, April, pp. 51-54, 1976.

"The Los Angeles Conference Equipment Exhibit," *Journal of the SMPTE*, vol. 84, no. 11, Nov. pp. 868-886, 1975.

"The N. A. B. Convention," *Broadcasting*, vol. 1, no. 1, October 15, pp. 18, 1931.

"The official NAB agenda," *Broadcasting*, March 26, pp. 40, 1973.

"The Winter Television Conference Denver, January 24 and 25," *Journal of the SMPTE*, vol. 83, no. 2, Feb., pp. 130-132, 1974.

Toobin, Jeffrey, *American Heiress*, New York, Doubleday, 2016.

"Transcript of the Panel Discussion on Electronic Newsgathering," *Television Newsgathering: 10th Annual SMPTE Winter Television Conference*, 1976, 129-164.

"Twenty-Fifth Anniversary: Society of Motion Picture Engineers," *Journal of the SMPTE*, vol. 37, no. 1, July, pp. 3-4, 1941.

United States v. Zenith Radio Corporation, 12 F.2d 614 (N.D. III. 1926)

"Use Both Now . . . Watch Tape's Future," *Broadcast Management/Engineering*, vol. 10, no. 1, Jan., cover, 1974.

"Video tape-film issue rekindled at SMPTE," *Broadcasting*, Oct. 30, pp. 44, 1972.

Vlahos, Petro, "Motion Picture Technology - From the Past to the Future," *SMPTE Journal*, vol. 106, no. 6, June, pp. 410-412, 1997.

"Watergate tape points to White House complicity in challenges to Post-Newsweek," *Broadcasting*, vol. 86, no. 20, May 20, pp. 25, !974.

"Whitehead Asserts Nixon Bill Does Not Seek to Curtail Television Freedom," *New York Times*, vol. 123, no. 41,991, Jan. 11, pp. 41, 1973.

Wilson, Anton, "Report From the 116th SMPTE Technical Conference and Equipment Exhibit," *American Cinematographer*, vol. 56, no. 2, Feb., pp. 184, 1975.

Zucchino, P. M., Lowrance, J. L., "TV Camera for the Command Module of the Apollo Spacecraft," *RCA Engineer*, vol. 10, no. 5, Feb.-March, pp.18-22, 1965.

INDEX

B

O

Oakland Unified School District 132

Ogle, Jack 214

One from the Heart 279

Ota City 18, 22, 23, 68, 85, 90, 95, 156, 166, 173, 201, 236

Owen, Henry 243, 244, 248, 251, 252

P

Paik, Woo 297

Panasonic 283, 284, 290

    M-II 290

Panavision 281, 306, 310, 311

    Genesis 310

Paramount Studios, see Army Pictorial Center

Patterson, Floyd 188

Pennebaker, D. A. 125, 279

Perry, Nancy Ling 131, 132

Perskyi, Constantin 34, 312

Philbin, Regis 285

Phillips Norelco 18, 151, 189, 223, 265, 299

    PCP-90 22, 84, 88, 102, 174, 189, 265

    LDK 11 189

Photokina 294

Photomaton Parent Corporation 57

Photoshop 294

Pinewood Studios 265

Pioneer 10 273, 296

Pirone, Tony 314

Pitts, Freddie 200

S

X

Made in the USA
Columbia, SC
11 October 2022

69067164R00207